iPod® & iTunes®

PORTABLE GENIUS
3rd EDITION

iPod® & iTunes®

PORTABLE GENIUS
3rd EDITION

Jesse David Hollington

WILEY

John Wiley & Sons, Inc.

iPod® & iTunes® Portable Genius, 3rd Edition

Published by
John Wiley & Sons, Inc.
10475 Crosspoint Blvd.
Indianapolis, IN 46256
www.wiley.com

ISBN: 978-1-118-16628-4

Manufactured in the United States of America

10 9 8 7 6 5 4 3 2 1

For general information on our other products and services or to obtain technical support, please contact our Customer Care Department within the U.S. at (877) 762-2974, outside the U.S. at (317) 572-3993 or fax (317) 572-4002.

Library of Congress Control Number: 2011945576

WILEY

About the Author

Jesse David Hollington is the Applications Editor for iLounge.com, a site about all things iPod, iPhone, iPad, and iTunes. He covers iPhone and iPad applications, writes technical articles and tutorials, and pens a weekly Ask iLounge column responding to readers' questions. Outside of the world of iPods, Jesse is also an IT consultant in the networking and collaborative services space and is an officer in the Canadian Forces Reserve working with Air Cadets in his spare time. Jesse lives in Toronto, Ontario, Canada with his wife Nina and their daughter Victoria.

Credits

Senior Acquisitions Editor
Stephanie McComb

Executive Editor
Jody Lefevere

Project Editor
Cricket Krengel

Technical Editor
Paul Sihvonen-Binder

Copy Editor
Beth Taylor

Editorial Director
Robyn Siesky

Vice President and Executive Group Publisher
Richard Swadley

Vice President and Executive Publisher
Barry Pruett

Business Manager
Amy Knies

Senior Marketing Manager
Sandy Smith

Project Coordinator
Sheree Montgomery

Graphics and Production Specialists
Andrea Hornberger

Quality Control Technician
Melanie Hoffman

Proofreading
Melissa D. Buddendeck

Indexing
Potomac Indexing, LLC

To Nina and Victoria, the two most important people in my life.

Acknowledgments

My sincerest thanks go out to the many people who have continued to provide their support and encouragement as I've worked through completing this Third Edition. As always, the support and guidance from my colleagues at iLounge has been invaluable: Jeremy Horwitz, Dennis Lloyd, Charles Starrett, Bob Levens, and Nick Guy — not only with this book, but also in my work writing about the world of iTunes and iPods in general over the years. Many thanks also to my good friend and my daughter's surrogate "big sister" Kathryn Shumelda for being around to hang out with Victoria and take her out for long walks when deadlines were fast approaching. Thanks to my editors, Stephanie McComb and Cricket Krengel, for their support and patience in accommodating shifting deadlines and eleventh-hour Apple announcements. Last but far from least, my deepest gratitude and appreciation goes out to my loving wife Nina for her support, encouragement, and patience as I juggled all of the obligations of writing a book, handling a day job, and being a husband and father in the midst of both of our very busy schedules.

Contents

chapter 1

What Do I Really Need to Know about iTunes?   2

chapter 2

What Do I Need to Know about Purchasing Content Online?   18

How Should I Organize My Content? 48

chapter 5

How Can I Use Playlists to Manage My Library? 102

chapter 4

How Do I Play My Content in iTunes? 80

chapter 6

How Do I Manage Podcasts,
Audiobooks, and iTunes
U Content? 142

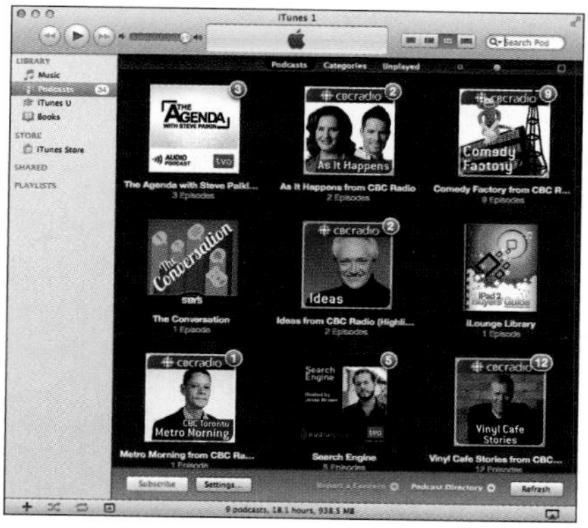

How Do I Manage the
Content on My iPod? 142

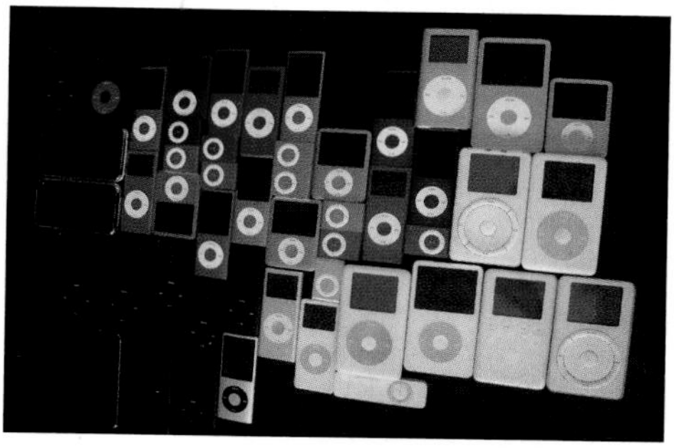

chapter 8

How Do I Get the Most Out
of My iPod?   192

chapter 9

How Do I Get My Own Movies
onto My iPod?   226

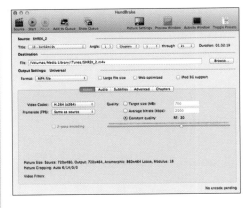

chapter 10

How Do I Get Content from My iPod Back to My Computer?   244

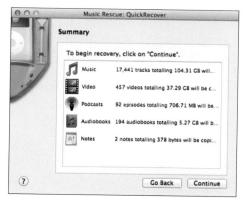

chapter 11

How Do I Play Content on an Apple TV?   262

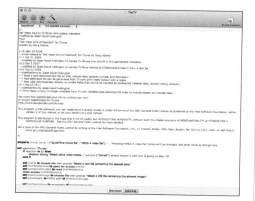

Introduction

Ten years ago, Apple Computer surprised the world by announcing that it would be stepping into the world of digital media, introducing a new portable media player that it chose to simply name iPod. At that point in time, the digital media player marketplace was just beginning to mature, and Apple was far from the first company to introduce such a product; however Apple in its typical fashion provided something different in its approach — not a standalone device that left the user to tackle the complexities of getting and loading on digital content, but instead an integrated solution with all of the pieces necessary to make the experience work: a Mac application to manage the content and later an online digital media store to make it easy for users to purchase and download content from the comfort of their own homes. Uniquely Apple, this approach allowed the average user to simply enjoy the experience of listening to their music instead of getting bogged down in the technical management required by most other digital media players.

The result of this accessibility to the average consumer was that the iPod quickly went from being a niche product for Mac users to a household name synonymous with portable digital media players. Support for Windows was added, the reach of the iTunes Store grew, and eventually the little music player expanded to support TV shows, movies, and even games. Not content with stopping there, Apple moved into the living room with the Apple TV, and then completely redefined another entire industry by brining the elegance and simplicity of the iPod approach to the mobile phone market with the iPhone and then the mobile computing marketplace with the iPad.

Today, Apple continues to enjoy overwhelming success in the market, with sales of over 320 million iPods, 146 million iPhones, and 40 million iPads along with over 16 billion songs sold on the iTunes Store. Ironically, as the now venerable iPod passes its tenth anniversary it's interesting to reflect that a device that many had dismissed as little more than a fad when it first debuted has had such an overwhelming success by creating something that speaks to the average user. Put simply, the iPod is a device that for the most part just works like it should and allows you to spend more time enjoying your media content and less time managing it.

Out of the box, the iPod and iTunes are relatively straightforward to use; this is after all the primary strength of the brand. However, one would be mistaken in assuming that iTunes is nothing more than a conduit to manage content on an iPod. While Apple has done an excellent job of making iTunes simple for the average user, there is a lot of hidden power under the hood of the iTunes application, making it one of the best media management solutions available, even for users who don't own an iPod or any other Apple device.

This book assumes that you understand the basics of media management and how to use iTunes itself and takes you deeper into the aspects of iTunes and the iPod that are hidden beneath the surface, exploring the real power of iTunes and how it interacts with your iPod, iPhone, iPad, and Apple TV devices. By fully exploring what iTunes has to offer, you can discover how to better manage and get more enjoyment from your digital media collection.

What Do I Really Need to Know about iTunes?

About iTunes

iTunes 10

iTunes 10.5.1 (42)
64-bit

Copyright © 2000–2011 Apple Inc. All rights reserved.
Apple, the Apple logo, iTunes, and the iTunes logo are
trademarks of Apple Inc., registered in the U.S. and other
countries.

MPEG Layer-3 audio coding technology licensed from
Fraunhofer IIS and THOMSON multimedia.

Managing a library of music and other media content can be challenging, and iTunes is a powerful tool for this, even if you're not planning to use an iPod or iPhone right away. A good understanding of how iTunes manages your digital media collection helps you to get the most out of your digital media experience and allows you to spend more time enjoying your media collection rather than managing it.

Understanding iTunes

iTunes is essentially the only game in town to get the most out of all of the media features on your iPod, iPhone, or iPad, but even for non-iPod users, it can be a great tool for managing an ever-increasing library of digital content. It's important to keep in mind that iTunes takes a different approach to managing content compared to many other applications. If you're already familiar with another media-management application it's very important that you understand a bit about how iTunes works under the hood before you begin building a library. This will help you to get the most benefit out of iTunes and avoid creating extra work for you in the future.

Types of audio content supported by iTunes

A popular misconception among non-iPod owners is that all of the content that you put into iTunes must come from the iTunes Store. Nothing could be further from the truth. Not only does iTunes support any standard audio CD that you give it, but it also supports the MP3 format — the most popular digital audio format available on the Internet today.

In addition to the MP3 format, iTunes provides support for the Advanced Audio Coding (AAC) format. Contrary to another common misconception, this is not an Apple-proprietary format but is actually an MPEG standard audio format originally designed to replace the MP3 format. It is also the standard audio format used by other devices, such as the Sony PlayStation 3 and the Nintendo Wii, and many other portable music players and cellular phones support this format.

Content that you do purchase from the iTunes Store comes in AAC format, and iTunes imports your CDs in this format by default, but you can import any standard MP3 file directly into iTunes without needing to convert it first, and you can play these same files on your iPod, iPhone, iPad, or Apple TV without having to worry about converting them to another format. Changing your default import format for CDs is discussed later in this chapter.

Note

Windows users may be familiar with the Windows Media Audio (WMA) format, which is the default format used by the Microsoft Windows Media Player application and many Windows-compatible portable media players. Although iTunes does not support the WMA format directly, the Windows version of iTunes offers to automatically convert any *unprotected* WMA files to your preferred format as you import them, as discussed later in this chapter. Note that this option is not available to Mac users, as Mac OS X does not include the necessary WMA components.

iTunes also provides support for several other less-commonly used formats, including Apple Lossless format, Waveform audio format (WAV), and Audio Interchange File Format (AIFF). These lossless formats preserve the full original sound quality of the source, but they also consume a lot of storage space as a result.

Understanding lossless and lossy

Digital music formats fit into two broad categories: *lossless* and *lossy*.

Lossless, as the name implies, refers to those formats that preserve the full sound quality of the original recording. Common lossless formats include WAV, AIFF, and Apple Lossless. The WAV and AIFF formats are essentially a direct copy of the audio from an original CD, while the Apple Lossless format performs lossless compression on the audio file to reduce the size slightly, although still without losing any of the original audio fidelity. This is the same way in which a Zip file on your computer works — when you zip up a document or other file, the size is reduced, but you don't lose any of the actual information.

The problem is that even with compression, lossless files are generally still very large — between 6MB and 10MB per minute of audio. To solve this problem, a number of lossy compression methods were developed.

The idea here is, because most people's ears cannot hear the full fidelity of most audio recordings, a simple analysis can be performed to throw out those sounds that are of a frequency above or below normal hearing range. By selectively discarding information that the average listener can't hear anyway, the remaining music can be stored in a much smaller file.

The most common lossy formats are MP3, AAC, and WMA. Each of these formats can be set to different bit rates, with the simple rule of thumb being that the lower the bit rate, the smaller the file but the lower the sound quality. Bit rates are expressed in kbps (short for *kilobits per second*), and although many audio enthusiasts prefer much higher bit rates, most users consider 128 kbps to be the lowest acceptable quality for a digital audio file.

Changing your default audio format

If you're importing existing media files that are directly supported by iTunes, such as MP3 or AAC files, these are simply left in their original format and cataloged into your iTunes library. No conversion ever takes place with an existing supported media file format during import.

However, when importing CDs or WMA files, it's necessary for iTunes to convert the audio into a supported digital media file format. Rather than pestering you each time, iTunes uses a default format that you set under your iTunes preferences. To set your import preferences, follow these steps:

1. **Open your iTunes preferences, click the General tab, and then click the Import Settings button.** A screen similar to the one shown in Figure 1.1 appears.

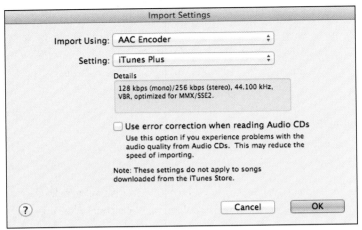

1.1 The iTunes Import Settings preferences dialog box

2. **Select the format you want iTunes to use for imports from the Import Using drop-down menu.** The format chosen here is used as the default for all conversion operations — importing from CD, converting WMA files automatically, or even converting tracks manually. The choices are

   - **AAC Encoder.** The default encoder used by iTunes. This lossy format provides reasonable quality at lower file sizes. This is the best-quality lossy encoder in iTunes, but the AAC file format is not as widely supported as MP3.

   - **AIFF Encoder.** An uncompressed, lossless format that is just a direct copy of the audio from a CD.

   - **Apple Lossless Encoder.** A lossless compression format. Files encoded using the Apple Lossless Encoder are the same quality as the original CD, but they are compressed to about 50 to 80 percent of their original size using lossless compression.

   - **MP3 Encoder.** The standard digital audio file format used by most content and digital audio software and hardware. This provides the widest range of compatibility with other software and hardware; however, the MP3 encoder in iTunes generally requires a slightly higher bit rate to be used than AAC to produce the same audio quality.

   - **WAV Encoder.** An uncompressed, lossless format that is just a direct copy of the audio from a CD.

Calculating Audio File Sizes

You can easily compute the size of an MP3 or AAC file based on the bit rate you've chosen. The bit rate is actually just the number of bits of data stored for each second of audio. So for a 256 kbps audio file, each second of audio requires 256,000 bits of data. Because there are 8 bits in a byte, with a given bit rate and length of a song you can figure out almost exactly how much space each track takes up if you want to do the math.

For example, for a 5-minute track encoded at 256 kbps

- 5 minutes = 300 seconds
- 256 kbps × 300 seconds = 76,800 kilobits of data
- 76,800 kilobits / 8 = 9,600K

For a quick approximate calculation, however, you can just multiply the bit rate by 7.5 and this tells you approximately how many kilobytes each minute of a song takes up.

Another good rule of thumb is to remember that a 192 kbps track is 50 percent larger than a 128 kbps track, and a 256 kbps track is twice the size of a 128 kbps track.

3. **Select a quality setting from the Setting drop-down menu.** For the MP3 and AAC lossy formats, select one of the predefined quality settings. Each quality setting corresponds to a specific bit rate for that format. If you want to set your own bit rate, select Custom and an additional dialog box opens to allow you to select a more specific bit rate. Note that this does not apply to AIFF, Apple Lossless, or WAV formats, as these formats provide the same quality as the original audio.

Note After you have imported your music into iTunes, you can view the size of your files by enabling the Size column in the View ⇨ Options menu in iTunes.

Types of video content supported by iTunes

iTunes also supports the organizing and viewing of your video content. Although the world of digital audio formats is much more well defined, with MP3 being the dominant standard, the world of online digital video content is a great deal murkier, with a wide variety of different formats out there and no clear standard.

iTunes uses QuickTime as its underlying video engine, so you can use any video format supported by QuickTime in iTunes. In a default configuration, this includes the QuickTime MOV format, as well as the H.264 and MPEG-4 video formats. A number of plug-ins are available for QuickTime, however, that extend this video playback to include numerous other popular formats, such as WMV and DivX.

Keep in mind that although iTunes supports any video format compatible with QuickTime, this is not the case with Apple media hardware. These devices are limited to the H.264 and MPEG-4 formats and have certain additional limitations on maximum resolutions and bit rates that are discussed in Chapter 9. Understanding these limitations becomes important if you plan to watch your video content on any device other than your computer.

How iTunes organizes and stores media

iTunes takes a considerably different approach from many other media-management applications in terms of how media content is organized on your computer. Basically, iTunes expects that you are performing all of your music and other media management using the iTunes application as the front end, and it takes care of all of the little details like file and folder management for you in the background.

Ironically, it's often the most experienced digital media users who have the hardest time coming to grips with how iTunes works. If you've been collecting digital media for a long time, even with another media-management application, you may have become used to managing your media collection through a file and folder structure. You've probably become quite comfortable with this organization and grown to expect that things are only ever where you put them and nowhere else.

However, the problem with a file and folder structure is that it's limiting by its very nature. Say you choose to organize your music into a folder structure by Artist and Album, with each song file named after the track. Now, how do you find all the music of a particular genre? How do you deal with songs from albums with various artists, such as movie soundtracks? For a few tracks, this may not be much of a challenge, but it can quickly become unwieldy as your library grows to thousands of songs — which it will.

Most digital audio formats already include room for tags stored within the files themselves to contain information such as the artist, album, song title, and genre. In most cases this information is already at least partially filled in for your existing media files — it merely needs to be read in and put to good use, which is essentially what iTunes does as you import your media files into your iTunes library. The information from the tags is stored in a database for quick access, and so iTunes can generally find a given track for you much faster than you could otherwise.

Genius

If you want to actually see a specific file, simply select the track in iTunes and choose File ➪ Show in Finder (Mac) or Show in Windows Explorer (Windows); iTunes opens the appropriate window to that location, with the selected file highlighted.

So what about the files themselves? Well, the point is that you don't really need to care where those files are located. There's no longer a need to deal with the original files — you can locate, play, copy, organize, and retag your media from within iTunes, and it takes care of all of the other trivial details like file storage for you automatically under the hood.

Genius

Need to copy a set of tracks? Try highlighting a single track or set of tracks in iTunes and then drag and drop them directly onto a Finder or Windows Explorer window. iTunes copies those files to that location.

Configuring Your Library Storage Settings

Armed with a basic understanding of the types of media that you can use in iTunes and how it's all stored, the next step is to actually get that content into iTunes. Of course, there's always a temptation to jump right in, but this is one of these situations where just a little bit of initial understanding and planning can help you avoid a whole bunch of headaches later.

Selecting a location for your iTunes media

By default, iTunes stores your media content under your *Music/iTunes/iTunes Media* folder. This folder is normally located on your system drive, and if you're importing a large library this may not be the ideal place for it. Even if you choose to leave your existing media files in their original locations, the iTunes Media Folder path is still used for tracks that you import from audio CDs as well as any content purchased from the iTunes Store, including podcasts.

Note

Prior to iTunes 9, the media folder was named *iTunes Music*. The *iTunes Media* folder in iTunes 9 and later serves the same function as before — Apple has simply acknowledged that many different types of content are stored here. If you've upgraded from an older version of iTunes, however, this folder will still be called *iTunes Music*.

Although iTunes stores its library database on the system drive by default, you can specify any location you want for the storage of your media content, and it does not need to be stored with

9

the actual database. You seldom need to be concerned with changing the database location — it doesn't grow particularly large. Your media content, however, can quickly take over your entire hard drive if you're not careful.

Note that it is possible to move your media content to another location in the future, and I discuss that in Chapter 12. However, moving the media content can still be a time-consuming process, and it's better to plan ahead and place it in a location where you want to keep it for the long run now.

To change the location of your iTunes media folder, follow these steps:

1. **Open your iTunes preferences and click the Advanced tab, as shown in Figure 1.2.**

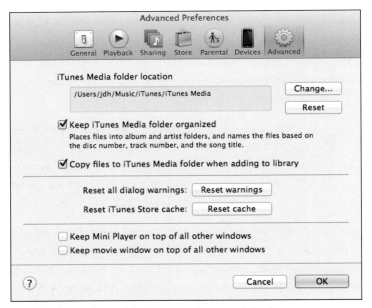

1.2 The Advanced tab of the iTunes preferences dialog box

2. **Click Change.**

3. **From the file browser dialog box that appears, specify a new folder location and click OK; this is the folder that contains your media content.** The actual library database remains in your Music folder.

4. **Back in the Advanced tab, click the check boxes to select the other options you want to apply with regard to your folder location.** There are two to choose from:

   - **Keep iTunes Media folder organized.** This option determines whether iTunes reorganizes content in your iTunes Media folder as you change the tags and other information. For example, if you change the Artist field for a track, iTunes moves that track into a new folder according to the new artist name. This only affects tracks that are already located in the iTunes Media folder.

- **Copy files to iTunes Media folder when adding to library.** When this option is selected, any existing files that you import into your iTunes library are copied to the iTunes Media folder. iTunes uses the copy for its library, but the original file is also left in its original location. If this option is not selected, iTunes simply references each file from its original location. It does not rename or move the file in any way, even if you later update the track information. Further, iTunes stores the full path to each file, and so if you rename or move the file later, iTunes will lose track of it, resulting in a broken link to the file. Note that content imported from CDs or downloaded from the iTunes Store (including podcast subscriptions) is always placed in the iTunes Media folder, regardless of this setting. Further, if you import a track that is already in the iTunes Media folder, it is moved or renamed if this option is selected because it's already in the iTunes Media folder.

5. **Click OK so that the new settings take effect.** The remaining options on the Advanced tab do not apply to your iTunes library storage.

The basic point that you should keep in mind here is that iTunes considers your iTunes Media folder to be its home folder. Anything in this folder can be reorganized and managed (subject to the options mentioned in the previous steps). Files outside of this folder location are never managed or reorganized by iTunes. In fact, if you remove a track from your iTunes library, iTunes doesn't even offer to delete the file if it's not already located in your iTunes Media folder.

Keep in mind that if you're concerned about maintaining your own file system organization and choose not to copy files into your iTunes Media folder when importing them, you should ensure that your file and folder layout is already set up the way you want it. Moving or renaming files is more difficult after they've been imported. Unless you have a very specific reason to maintain your own file and folder organization, personally I strongly recommend letting iTunes manage your file organization for you. You save a lot of time and hassle in the long term, particularly if you ever need to move your library to another drive or another computer, and after all, aren't computers supposed to make our lives easier?

Note If you have selected the option to do so, iTunes *copies* files into your iTunes Media folder during import, and so if you're importing a large number of media files, you need to make sure that you have enough hard drive space for this. Alternatively, you can move all of the files into the iTunes Media folder manually before adding them to your iTunes library. If they're already in your iTunes Media folder, then iTunes just imports them in place and reorganizes them as necessary.

Adjusting your CD import settings

Importing an audio CD into iTunes is normally as simple as putting the CD into your computer's CD drive. With default import settings, iTunes simply asks you if you want to import the CD and then does this for you. If you want to be a bit more selective about what you import from the CD, however, you can either adjust your import settings to not automatically prompt you or simply select No when asked to import your newly inserted CD.

If you choose No, iTunes displays the CD in your Source list on the left-hand side and a list of the tracks it contains, as shown in Figure 1.3.

1.3 The iTunes CD track listing

Note

Many audio enthusiasts consider the quality of the iTunes built-in MP3 encoder to be less than acceptable. If you're concerned about audio quality and want to use the MP3 format for your imported music, you might want to consider ripping your CDs using a third-party tool, such as Exact Audio Copy (EAC) from www.exactaudio copy.de and then converting them to MP3 using the popular L.A.M.E. conversion tool, which can be downloaded from http://lame.sourceforge.net. The result is a standard MP3 file that you can just import directly into iTunes.

From here, you can choose specific tracks that you want to import simply by placing a check mark beside them and unchecking the tracks that you do not want to import — a useful feature if you only want to grab a single track or two from a CD, rather than importing the entire disc.

Changing CD track information

When you insert a CD, iTunes tries to look up the correct track information for it by using the Gracenote CD Database (CDDB). You can turn this behavior off by deselecting the Automatically retrieve CD track names from Internet option in your General preferences.

Note If you're not connected to the Internet when you insert your CD, or iTunes doesn't retrieve the track information for some other reason, you can force it to try again by choosing Advanced ⇨ Get Track Names.

For most commercial CDs, it does a pretty reasonable job, but keep in mind that the information that goes into CDDB is based on user submissions, and it's only as accurate as the information provided by end users like you. If you notice an error, you can easily correct it before importing your CD simply by editing the information in the CD track listing as you would for any other file in iTunes. Follow these steps:

1. **Select a CD track.**

2. **Choose File ⇨ Get Info from the iTunes menu.** You should see a dialog box similar to the one shown in Figure 1.4.

3. **Fill in the correct information for that track.**

4. **Click OK.**

If you want to change an entry for several tracks at once, such as for an incorrectly spelled album name, you can simply select all of the tracks you want to change and follow the previous steps to edit the common properties for all of them.

Genius When editing the properties for an individual track, you'll notice a pair of Previous and Next buttons at the bottom-left corner of the window. If you're changing information on multiple tracks, you can use these buttons to quickly navigate through the entire set of tracks. You can even use the keyboard shortcuts ⌘+P and ⌘+N, respectively, on a Mac, or Ctrl+P and Ctrl+N in Windows.

1.4 The iTunes CD track properties window

If you've corrected some obvious error in the track information from CDDB, why not share your experience with the rest of the world? Follow these steps to submit your own information to CDDB:

1. **With the CD still inserted in your computer, choose Advanced ⇨ Submit CD Track Names to submit your changes to the CDDB database.** You should see a dialog box similar to the one shown in Figure 1.5. Note that as long as the CD is still inserted, you can also display this dialog box at any time by right-clicking the CD in the iTunes Source list and choosing Get Info. After you eject the CD, the option is grayed out.

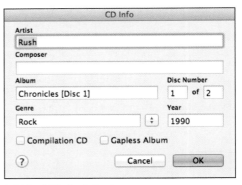

1.5 The CD Info dialog box

2. **Fill in the requested information in the dialog box for the CD.** At a minimum, you should include the artist, album, and genre information.

3. **If the album has more than one artist, type Various Artists in the Artist field and click the Compilation CD check box.** Note that the Compilation CD check box is only for albums with multiple artists, not albums that are merely special collections of a single artist's work.

4. **If the CD is designed to be played back with no breaks of silence in between tracks, click the Gapless Album check box.** More on gapless playback is discussed in Chapter 4.

Keep in mind that your submission won't appear immediately because there's a review process for user-submitted changes, but it can certainly help the CDDB team to keep its information accurate.

Importing your existing media files

If you already have a collection of media files lying around on your computer, you can import them directly into iTunes. iTunes does not offer any means of converting from another media-management application, such as Windows Media Player, but if your files are correctly tagged, most of the information you need is already contained within the actual files.

Note iTunes can be strangely unhelpful when you try to import unsupported file formats, particularly where video files are concerned. If a file format is incompatible and cannot be imported into iTunes, you often get no feedback — it just doesn't appear in your library.

The easiest and most obvious way to get the tracks into iTunes is simply by dragging and dropping a track onto the iTunes window. You can also do this with complete folders.

If you're importing a lot of content, and drag-and-drop doesn't work for you, then you can use the Add To Library option found under the iTunes File menu. Follow these steps:

1. **Choose File ⇨ Add to Library.** You are presented with a standard file browser dialog box.

2. **From the file browser, select the media files or folder that you want to import into iTunes.**

3. **Click OK.**

Note iTunes for Windows offers two options on the File menu: Add File to Library and Add Folder to Library. These function in exactly the same way that the Mac's single Add to Library option does, although you need to select the appropriate option depending on whether you're adding individual files or an entire folder.

15

Importing playlists from another application

If you've come from another media-management application, chances are that you've collected more than a few playlists in your time over there. Although iTunes doesn't offer a direct conversion option, if your playlists are in the M3U format, or can be exported into this format (most common media players can do this), then you can import them into iTunes manually. Follow these steps:

1. **Make sure that the media files on the playlist you are importing are already imported to your library.** If the media files are not already imported, your imported playlist may not function correctly.

2. **Export your playlists into an M3U format from your existing media player.**

3. **In iTunes, choose File ⇨ Library ⇨ Import Playlist.** A file browser dialog box appears.

4. **Browse to and select the saved M3U file on your computer.**

5. **Click OK.** Your M3U file is imported into iTunes as a new playlist with the name of the M3U.

What Do I Need to Know about Purchasing Content Online?

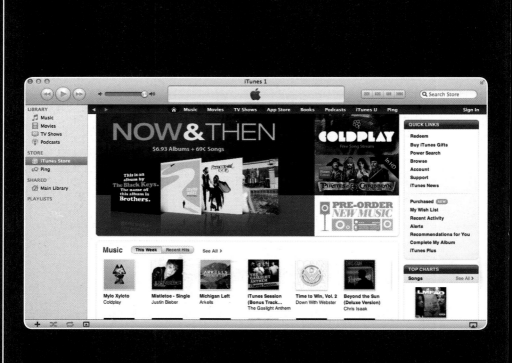

Although many iTunes users still get their music the traditional way by purchasing CDs, many online music stores offer a massive selection of music and other media content that can be purchased through the convenience of your computer. Not all online media stores are the same, however, and it is important to understand the differences and limitations among them so that you can make an informed purchase and get the most out of your digital media experience.

Getting the Most Out of the iTunes Store

The first and most obvious source of content for your iPod, iPhone, or iPad is the Apple online media store, which you can access directly from within iTunes. The iTunes Store began as a music-only store exclusive to Mac users in the United States. Today, however, it has expanded to support both Mac and Windows users in more than 90 countries and includes a wide variety of media content such as music, audiobooks, podcasts, music videos, movies, TV shows, and even games and other applications for your iPod or iPhone. Although using the iTunes Store is not at all necessary for you to enjoy your iPod, it can be a very convenient source of additional content.

How to set up an iTunes Store account

Although you can browse the iTunes Store and even preview content without setting up an account or being signed in, you need an account to actually purchase anything from the store. To set up an iTunes Store account, you need to specify a payment method. This can be a credit card, a PayPal account (if you're in the United States), or an iTunes Store gift card or gift certificate. This last option is especially useful if you do not have a credit card because you can actually fund iTunes Store purchases simply using prepaid gift cards, which can be purchased at any Apple Store and many other retailers. Some restrictions exist on what gift cards can be used for, but they're generally fine for purchasing music and video content.

To create an account on the iTunes Store, follow these steps:

1. **Chose Store ⇨ Sign In from the iTunes menu.** You should see a dialog box similar to the one shown in Figure 2.1.

2. **Click Create New Account.** The main iTunes window shows a Welcome screen similar to the one shown in Figure 2.2.

2.1 The iTunes Store sign-in dialog box

3. **Click Continue.** The iTunes Store Terms and Conditions are displayed, similar to Figure 2.3. These are specific to the country that you are registering for an iTunes Store account in. If your billing address is in another country from that which is displayed, you can click where indicated to change your selected country.

2.2 The iTunes Store Welcome screen

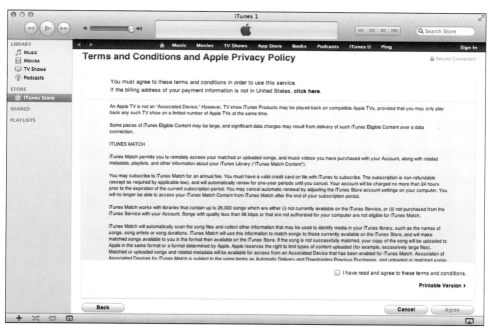

2.3 iTunes Store Terms and Conditions

4. **Click the check box that indicates that you have read and agree to the iTunes Terms and Conditions and then click Continue.**

5. **Fill in your personal information on the remaining screens.** If you are using an iTunes gift card or gift certificate to create the account, you can specify this on the payment method screen instead of providing credit card information, as shown in Figure 2.4.

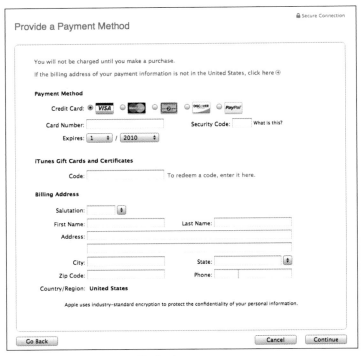

2.4 Specify iTunes Payment Method

Caution

iTunes gift cards and gift certificates may only be redeemed at the iTunes Store for the country where they were purchased. This is something to be aware of if you travel to other countries. Gift cards purchased while abroad may end up being of no use to you once you arrive home.

Note

Apple sells themed gift cards for specific types of content, such as iBooks or Apps. Despite this branding, all gift cards translate to store credit and can be used to purchase any type of content on the iTunes Store.

Making Allowances

The iTunes Store provides a useful feature for parents who do not want to give their off-spring carte blanche on the iTunes Store by setting up an account with a credit card. Instead, you set up an iTunes Store account normally for yourself and then set up an allowance under the Buy iTunes Gifts section of the iTunes Store. Your son or daughter receives an e-mail with the allowance amount and instructions on setting up his or her own iTunes Store account. Once this is set up, on the first of each month the specified amount is automatically billed to your credit card through your own iTunes Store account and credited to your child's iTunes Store account. The effect is the same as buying a gift card for the account, except that the money is added automatically on a monthly basis.

Of course, you can modify or cancel an allowance at any time, and you can still purchase gift certificates to supplement the allowance credit for those special occasions when you want to give a bit more.

What you can do with content purchased from the iTunes Store

Traditionally, almost all of the content that you purchased from the iTunes Store was protected by the FairPlay digital rights management (DRM) system from Apple. Although Apple has removed DRM protection from its music catalog in recent years, other content such as audiobooks, movies and TV shows retain the same DRM protection and accompanying restrictions. The bad news is that this puts some limitations on what you can actually do with some of the content you purchase, but the good news is that the iTunes restrictions are actually some of the most generous of any DRM-laden online media store.

Note

There is a distinction between iTunes Store Gift Cards and Apple Store Gift Cards. Apple Store Gift Cards may be redeemed for Apple product purchases at all Apple retail stores and the Apple Store (which is online), but cannot be used on the iTunes Store, although you can purchase an iTunes Store Gift Card from the Apple Store. Likewise, an iTunes Store Gift Card can only be used to purchase media content on the iTunes Store, and cannot be used at the Apple Store or Apple retail stores.

Basically, the restrictions on DRM-protected iTunes Store purchases are as follows:

- **You can play back your purchased content through iTunes on up to five authorized computers.** Note that this limit is based on five computers authorized at any given time, and these authorizations can be moved to other computers, which I discuss a bit later in this chapter.

- **You can transfer your purchased content to an unlimited number of iPods, iPhones, or iPads from any one of your five authorized computers.**

- **You can transfer your purchased content to up to five first-generation Apple TV devices.**

- **You can burn individual audio tracks to audio CDs an unlimited number of times.** The only restriction on burning audio tracks is that you can only burn the same playlist a maximum of seven times. This is presumably to prevent mass reproduction of the same CD.

- **You cannot convert a copy-protected iTunes Store purchase to another format (for example, AAC to MP3), at least, not directly.** You can get around this for music by burning your purchases to CD and then importing them in your preferred format, but this is a time-consuming process and can result in a potential loss in audio quality as the files are recompressed. Note that this does not apply to music tracks purchased after June 2009.

- **You cannot play this content on a non-Apple device.** Apple has not licensed its FairPlay DRM to any third parties.

- **You cannot burn movies, TV shows, or music videos to DVD.**

In 2007, Apple introduced iTunes Plus content to the iTunes Store, which was made available in conjunction with certain music labels that were willing to sell their content without digital restrictions. iTunes Plus content comes in a higher-quality 256 kbps AAC format, and contains no DRM restrictions whatsoever. Purchased tracks are still tagged with your iTunes Store account information for tracking purposes, but you can otherwise use them on any device supporting the AAC format, freely convert them to another format such as MP3, and use them on as many different devices as you please, whether or not they are made by Apple.

In January 2009, Apple announced that it was converting the remainder of the iTunes Store music catalog over to the iTunes Plus format, a process that was completed by mid-2009. All music purchased from the iTunes Store today is now DRM free; however, users with tracks in their library purchased prior to that time may need to pay a nominal per-track fee to convert them into the new iTunes Plus format in order to remove the DRM.

Genius

Purchased content redownloaded via iTunes in the Cloud, discussed later in this chapter, is always in iTunes Plus format, regardless of the format it was originally purchased in.

Despite the removal of FairPlay DRM on music tracks on the iTunes Store, other types of content such as movies and TV shows remain DRM protected and subject to the restrictions noted earlier.

Purchasing items with bonus content

With the release of iTunes 9 in the fall of 2009, Apple also introduced two new types of bonus content to the iTunes Store:

- **iTunes LP.** This is a bonus package available with specific albums that provides additional rich-media content such as interactive liner notes, lyrics, performance videos, and photos.

- **iTunes Extras.** These are included with specific movies to provide additional content similar to that found on commercial DVDs such as deleted scenes, interviews, director's commentary, and cast and crew information.

Albums and movies that include bonus content are identified on the iTunes Store by a specific icon. iTunes LPs and iTunes Extras are downloaded automatically with their accompanying purchased album or movie. At this time, these features can only be viewed directly on your computer or on the first-generation Apple TV; the iPod, iPhone, and iPad do not support or provide any capability for syncing this content, nor does the new second-generation Apple TV released in September 2010.

Creating an iTunes Store Wish List

One of the problems with the iTunes Store is that sometimes it's a bit too easy to go on a shopping spree. The iTunes Store uses a one-click purchasing system, which means that as soon as you see something you like, you click the button, and it is immediately purchased, billed to your account, and downloaded to your computer. Although this is very convenient, if you're a compulsive buyer such convenience may be hard on your monthly credit card bill.

Fortunately, the iTunes Store provides a Wish List feature that you can use to keep track of items that you may want to purchase later without having to immediately go for the Buy Now button.

Note Previous versions of iTunes also offered a Shopping Cart method for purchasing items from the iTunes Store. Sadly, this option was removed in iTunes 9.

To add items to your iTunes Store Wish List, follow these steps:

1. **Locate an item on the iTunes Store that you want to add to your Wish List.** You can search for a specific item or simply browse through the store.

2. **Click the small triangle to the right of the Buy button.** A drop-down menu appears similar to Figure 2.5.

3. **Choose Add to Wish List.** The selected item is added to your iTunes Store Wish List.

You can view your iTunes Store Wish List page by selecting the My Wish List option from the main iTunes Store home page, as shown in Figure 2.6. Note that the number of items on your Wish List is displayed to the right of the My Wish List option.

Items can be purchased from your Wish List page in the same manner as any other iTunes Store page.

2.5 iTunes Store Buy Options

2.6 iTunes Store Quick Links

Creating an iTunes Store playlist

As an alternative to using the iTunes Store Wish List, you can create a normal playlist in iTunes to use as a wish list and add tracks to it directly from the iTunes Store. Follow these steps:

1. **Create a new playlist by choosing File ⇨ New Playlist from the iTunes menu.** An untitled playlist appears in your Source list with the name selected for editing.

2. **Type a name for the new playlist and press Enter.** Call it whatever you like.

3. **Visit the iTunes Store and enable the Browser View by choosing View ⇨ Column Browser ⇨ Show Column Browser.**

4. **Browse for tracks that you want to add to your iTunes Store Wish List.**

5. **Drag and drop these tracks from the iTunes Store window to the iTunes playlist that you created in Step 1.**

6. **Select the playlist in iTunes, and you should see that the tracks have been added as iTunes Store references, similar to Figure 2.7.**

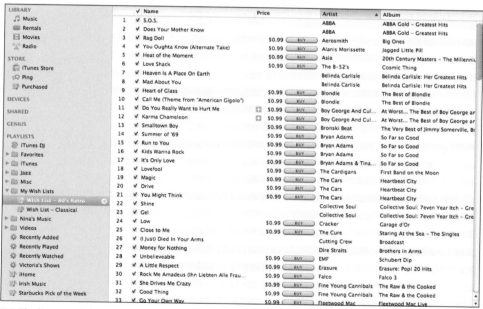

2.7 Playlist containing iTunes Store Items

You can preview iTunes Store tracks directly from your playlist simply by double-clicking on them, or purchase the track by clicking the Buy button that appears to the right of the track name column. Purchased items automatically replace the iTunes Store link in the playlist.

Sharing iTunes Store items on Facebook and Twitter

iTunes 9 introduced a new feature allowing you to share links to your favorite iTunes Store items to either your Facebook page or your Twitter stream.

1. **Locate an item on the iTunes Store that you want to share on Facebook or Twitter.**
   You can search for a specific item or simply browse through the store.

2. **Click the small triangle to the right of the Buy button.** A drop-down menu appears similar to Figure 2.8.

3. **Choose Share on Facebook or Share on Twitter.** Facebook or Twitter opens in your browser with information and an iTunes Store link for the selected item already filled in, similar to Figure 2.9.

2.8 iTunes Store buy options

2.9 Sharing an iTunes Store item on Facebook

Getting Social with Ping

With the release of iTunes 10 in September 2010, iTunes takes sharing your musical tastes and discovering new music on the iTunes Store to a whole new level. iTunes 10 introduces a new music-centric social network known as Ping. Integrated completely into the iTunes app, Ping simply appears as a new section prominently displayed immediately below the iTunes Store on the left side of your iTunes window. Selecting the Ping section in iTunes or responding to a Ping friend request from outside of iTunes opens the main Ping page in the iTunes Store and gives you the option to enable Ping, as shown in Figure 2.10.

2.10 Ping welcome screen

Setting up Ping

Enabling Ping requires that you sign in with your iTunes Store Apple ID and password, after which you are prompted to set up your Ping profile, as shown in Figure 2.11.

Caution

As indicated in fine print below the Name fields, the process of setting up a Ping profile also replaces your nickname with your real name on any previous reviews that you have left on the iTunes Store. You can view and manage your reviews in your iTunes Store account settings to remove any that you may not want associated with your real name.

After filling in your personal details, you must then choose your privacy preferences for your Ping account. Ping uses a one-way "follower" model similar to Twitter, allowing users to follow each other without requiring a reciprocal relationship. The Privacy options are as follows:

- **Allow people to follow me.** This allows any other user to view your Ping profile and follow you. You are not notified of new followers — they simply appear in your followers list.

2.11 Creating a Ping profile

- **Require my approval to follow me.** Other Ping users can find your profile and view basic information, such as your name, but must send a request to follow you. You are notified by e-mail of new follow requests and must approve them individually before those users can follow you and see your full profile.

● **Don't allow people to follow me**. Your Ping profile is essentially hidden. You can still follow other members, but they cannot find your profile in a search or even request to follow you. Your name still appears in reviews of iTunes Store content and comments on other users' Ping profiles, however.

After you set up your Ping user profile, you are taken to the Ping home page and offered some recommendations on artists and other users who you may want to follow as well as a search field to locate other users and artists to follow. Once you're following some other users, your home page also displays a list of recent activity from those users who you are following, including other users who they have started following and items that they have recently commented on or indicated that they like, similar to Figure 2.12.

After you've enabled Ping, Like and Post buttons are displayed beneath the album artwork and purchasing options for music on the iTunes Store and also appear on the drop-down menu for the Buy button, similar to the Facebook and Twitter sharing options discussed previously in this chapter. Clicking the Like button allows you to simply indicate that you like a specific item without further comment, while the Post button allows you to actually make a comment on the album or track. Tracks you like and any comments you post appear on your Ping profile page and in your Ping stream to your followers.

2.12 Ping home page

Note

At this time, Ping is intended to be a music-centric social network, and the Like and Post buttons are limited to music content only. Other content, such as movies, TV shows, podcasts, and apps do not have any Like or Post options available, although any reviews that you post on any item in the ITunes Store displays your full name and appears in your My Reviews page.

Renting Video Content from the iTunes Store

In January 2008, Apple announced that it would begin offering movie rentals through the iTunes Store, akin to the video-on-demand services that many cable operators offer. Of course, unlike purchased content, which you get to keep in your iTunes library in perpetuity, rentals eventually must be returned to the store.

The Apple solution to this problem was relatively straightforward. Although you purchase rentals through iTunes in much the same way as any other type of content, these rentals simply expire after a specific time frame. When you rent a movie, you can store it in your iTunes library or on an Apple media device, such as an iPod or Apple TV for up to 30 days, after which it is automatically deleted whether you have watched it or not.

After you actually "break the seal" and start watching a rented movie, it expires in 24-48 hours depending on which country you're in, whether you have actually finished watching it or not. You can, however, watch the movie as many times as you want within that time period, and, in fact, if you begin watching a movie even one minute before it is due to expire, you are permitted to continue watching it, and even pause, rewind, and fast-forward through the movie. The expiry is enforced only when you actually stop watching the movie or leave it on pause for an extended period of time.

The other major difference in how rentals are handled as compared to purchased content is that a rental can only be stored on a single Apple device at a time. So if you rent a movie on your computer using iTunes and want to watch it on your iPod, you must move it to the iPod. If you later decide that you want to finish watching it on your computer, you must move it back. You must also be connected to the iTunes Store when moving rented content between devices so that the necessary authorization information can be updated.

Note also that movie rentals do not include iTunes Extra content, and although high-definition movies can be rented directly in iTunes, unlike a purchased movie, a rented movie does not include the standard-definition version.

Note Movies can be rented directly from Apple TV, iPhone, iPod touch, and iPad devices. Movies rented on older iPhone or iPod touch devices can be moved back to iTunes; however, movies rented on an Apple TV, iPad, iPhone 4/4S, or fourth-generation iPod touch can only be watched on the device they were rented on — they cannot be transferred to iTunes or to other devices.

Working with Season Pass for TV shows

If you purchase current TV content through iTunes, you may have noticed that some shows have a Season Pass option listed beside them, whereas others merely have an option to buy the season outright.

A Season Pass is a feature of the iTunes Store that is offered for some TV shows that allows you to buy all of the current episodes and future episodes from a given season in a single transaction. When you purchase the Season Pass, all of the available episodes for that season are downloaded immediately. As new episodes become available, they are automatically downloaded to your designated iTunes library, saving you the trouble of having to visit the iTunes Store each week to check for and get the latest episodes.

Setting iTunes to automatically download new episodes

To get the most out of a Season Pass, you should enable the setting in your iTunes preferences to automatically download prepurchased content as it becomes available. Follow these steps:

1. **Open your iTunes preferences and click the Store tab, as shown in Figure 2.13.**

2.13 The Store tab of the iTunes Store preferences dialog box

2. **Select Automatically download pre-orders when available.**

3. **Click OK.**

As new episodes become available in your Season Pass, they are automatically downloaded to your iTunes library and become available for viewing through iTunes or on any other device you are synchronizing them to.

Managing your Season Passes

From your iTunes Store account page, you can view a list of your current Season Passes. This screen also allows you to check for any pending episodes that have not yet been downloaded and control whether or not you receive e-mail notifications when new episodes are available for a given Season Pass. Follow these steps:

1. **Choose Store ⇨ View My Account from the iTunes menu.**

2. **Type your iTunes Store account name and password when prompted.** You are taken to your iTunes Store account information screen, similar to Figure 2.14.

3. **Click the Manage link beside the Passes entry.** You are shown a page listing all of your current and completed Season Passes, similar to Figure 2.15.

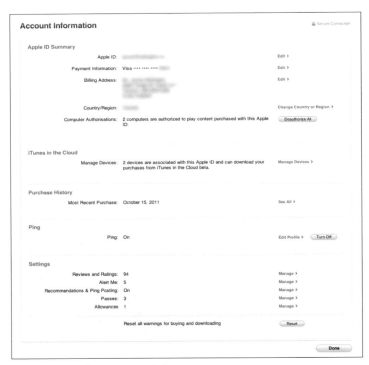

2.14 An iTunes Store account information screen

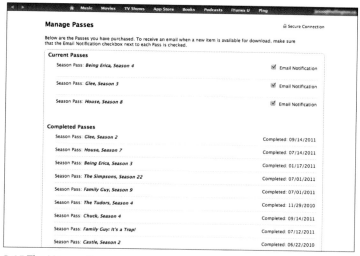

2.15 The Manage Passes screen

4. **Select or deselect the Email Notification check box to turn e-mail notifications on or off for a given Season Pass.**

5. **If a Season Pass shows any episodes awaiting download, clicking the notification checks for and downloads any missing episodes.**

6. **Click Done to return to the iTunes Store account information screen and save any changes to the Email Notification settings.**

Note

You may find that the information on the Manage Passes screen about Season Passes and pending episodes is not entirely accurate. Season Passes sometimes remain listed as current after they have ended, and sometimes a Season Pass even shows new episodes available that have already been downloaded. These are simply display issues that should not affect how your Season Passes actually work.

Purchasing high-definition content

You can purchase certain TV shows and movies in high-definition (HD) format from the iTunes Store, where available. These are purchased in the same way as standard-definition (SD) videos, except that they are slightly more expensive and include both a 720p high-definition version that you can watch on your computer, Apple TV, iPad, iPhone 4/4S, or fourth-generation iPod touch and a standard-definition version that is also compatible with older iPhone and video-capable iPod models.

When you purchase an HD TV episode or movie, both versions are downloaded to your computer; however, they appear as a single entry in your iTunes library. By default, the HD version is used when watching the episode on your computer, Apple TV, iPad, iPhone 4/4S, or fourth-generation iPod touch and the SD version is automatically selected if you choose to sync the TV show to an older iPod or iPhone model. Selecting HD and SD content for playback in iTunes is discussed in more detail in Chapter 4.

Note

Note that when renting HD movies from iTunes only the HD version is downloaded, and can therefore only be viewed on your computer, Apple TV, iPad, iPhone 4/4S, or fourth-generation iPod touch.

Subscribing to podcasts from the iTunes Store

With the exception of a few weekly promotional items, much of the content available directly from the iTunes Store comes at a cost. However, the iTunes Store also provides a gateway to a large amount of free content in the form of podcasts.

Podcasts are independently produced programs similar in concept to radio shows and cable-access TV shows. Some podcasts are simply produced by individuals, while others are podcast versions of popular radio programs made available by the broadcasters themselves. These days, you can find podcasts on a wide variety of subjects, from arts and music to science and technology to business and finance.

Apple doesn't provide podcasts directly from the iTunes Store. Instead, it simply provides a directory of podcasts to allow you to quickly and effectively locate podcasts that may be of interest.

Subscribing to podcasts

You search for and subscribe to podcasts through iTunes in much the same way as you purchase music. Follow these steps:

1. **Browse the iTunes Store to find a podcast that interests you.** If you click the title of the podcast, you should see a summary screen similar to Figure 2.16.

2. **Click Subscribe Free if you want to subscribe to the podcast to receive new episodes on a regular basis.** The current episode(s) are downloaded immediately, and any new episodes are automatically downloaded as they become available. Some podcasts publish new content very infrequently, while others are updated daily, so be sure you know what you're getting into before subscribing to a podcast.

2.16 A podcast information screen

3. **If you want to download only one or two specific episodes of a podcast, click the Free button beside the specific podcast episodes that you want to download.** The selected episodes are downloaded immediately, but you are not subscribed to the podcast, and so new episodes are not downloaded unless you revisit this page and select them manually.

Viewing your podcast subscriptions

You can find a listing of all podcasts that you have downloaded or subscribed to by selecting the Podcasts listing in iTunes.

As shown in Figure 2.17, podcasts for which you have downloaded individual episodes have a Subscribe button next to the podcast series title, allowing you to subscribe to the entire podcast if you like. For episodes that have not yet been downloaded, a Get button displays to allow you to manually download these additional episodes, and a Get All button displays to allow you to download all episodes.

To unsubscribe from a podcast, simply delete the podcast series title from this listing in the same way as any other item in your iTunes library. All podcast episodes are removed and iTunes no longer looks for and downloads new episodes. As an alternative, you can keep the podcast series in your library and simply turn off automatic updating as described in the next section.

2.17 The iTunes Podcasts listing

Managing podcast download settings

You can set how often iTunes checks for new episodes of any podcasts you're subscribed to, and how many episodes are automatically downloaded, by visiting your iTunes preferences. Follow these steps:

1. **Select Podcasts from the iTunes Source list.** The Podcasts listing appears.

2. **Click Settings at the bottom of the Podcasts listing screen.** The Podcast Settings dialog box appears, as shown in Figure 2.18.

2.18 The iTunes Podcast Settings dialog box

3. **From the Check for new episodes drop-down menu, select how often you want iTunes to automatically check for new podcast episodes.** Options are Every hour, Every day, Every week, or Manually. You can also select how many episodes to download when new episodes are available by selecting a specific podcast subscription from this drop-down menu. Managing podcasts is discussed further in Chapter 6.

4. **From the When new episodes are available drop-down menu, select how many new episodes you want to download.** Options are as follows:

    ●   **Download all.** Downloads all new episodes that have become available since the last time iTunes checked for new episodes.

    ●   **Download the most recent one.** Downloads only the most recent episode. Other episodes are still listed under the podcast subscription in iTunes so that you can download them manually if you want them by clicking the Get button from the podcast listing in iTunes.

    ●   **Do nothing.** The podcast listing is updated to show the new episodes, but you need to download them manually using the Get button from the podcast listing in iTunes.

Authorizing and deauthorizing your computer

As I mentioned earlier in this chapter, older music tracks and all audiobooks, TV shows, and movies purchased from the iTunes Store are protected by digital rights management (DRM), which controls how and where this content may be used. To play back this protected content in iTunes, you must ensure that your computer is authorized for the iTunes Store account that was used to purchase this content.

Authorizing iTunes on your computer

Normally, when you first purchase content from iTunes on a given computer, that computer is automatically authorized for your iTunes Store account. If you transfer purchased content to another computer, however, you need to specifically authorize it before you can play that content or transfer it further to an iPod, iPhone, or iPad.

iTunes should normally prompt you to authorize your computer the first time that you attempt to play back a track that requires authorization; however, you can also authorize your computer manually. Follow these steps:

1. **Choose Store ⇨ Authorize Computer from the iTunes menu.** An iTunes Store Authorize Computer dialog box appears, as shown in Figure 2.19.

2. **Type your Apple ID and password.**
   Your Apple ID is the login name used to access your iTunes Store account.

3. **Click Authorize.** Provided you have not already reached your five-computer limit, iTunes should respond with a message that your authorization was successful and indicate how many authorizations have been used, as shown in Figure 2.20.

2.19 The iTunes Store Authorize Computer dialog box

If you are using more than one iTunes Store account on a single computer (for different family members, for example), then you must repeat this process for each additional iTunes Store account that you have purchased content from.

2.20 The iTunes authorization is successful.

Note Reauthorizing an existing computer does not use up any additional authorizations, provided that the software and hardware configuration has not changed. iTunes still displays a dialog box to indicate how many authorizations have been used, but the number should remain the same each time.

Deauthorizing iTunes on your computer

Because you are limited to a total of five computers that may be authorized at any given time, you should always deauthorize a computer for your iTunes Store account before selling it or reinstalling your operating system. Deauthorizing a computer is about as simple as authorizing it in the first place. Follow these steps:

1. **Choose Store ⇨ Deauthorize Computer from the iTunes menu.** The iTunes Store Deauthorize This Computer dialog box appears, as shown in Figure 2.21.

2. **Type your Apple ID and password.**
   Your Apple ID is the login name used to access your iTunes Store account.

2.21 The iTunes Store Deauthorize This Computer dialog box

3. **Click Deauthorize.** iTunes responds with a dialog box indicating that the deauthorization is successful.

Note

Always ensure that you deauthorize your computer before reinstalling the operating system, taking it in for service, or performing major hardware upgrades on it. iTunes stores its authorization based on your specific configuration, so any major changes require the computer to be reauthorized as if it were new. Further, because the old configuration is gone, you have no way of deauthorizing the old computer. You could quickly reach your five-computer authorization limit if you regularly reinstall your operating system or upgrade your computer without deauthorizing first.

Resetting your authorization count

iTunes limits you to a maximum of five computers that may be authorized for an iTunes Store account at any given time. Although I explained earlier how you can deauthorize a computer, that only works if you still have the computer in your possession, and you have not reinstalled the operating system.

It's not uncommon for iTunes users to get into trouble by not realizing that they need to deauthorize a computer before they reinstall their operating system or perform a major hardware upgrade. Further, even the most diligent user sometimes encounters circumstances beyond his or her control. Sometimes a computer just dies and there is really no way you can get at it to deauthorize it, and, of course, it's not uncommon for many computer repair shops to just reinstall the operating system on your behalf without realizing that iTunes needs to be deauthorized first.

Fortunately, Apple offers a solution: You can reset your authorization count and all of your authorizations from your iTunes Store Apple Account Information page. Note that once you do this, any computers that you want to continue using iTunes on must be reauthorized manually by following the steps earlier in this chapter.

1. **Choose Store ⇨ View My Account from the iTunes menu.**

2. **Type your iTunes Store account name and password when prompted.** You are taken to your iTunes Store Apple Account Information page, similar to Figure 2.22.

3. **Beside Computer Authorizations, you can see information on how many computers are authorized for this account.** A Deauthorize All button appears beside this entry.

4. **Click Deauthorize All.** You are prompted to confirm that you want to deauthorize all of your registered computers.

2.22 The iTunes Store Apple Account Information page

5. **Click Deauthorize All Computers in the confirmation dialog box.** Your authorization count is reset to zero. Note that any computers that you still plan to use with iTunes need to be reauthorized manually.

Keep in mind that you can only do this once per year, and so this should not be considered a practical alternative to deauthorizing your computer manually; however, it can save you the trouble of having to contact iTunes Store customer service if you find yourself in a situation where you've used up all of your authorizations on only one or two computers.

Downloading Content from iTunes in the Cloud

In June 2011 Apple debuted its new iCloud online service, which, among other things, introduced the capability to redownload certain types of previously purchased content from the iTunes Store. Users had always been able to redownload their previously purchased applications, as these were exclusively under Apple's control; however, licensing restrictions with various content providers and copyright holders had previously precluded Apple from offering the capability to redownload items, such as music without repurchasing that content again.

Depending on what country you're in, with iTunes 10.3 or later you can now redownload any music, TV shows, or iBooks that you have previously purchased from the iTunes Store at no additional charge. To access and redownload your prior purchases

1. **From the iTunes Store, click the Purchased link in the Quick Links bar at the top-right corner, as shown in Figure 2.23.** The Purchased content section appears, similar to Figure 2.24.

2. **Select the type of content you would like to redownload, such as Music, TV Shows, Apps, or Books.** Note that the type of content available may vary depending on which country you are in.

3. **Choose All or Not In Library from the top-right corner to view a list of all available content that you have previously purchased or only display that content that is not already in your iTunes library.**

4. **For music or TV shows, select an artist or show from the left-hand column.** The right-hand panel updates to display only the content for the selected artist or show. You can also search for a specific item by entering text in the search field at the top of this list. Apps and books simply display a thumbnail view of purchased content with no additional filtering options, as shown in Figure 2.25.

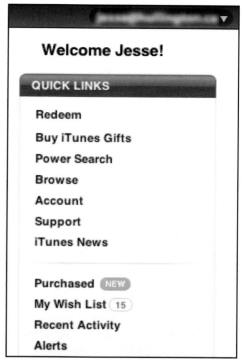

2.23 iTunes Store Quick Links

5. **Click the iCloud download button to the right of the items you want to redownload.** iTunes begins redownloading the selected items. Note that the iCloud button is only available for items that are not already in your iTunes library.

Note You can only redownload content from one iTunes account to a given computer within a 90-day period; after you have redownloaded something from iTunes in the Cloud, you must wait 90 days before you can redownload content from a different iTunes Store account. This restriction does not apply to apps, however.

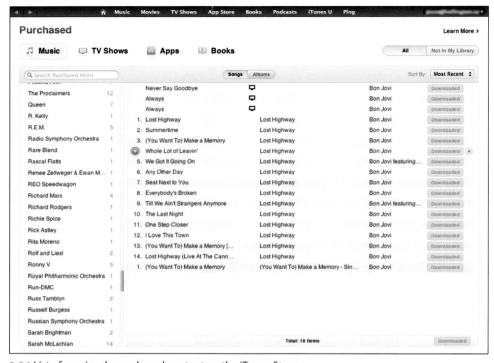

2.24 List of previously purchased content on the iTunes Store

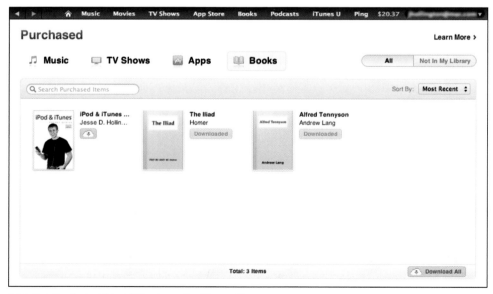

2.25 Previously purchased iBooks on the iTunes Store

Automatically downloading content purchased from other computers or devices

iTunes in the Cloud also allows you to configure iTunes to automatically download apps, music, or books purchased with the same iTunes Store account from another iTunes library or iOS device. To configure this

1. **Open your iTunes preferences and click the Store tab, as shown in Figure 2.26.**

2. **Select the types of content you want iTunes to automatically download when purchased from another iTunes library or iOS device.**

3. **Click OK.**

Note iTunes can only automatically download content from a single iTunes Store account, and you must wait 90 days before configuring a different account. The 90-day restriction does not apply to apps, however.

2.26 The Store tab of the iTunes Store preferences dialog box

Using Other Digital Media Stores

Although the iTunes Store was among the first online media stores to provide iTunes- and iPod-compatible content, and is still the top online music retailer in the world, it is not the only game in town. Many other online music stores have emerged in the past few years, and with the music industry relaxing its attitude toward DRM restrictions, many of these stores are now iTunes and iPod compatible.

Types of supported digital media stores

The first and most important thing to keep in mind when shopping around for other online music stores is to look at the format in which they provide their content. In the days when almost all online media content was sold with DRM restrictions, the iTunes Store really was the only option for iTunes and iPod users because Apple had not licensed its FairPlay DRM to third parties. The result was that most other online media stores sold music in the Microsoft PlaysForSure Windows Media Audio (WMA) DRM format, which was completely incompatible with iTunes and the iPod.

Although some online media stores are still only providing music in the protected WMA format, the good news is that many of these stores are starting to abandon this format in favor of the more open-standard MP3 format, which includes no DRM protection and can be played on just about any digital audio player on the market, including software and hardware devices from Apple.

Other online stores are normally accessed through your Web browser, and purchased tracks are downloaded as standard MP3 downloads. These files are then imported into your iTunes library in the same way as any other MP3 file.

Some good examples of online music stores that now sell music in an unprotected MP3 format are Amazon.com, Walmart.com, Napster, Rhapsody, and eMusic.com. Unfortunately most of these are only available to users in the United States at this time.

Purchasing audiobooks from Audible.com

If you like listening to audiobooks, an alternative source of content to the iTunes Store is Audible.com, one of the first and largest online audiobook providers. In fact, much of the audiobook content that is available on the iTunes Store actually comes from Audible and is merely resold by iTunes.

Generally for one-time purchases, the prices of audiobooks on Audible are not much different from the iTunes Store. However, for an audiobook enthusiast, Audible offers subscription plans that are economical because you can generally get several audiobooks per month for a fixed monthly price, regardless of individual cost.

The Audible content is protected by its own proprietary DRM similar to content purchased from the iTunes Store, with slightly tighter restrictions: Only three computers can be authorized to play back Audible content.

Purchasing audiobooks from Audible.com is handled through the Audible Web site, where you sign up for an account independently of your iTunes Store account and download content directly through your Web browser. For Mac users, Audible content is downloaded directly into iTunes from the Audible Web site. Windows users require an additional Audible Download Manager plug-in, available from the Audible Web site.

Note

Your Audible account is authorized separately from your iTunes Store account, and the number of authorized computers is limited to three. As with your iTunes Store authorizations, always ensure that you deauthorize your Audible account by choosing Advanced ⇨ Deauthorize Audible Account before selling, upgrading, or performing other maintenance on your computer.

Note

Audible content can be played in iTunes and on the iPod, iPhone, and iPad. Notably, however, the Apple TV is not compatible with the DRM used by Audible because of licensing restrictions, so you will not be able to listen to your Audible.com audiobooks on an Apple TV.

If you have your iTunes library loaded up with your music, videos, and other content, now you need to know how to make the best use of that content. The best place to start is by organizing it so that you can find it and use it. iTunes is an outstanding media-management application, but getting the most out of it requires that you take the time to properly label and catalog your content and organize it in the way that works best for you.

Organizing Music Content

Despite the added capabilities of modern versions of iTunes to handle video and other types of content, you are probably going to find that the majority of your content is still actually music and that you spend most of your time working with your music collection.

As I mentioned in Chapter 1, iTunes uses a tag-based system to keep track of your music rather than relying on a file and folder structure. As a result, it is absolutely essential that your music be tagged properly if you are going to get the most out of your iTunes experience. Music imported from CDs or purchased from online music stores normally has this information filled in for you, but music from other sources may not. Further, you may find that you don't like the way a particular field is filled in and want to change it to your liking.

Filling in required tags

For music content, three tags are required for your music to be properly organized by iTunes and on your iPod. These are the Name, Artist, and Album fields. iTunes organizes your music, both within its own menus as well as within the underlying file system, based on these three tags. Although iTunes doesn't force you to fill in the Artist and Album fields, you may find your music very difficult to locate, particularly on your iPod, if these fields are left blank.

To fill in the artist and album information for a single track, follow these steps:

1. **Select the track that you would like to edit.**

2. **Choose File ⇨ Get Info from the iTunes menu.** A dialog box similar to Figure 3.1 appears.

3. **Fill in or edit the Name, Artist, and Album fields with the appropriate information.**

4. **Click OK.**

Genius

You can also edit name, artist, and album track properties from the iTunes track listing. Simply click twice (two single clicks, not a double-click) on the field that you want to edit and type the new information.

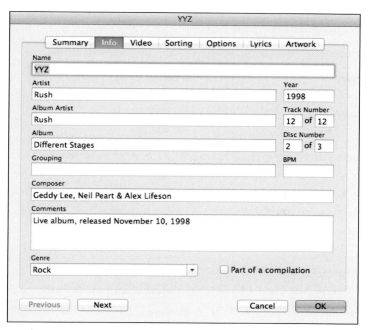

3.1 The iTunes Track Properties dialog box

Filling in optional tags

In addition to the standard tags that are required to organize your music, you have probably noticed that there are a lot of additional properties for any given track. Some of these fields are used to aid in sorting and organizing your music, while others are simply for reference purposes.

- **Year.** This should contain the year the track or album was produced. Most tracks downloaded from CDDB or the iTunes Store contain the album year in this field, regardless of when the original song may have been produced. This can be used for sorting.

- **Album Artist.** This should contain the name of the artist for the album as a whole. This is generally used for albums with guest artists or featured artists to indicate the primary artist for the album. For single-artist albums, it is usually either blank or the same as the Artist field for all of the individual tracks. This is used primarily for grouping and sorting. iPod and iOS devices use this field in different ways; I discuss this in more detail in Chapter 8.

- **Track Number.** This would contain the number of the track from a CD or album and the total number of tracks. This is used primarily for sorting both in iTunes and on the iPod to list tracks in their proper album order when viewing an album listing. If this field is blank, tracks are sorted within each album alphabetically instead of by track number.

- **Disc Number.** For multidisc albums, this field contains the disc number that this track is from and the total number of discs. Like Track Number, it is used primarily for sorting of multidisc albums to ensure that tracks appear in their proper order.

- **Grouping.** This field is used primarily for classical works to group movements of the same work together during playback. The Grouping in this case would specify the name of the overall work for each movement. For example, if you have a recording of Beethoven's Fifth Symphony, each of the four movements is an individual track with the title of the movement itself as the track number, but all four tracks would contain "Beethoven: Symphony No. 5 in C minor, Op 67" in the Grouping field.

- **BPM.** This field is used to enter the tempo of a track in beats per minute. It is normally blank and is used primarily for reference purposes and as a criterion for Smart Playlists. Third-party tools are available to assist in entering this information into your tracks.

- **Composer.** This field lists the composer of a work. Depending on the work in question, this may be the same as the artist, or it may indicate the lyricist, songwriter, or classical composer. Music can be grouped and searched for by composer as another level of organization in iTunes and on the iPod. This is particularly useful for classical music listeners, although many contemporary tracks downloaded from the iTunes Store also contain information in this field.

- **Comments.** This is a free-form field where additional comments may be entered. This is used primarily for reference purposes, although you can also search this field and use it in Smart Playlists.

- **Genre.** This lists the genre of the track in question. You can select from one of the existing genres or simply type your own.

- **Part of a compilation.** This indicates that this track is part of a multiartist compilation album. This feature is covered in more detail later in this chapter.

Although some of the tags stored within your tracks are primarily informational, almost all of them may be searched for within iTunes, providing an easy way to quickly locate groups of tracks based on this additional information. Further, these tags can be used in Smart Playlists to provide a very effective way of selecting and managing the content you listen to. Smart Playlists are discussed in more detail in Chapter 5.

The Beat Goes In

A very useful field in your iTunes library is the BPM, or Beats Per Minute, field. This is often ignored by iTunes users because they either do not understand it, or they simply don't know of any easy way to get information into it. The field itself is used to store a number representing the tempo of each song expressed as an average number of beats per minute. Although you can technically put any number you want in this field, it is most effective when you use numbers that represent the tempo of your music as closely as possible because you can then easily build Smart Playlists that automatically select music based on tempo — for example, you could easily generate an upbeat workout mix or a mix of slow music to relax by.

The trick to making the most use of this is getting valid information into the BPM field. Fortunately, third-party tools handle this for you by analyzing your music library and updating the field directly. Some of the more popular options include the following:

- **MixMeister BPM Analyzer (www.mixmeister.com/bpmanalyzer).** A free tool available in both Mac and Windows flavors, this will quickly analyze any set of MP3 files you throw at it and write the results directly into the BPM field. Unfortunately, AAC files are not supported.

- **iTunes-BPM (www.blacktree.com, under More Projects).** Another free tool for Mac users that takes a slightly different approach by simply displaying a window that you click on in time to the beat of the song while actually listening to your music. The result is calculated and added to your iTunes library. The advantage is that it supports any format that iTunes can play, including DRM-protected iTunes Store files. The obvious disadvantage is that it's only slightly less arduous of a task than manually typing values into the BPM field yourself.

- **Tangerine (www.potionfactory.com).** A $25 shareware tool similar in concept to MixMeister BPM, but only available for Mac users. This tool has the advantage of supporting both MP3 and unprotected AAC formats and can automatically read and analyze your iTunes library and write the BPM information directly back in.

- **beaTunes (www.beatunes.com).** A $32 shareware tool for both Mac and Windows that not only performs BPM analysis but can also handle other iTunes library analysis and cleanup functions, such as correcting inconsistent artist names. Also supports both MP3 and unprotected AAC formats.

Tagging multiple tracks simultaneously

Tagging individual tracks is sometimes necessary to get information like track names and numbers correct, but when putting information into common fields such as Album and Artist, editing multiple tracks at once is more effective. Follow these steps:

1. **Select the tracks you would like to edit.** As with any other application, you can use the Shift key to select a range of tracks and the ⌘ key (Mac) or Ctrl key (Windows) to select multiple noncontiguous tracks. You can also press ⌘+A (Mac) or Ctrl+A (Windows) to select all of the tracks currently displayed.

2. **Choose File ⇨ Get Info from the iTunes menu.** If this is the first time you have done this, you may receive a prompt asking you if you want to edit the properties for multiple items. If this dialog box appears, click Yes to continue. The Multiple Item Information dialog box appears, as shown in Figure 3.2.

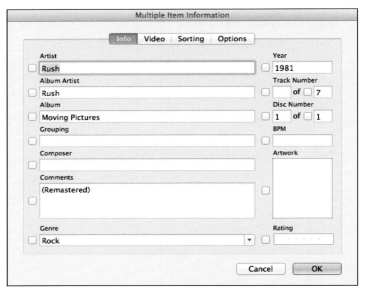

3.2 The iTunes Multiple Item Information dialog box

3. **Fill in the properties that are common to all of the selected tracks.** Note that properties that are the same for all tracks are filled in already, but you can modify them by typing over them.

4. **Ensure that the check boxes beside any fields you want to modify are selected.** These boxes are selected automatically when you modify a field, but you may need to select the check box yourself if you want to clear a field for all of the selected tracks.

5. **Click OK to save your changes.**

Genius

If you have a situation where an artist or album appears twice on your iPod or in iTunes, it is probably because there are invisible differences in the artist or album name between the tracks. The most common cause of this is a space character at the end of an artist or album name. To fix this, select tracks from a given artist or album, and then edit the properties of them all together and retype the artist or album name. This ensures that the information is the same across all tracks.

Filtering and browsing your iTunes library

Although you can easily sort and search for tracks within your iTunes library from the Music view, this process is made much easier by turning on the Column Browser view, which allows you to quickly filter your track listing by genre, artist, and album.

To turn on this view, simply choose View ⇨ Column Browser ⇨ Show Column Browser. The iTunes Column Browser appears at the top of your track listing, similar to Figure 3.3.

3.3 The iTunes Column Browser

With the Column Browser displayed, simply click the information with which you want to filter. The selections in each column work from left to right, so selecting a genre limits the artist listing to only the artists within that genre; likewise, selecting an artist from the second column limits the album listing to only albums by that artist. By default, the Column Browser includes only Genre, Artist, and Album columns; however, you can also add additional columns such as Composer and Groupings from the View ⇨ Column Browser menu.

Genius

You can also press ⌘+B (Mac) or Ctrl+B (Windows) to quickly toggle the iTunes Column Browser on and off.

The iTunes Column Browser can be turned on for almost any listing, including any of the categories in your main iTunes library (such as Music, Movies, and TV Shows) or even within your playlists. Note that the Browser view is set separately for each category; for example, you can have it turned on for your Music listing, but off for your TV Shows.

Recent versions of iTunes also provide the capability to display the Column Browser on the left side of the track listing, as shown in Figure 3.4. This can be set in the View⇨Column Browser submenu.

3.4 The iTunes Column Browser on the left

Genius

If you are editing all of the tracks for an artist or album, speed up the track selection process by selecting the artist or album from the Column Browser view so you can change the information for all tracks by that artist or in that album. There is no need to select the individual tracks, and you can even select multiple artists or albums in this manner to edit all of the tracks together.

Organizing compilation albums

Some of the albums that are in your iTunes library may not have tracks that are all performed by the same artist. These are called *compilations* and include such albums as movie soundtracks and compilations of music from an era or a theme (such as a Best of the '60s album). Because iTunes and the iPod group music primarily by artist, it can be inconvenient to have a bunch of one-hit wonders cluttering up your artist list, and of course, this can also make these albums more difficult to locate.

The solution is to mark these albums as part of a compilation in their track properties and then tell iTunes and your iPod to group your tracks based on these compilation settings.

Marking tracks as part of a compilation

To mark tracks as belonging to a compilation, follow these steps:

1. **Select the tracks you would like to edit.** As with any other application, you can use the Shift key to select a range of tracks and the ⌘ key (Mac) or Ctrl key (Windows) to select multiple noncontiguous tracks. You can also press ⌘+A (Mac) or Ctrl+A (Windows) to select all of the tracks currently displayed.

2. **Choose File ⇨ Get Info from the iTunes menu.** The Multiple Item Information dialog box appears.

3. **Click the Options tab, as shown in Figure 3.5.**

4. **From the Part of a compilation drop-down menu, select Yes.** Note the check box that appears to the left of this field, indicating that it is going to be changed for all selected tracks.

5. **Click OK to save your changes.**

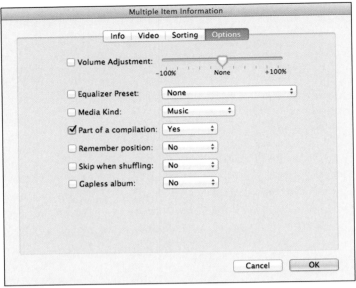

3.5 The iTunes Multiple Item Information dialog box

Setting iTunes to group compilations

After you mark your tracks as part of a compilation, you need to tell iTunes to actually use this field and group your tracks accordingly. This option is toggled by choosing View ➪ Column Browser ➪ Group Compilations. In older versions of iTunes, this setting was found in iTunes Preferences.

Genius

In iTunes 9.1 and later, you can now use the Album Artist field when grouping compilations. This option can be particularly useful for albums that are primarily by a single artist but contain several featured artists. Select this option by choosing View ➪ Column Browser ➪ Use Album Artists.

Adjusting the column headings

iTunes provides a default column listing to get you started, but you can actually view almost any one of the track properties discussed earlier in this chapter within the normal iTunes column view, and you can even sort by any of these properties simply by sorting on the appropriate column heading.

To add or remove a column, follow these steps:

1. **Select the listing in the iTunes Source list that you want to modify.** You may choose either a category from the main iTunes library (such as Music, Movies, or TV Shows) or a playlist. View options are set individually for each listing.

2. **Choose View ⇨ View Options from the iTunes menu.** The View Options dialog box appears, as shown in Figure 3.6.

3.6 The iTunes View Options dialog box

3. **Select the columns that you want displayed.**

4. **Click OK.**

After the additional columns are added, you can reorder them simply by dragging the column headings to the left or right on the listing. Note that the Name column must always remain on the far-left side, however.

Genius

You can also add and remove columns simply by right-clicking the column headings and choosing the columns from the contextual menu.

Sorting your library

You probably already know how to perform basic sorting on your iTunes library: Simply click the column headings you want to sort by, and that's about it. However, iTunes also offers a few hidden sorting options to help you get a bit more control over how your tracks are sorted.

Album by Artist and Album by Artist/Year

The Album column in iTunes actually hides a little-known option. Clicking the Album column heading toggles the heading from merely Album to either Album by Artist or Album by Artist/Year. The column itself contains the same information, but the nature of how your tracks are sorted changes.

- **Album.** This simply sorts your track listing alphabetically by album name. This is the default when sorting on the Album column.

- **Album by Artist.** This sorts your track listing first alphabetically by artist, and then alphabetically by album within each artist. iTunes is also clever enough to recognize albums with multiple artists and compilations based on the value of the appropriate tags, and sorts these separately at the bottom of your track listing.

- **Album by Artist/Year.** This first sorts your track listing alphabetically by artist, and then groups each album within each artist by the year of release, based on the Year tag. If you have tracks in the same album with different years, they are sorted based on the oldest track.

Because iTunes doesn't otherwise offer the capability for secondary or multicolumn sorting, this feature provides a couple of practical predefined sorting and grouping options.

Overriding sorting for individual tracks

When sorting information in your library, iTunes normally sorts numbers and letters separately. Further, starting in iTunes 7.3, Apple made the decision to change the default behavior to always sort numbers at the bottom of a listing rather than at the top. This change confused many iTunes users, because it seems to differ from how most other computer applications work, but it can be easily overridden by specifying individual sorting values for your tracks.

For example, say you have the album *2112* by the band Rush. By default, if you sorted by album, iTunes sorts these tracks at the very bottom of your album listing, as the album name starts with a number. You could change the album tag to read "Twenty One Twelve" and the album would sort correctly based on the phonetic pronunciation of the album, but, of course, no self-respecting Rush fan could ever possibly do such a thing.

Instead, iTunes provides the capability to type different tag information to be used only for sorting purposes, so that you can spell out exactly how you want your tracks sorted without affecting how the information is shown in iTunes or on your iPod. Follow these steps to adjust the sorting fields:

1. **Select an individual track or group of tracks from an album or artist that you want to modify.**

2. **Choose File ⇨ Get Info from the iTunes menu.** The iTunes track properties dialog box appears.

3. **Click the Sorting tab from the top of the dialog box.** The Sorting options are displayed, as shown in Figure 3.7.

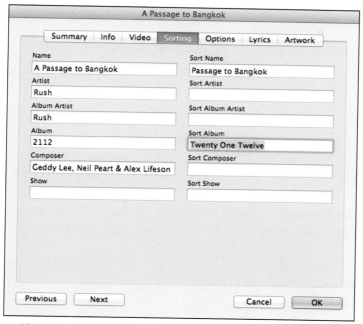

3.7 The Sorting tab of the iTunes track properties dialog box

4. **Type text based on the way you want the track sorted into the appropriate Sort field.** In Figure 3.7, "Twenty One Twelve" has been typed in the Sort Album field. This tells iTunes to sort this track internally based on this value, but the album name is still displayed as 2112.

5. **Click OK.** The selected track is sorted based on the new value in the Sort fields, but is still displayed with the appropriate information.

Using the Grid and Cover Flow views

In addition to the standard track listing view, iTunes offers two other ways of viewing your iTunes library: Grid view and Cover Flow view.

You can select these views either by choosing them from the iTunes View menu or by clicking the View buttons found in the top-right corner of the iTunes window.

The Grid view, shown in Figure 3.8, displays your tracks in a grid layout grouped by album, artist, genre, or composer, with the album artwork shown for each category.

You can switch to a different grouping by clicking the buttons shown at the top of the screen. Further, when viewing by categories such as artist or genre, moving your mouse over the artwork scrubs through the covers within each category (for example, all covers for a specific artist or within a specific genre). Sorting is also available in Grid view from the iTunes View menu or by right-clicking the category headings.

3.8 The iTunes Grid view

Note

If the grouping buttons do not appear at the top of the screen in Grid View, select View ⇨ Grid View ⇨ Show Header to display them.

You can choose to use either a dark or light background for Grid View in your iTunes Preferences.

The Cover Flow view, shown in Figure 3.9, is similar in concept to the Grid view in that it is intended to group your tracks and display them in their respective albums. The Cover Flow view provides an experience similar to that of flipping through a CD rack. You can change the columns and sort order that display below the Cover Flow browser, but it works best when sorted by the Album column in order to keep your tracks grouped together. Note that the iTunes Column Browser is not available in Cover Flow view.

3.9 The iTunes Cover Flow view

Note When browsing your TV shows or podcasts in Grid view, a number is also shown over each item grouping to indicate the number of new items in each category.

Rating tracks and albums

Rating tracks in iTunes is a fun and easy way to mark those songs that you particularly like versus those that you plan to delete. At a basic level, you can rate any track by clicking in the rating column in your iTunes track listing. The main advantage of ratings is their use in building effective Smart Playlists, which are discussed in more detail in Chapter 5.

Genius

The Cover Flow view offers one additional cool feature. With the Cover Flow view active, choose View ⇨ Full Screen from the iTunes menu to switch to a full-screen Cover Flow view. This looks absolutely stunning on a large screen such as an Apple LED Cinema Display or 27" iMac and can be great for letting your friends browse through your music collection when throwing a party.

Rating tracks while listening to them in iTunes

Although you can rate a track simply from the iTunes track listing, this can be too much trouble if you're listening to iTunes in the background while working on something else. Although a number of third-party tools have been written to assist with this, iTunes itself offers the capability to rate tracks right in your Dock or System Tray.

To rate a song while you're listening to it in iTunes, follow these steps:

1. **Right-click on the iTunes icon on your Dock (Mac) or System Tray (Windows).**

2. **Choose Rating from the context menu.**

3. **From the Rating submenu, select the number of stars you want to assign to the currently playing song.**

Rating albums

In iTunes 7.4, Apple added the capability to rate entire albums in addition to individual songs. An Album Rating column can be added to the iTunes track listing to show the album rating on each track, or you can see the album rating shown directly beside the album artwork in Album List view, as shown in Figure 3.10. You can switch to the Album List view from the View menu or by using the View buttons found in the top-right corner of the iTunes window.

If you have not set a specific rating for an album, a default rating is assigned based on an average of all rated tracks within that album. This is shown in the form of unfilled stars to indicate that it is an automatically generated rating as opposed to one that you have specifically assigned yourself. Note that tracks with no rating are not counted in this average, and so an album with ten tracks of which one has been given a five-star rating shows a five-star default rating for the entire album.

3.10 Album ratings shown in the Artwork column

To set your own rating on an album, simply click the number of stars you want to assign. Ratings you assign yourself are shown as solid black stars, in the same way as track ratings are shown. When you assign a rating to an album, any unrated tracks within that album are assigned the album rating as a default, again shown as hollow stars instead of solid black stars.

Adding lyrics to your music

If you're a person who likes to sing along with your iPod or wants to take a look at those lyrics that you can't quite make out when listening to a song, then you may want to consider adding lyrics to your songs in iTunes. Although the feature doesn't do much for you in iTunes itself, adding lyrics to your tracks ensures that while you're on the go with your iPod or iPhone, you can easily pull up the lyrics for whatever song you happen to be listening to.

Adding lyrics manually

If you're only concerned with adding lyrics to a few of your favorite tracks, you can do this manually in iTunes without any third-party tools. There are many sources on the Internet where you can find lyrics for your favorite songs, and Google is a good place to start looking. When you find the lyrics, you can just paste them straight into the track in iTunes. Follow these steps:

1. **Select the track to which you want to add lyrics.**

2. **Choose File ⇨ Get Info to display the track properties.**

3. **Click the Lyrics tab to see the lyrics tag field, as shown in Figure 3.11.**

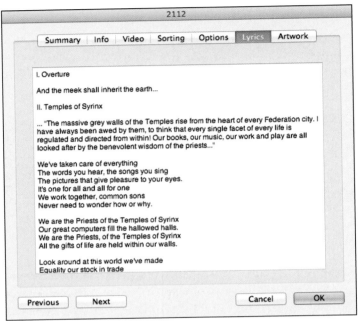

3.11 The Lyrics tab of the track properties dialog box

4. **Either type in the lyrics, or paste them in from your system Clipboard.**

5. **Click OK to save the lyrics.** The lyrics are attached to the track and synchronized with your iPod, iPhone, or iPad for viewing on the go.

Adding lyrics automatically

Although adding lyrics manually works for a few tracks here and there, if you're serious about lyrics, you'll want to look at a third-party tool that can scour the Internet for lyrics on your behalf and add them to your tracks.

A number of stand-alone applications are available that can look up lyrics and add them to your tracks as a group. Although a number of free lyrics apps have been available in the past, copyright licensing requirements for lyrics are requiring more developers to pay for access to lyrics information, with free online lyrics collections becoming more restrictive. Some free options such as Get Lyrical (http://shullian.com/get_lyrical.php) still exist and work for the time being, while other formerly free solutions such as GimmeSomeTune (www.eternalstorms.at/gimmesometune) are in the process of being rewritten as commercial software to continue accessing lyrics. Sadly, many other free lyrics tools no longer work at all.

If you're willing to pay for a commercial app for adding lyrics, iArt (www.ipodsoft.com) is a $10 solution for Windows users that can also add album artwork. Mac users can check out SongGenie (www.equinux.com/us/products/songgenie), a $30 app that can not only add lyrics and artwork, but also help identify unknown songs and fill in other tags for you.

Note

A number of older applications are also available to download lyrics; however, many of these do not work properly because they have not been updated for the latest version of iTunes or use online lyrics services that are no longer available. Always ensure that you get a relatively current version of any iTunes companion software to ensure maximum compatibility.

Organizing Video Content

Although iTunes started out as being "all about the music," these days there is much more to iTunes than just music content. Limited video support was added to iTunes 5.0 in 2004, but little was done with it until the release of the fifth-generation iPod with video in fall 2005. From that point on, video support in iTunes and on the iTunes Store has simply exploded, and iTunes has now become almost as adept at handling your videos as it is with your music collection.

Types of video content

iTunes organizes your video content into five general categories:

- **Movies.** As far as the iTunes Store is concerned, this category applies to feature-length films. Realistically, however, it can just as easily represent any video clip you have imported into iTunes. It is the default category for any newly imported video content and the most generic category of the three.

- **TV Shows.** As the name implies, this category is used for TV content. Content in this category is generally organized by typical TV show information, such as a show name, season, episode name, and episode number.

- **Music Videos.** This category identifies music videos and is organized in much the same way as your music is. Album, artist, and track name fields are all used here, and you can find your music videos in your Music section in iTunes listed right alongside your audio music tracks by the same artists.

- **Podcasts.** This special category is used for videos downloaded as part of a podcast subscription. I discuss podcasts in more detail in Chapter 6.

- **iTunes U.** This special category is used for videos downloaded as part of an iTunes U collection. I discuss iTunes U in more detail in Chapter 6.

Tagging video content

As with the music in your iTunes library, your video files must be properly tagged in order for iTunes and your iPod to properly organize your content so that you can easily find it.

Video tracks have the same basic tag information as audio tracks, and this information is edited in much the same way. However, there are also some video-specific fields that apply to different types of video content, not the least of which is the content type itself.

Any videos that you import into your iTunes library are automatically tagged as Movies by default. To change the video kind to either TV Show or Music Video, follow these steps:

1. **Select the individual video track or group of tracks that you want to modify.**

2. **Choose File ⇨ Get Info from the iTunes menu.** The standard track properties dialog box appears.

3. **Click the Options tab, as shown in Figure 3.12.**

4. **From the Media Kind drop-down menu, choose Movie, Music Video, or TV Show.**

5. **Click OK.** Depending on the video type, there may be additional fields that need to be filled in for the content to be organized and to display properly.

Note

You can also set the Media Kind to Podcast or iTunes U; however, this is normally only done for episodes that are downloaded as part of a podcast subscription or iTunes U collection. I discuss these types of videos in more detail in Chapter 6.

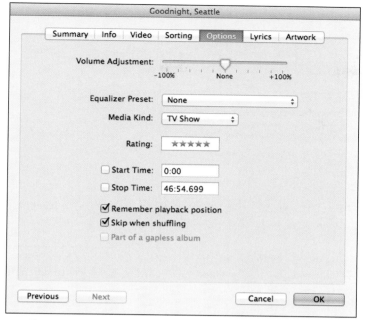

3.12 The Options tab of the iTunes standard track properties dialog box

Organizing movies

Movies are the simplest video content to tag and organize in iTunes. They are displayed in the Movies section and organized simply by the standard track name field. Other tags can be filled in to provide more sorting options and tags such as year, description, and genre are used to display additional information on the Apple TV and iPad. These additional tags are completely optional, however.

Organizing TV shows

TV shows, on the other hand, are much more complex to deal with properly in iTunes, and if the necessary fields aren't filled in, you may not be able to even see your TV shows listed on your iPod.

To fill in the proper TV show information, follow these steps:

1. **Select the individual TV show or group of shows that you want to modify.**

2. **Choose File ➪ Get Info from the iTunes menu to open the track properties dialog box.**

69

3. **Click the Info tab, as shown in Figure 3.13.**

4. **Type the name of the specific episode in the Name field, as shown in Figure 3.13.**

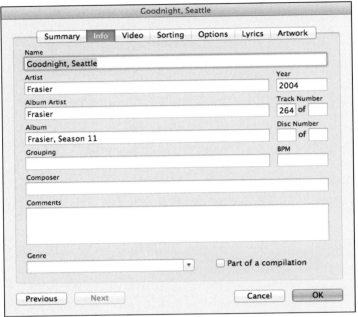

3.13 The Info tab of the iTunes TV show track properties dialog box

5. **Optionally, fill in the Artist, Album Artist, and Album fields.** The convention for these fields is to type the show name in the Artist field, and the show name and season number in the Album field. These fields are not strictly necessary for proper organization; however, TV shows purchased from the iTunes Store use this standard, and it is a good idea to fill these fields in for consistency.

6. **Click the Video tab, as shown in Figure 3.14.**

7. **Fill in the following fields in the video properties, using Figure 3.14 as an example:**

   - **Show.** Type the name of the TV show (for example, the TV series).

   - **Season Number.** Type the season number. iTunes uses this to group episodes into their appropriate seasons in iTunes and on the iPod and Apple TV.

   - **Episode ID.** Type the production episode ID or simply the episode number. This field is optional and may be left blank. It is used primarily for reference purposes, but is also used for sorting in the absence of the Episode Number field. You can type both letters and numbers in this field, as it is intended to follow a studio production-numbering system, which varies among different TV shows.

- **Episode Number.** Type the number of the episode within the season or within the series. Content purchased from the iTunes Store normally numbers episodes on a per-season basis; however, you can use a numbering system for the entire series here if you prefer. This field is simply used to sort episodes within each season. This field accepts numeric values only.

- **Description.** Optionally, you may type a description for the TV show that you want to see appear on the Apple TV, iPad, or in iTunes. This field is not yet used on the iPod or iPhone.

8. **Click OK to save your changes.**

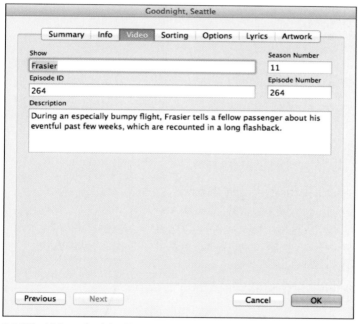

3.14 The Video tab of the iTunes TV show video properties dialog box

Organizing music videos

Music videos are tagged in the same way as music tracks are. They are organized by artist and track name and shown in the Music section of your iTunes library right alongside your audio tracks. Refer to the section on organizing music content earlier in this chapter for more information.

Adding more information to your videos

Although there are a number of video-related fields that iTunes can happily display for you, such as release date and content rating, it does not provide a way to actually put information into these fields yourself. These fields are regularly used by content purchased from the iTunes Store, but iTunes provides no way for users who want to encode their own content to fill in this information.

Fortunately, around the time that iTunes began supporting video content, an open-source tool known as AtomicParsley (www.atomicparsley.sourceforge.net) was released to handle updating the metadata directly within the underlying video files. AtomicParsley is a command-line tool and can be cumbersome to use, but a number of tools have been developed to provide a graphical interface for AtomicParsley.

For Mac users, Parsley is Atomically Delicious (www.them.ws/pad) and MetaX (www.kerstetter. net/index.php/projects/software/metax) are both good options to handle these tasks for you as well as modify some of the advanced metadata. The best part of all is that these tools are free.

A ported version of MetaX is also available for Windows users at www.danhinsley.com/metax/ metax.html; however the Windows version is a commercial application that sells for $10.

Note as well that Mac users can also take advantage of AppleScript, which provides another set of options for tagging videos in iTunes. You can find more on AppleScript in Chapter 14.

Some of the extra information that you may want to add to your own videos include

- **Content Rating.** This field allows you to specify an MPAA-style content rating for your movies or TV shows, such as PG-13 or TV-MA. Ratings are displayed within iTunes and on the Apple TV and iPad and can also be used to enforce parental controls on the Apple TV and iOS devices and may therefore be very important if you have children in the house. Note that this field currently cannot be set using AppleScript.

- **Release Date.** Although this field is largely informational, it is displayed on the Apple TV and iPad, and some users may want to have accurate release dates for their movies and TV shows. Note that this field currently cannot be set using AppleScript.

- **Cast and Crew.** This is a multivalued field that allows you to specify actors, directors, writers, and other principal movie credits. This is completely optional, but like Release Date, it is displayed on the Apple TV and iPad. This information is also displayed in iTunes beneath the Long Description. Note that this field currently cannot be set using AppleScript.

Many of the third-party tools mentioned earlier can fill in other information such as the TV network, copyright notices, encoding tool, and even rating annotations. These fields are not presently used in any meaningful way by iTunes or any of the Apple media devices.

Adding Artwork to Your Media

At one time, most of us were merely content to actually listen to our music, and with the early iPod models it was considered a bonus just to have a screen. Of course, this all began to change when Apple began putting color screens on its iPods a few years ago. Suddenly, with that shiny color screen, you wanted to see more than just the title of the song on a white background, and the ability to add and display album artwork came to iTunes and the iPod.

Where to find album artwork

Of course, if you purchase your music from the iTunes Store, it comes complete with artwork already provided, and there's rarely any need to change this. However, because you have probably ripped a large portion of your music from your own CD collection, you're likely going to need to fill in some of your own album artwork for these tracks.

Genius By default, iTunes shows the artwork for the currently selected item, but here's a hidden trick: Click the words *Selected Item* that appear above the artwork, and iTunes toggles between showing artwork for the selected item or the item currently playing.

There are a number of sources on the Internet where you can find album artwork, with the most obvious being online CD stores such as Amazon.com and Walmart.com. Depending on how and where you plan to use your album artwork, you may be concerned about getting the highest-resolution artwork images possible. This is especially important if you plan to display artwork on a device such as the Apple TV or iPad. You should go with an absolute minimum resolution of 600×600 for this purpose (which is the same resolution of artwork found in content purchased from the iTunes Store).

If you're only displaying artwork on an iPod screen or a lower-resolution computer screen, the resolution is going to be considerably less important, and you can probably get away with resolutions of around 200×200.

Genius

You can also add artwork for your movies and TV shows, which will be displayed on devices such as the iPad and Apple TV. The optimal format for TV show cover art is a square image similar to album art; however, the Apple TV and iPad are designed to display movie cover art in a rectangular 1.5:1 aspect ratio similar to a DVD cover image.

If you're concerned about getting the highest resolution possible and you have the original CD and a scanner, you can also scan in the artwork yourself to a JPEG file and add it from there.

Note

Keep in mind that album artwork takes up additional space within your media files. The additional space requirements are relatively small compared to the size of each track, but it can add up, so this is something to consider when adding higher-resolution album artwork. Expect to see about a 40K to 100K increase in size per file when adding artwork.

Adding album artwork manually

Although there are several ways in iTunes to add album artwork to a track, the simplest way is by using drag-and-drop. Follow these steps:

1. **Locate the artwork that you want to add.** Note that if you are finding artwork on the Internet, there is no need to actually download the file to your computer — simply leave the browser window open on that page.

2. **Locate and select the track(s) to which you want to add artwork.** Note that if you are adding artwork to an entire album, you can simply select the album from the iTunes library browser.

3. **Ensure that the artwork panel is displayed in the bottom-left corner of your iTunes window, as shown in Figure 3.15.** Click the fourth button in the bottom-left corner if it is not displayed.

4. **Drag the artwork image from your Web browser, or the image file from the Finder or Windows Explorer, directly into the artwork panel.** The artwork is added to all of the selected tracks. Note that if you are adding artwork to large media files such as video content for the first time, iTunes may take a few minutes to actually process the artwork because it must be written into the actual files.

Note that this method adds to any existing artwork that is already in your tracks, and secondary artwork images are generally of no use other than taking up space. If you have existing artwork in more than one track and want to replace it with the artwork you're adding, you need to use the Multiple Item Information dialog box instead. Follow these steps:

1. **Locate the artwork that you want to add.** Note that if you are finding artwork on the Internet, there is no need to actually download the file to your computer — simply leave the browser window open on that page.

2. **Locate and select the tracks to which you want to add artwork.** Note that if you are adding artwork to an entire album, you can simply select the album from the iTunes library browser.

3.15 The iTunes album artwork panel

3. **Choose File ⇨ Get Info to open the Multiple Item Information dialog box.**

4. **Drag the artwork image from your Web browser, or the image file from the Finder or Windows Explorer, directly into the Artwork panel in the Multiple Item Information dialog box.** A thumbnail of the artwork is displayed, as shown in Figure 3.16.

5. **Click OK to save your changes for all selected tracks.** The added artwork replaces any artwork that was already in these tracks. Note that if you are adding artwork to large media files such as video content for the first time, iTunes may take a few minutes to actually process the artwork because it must be written into the actual files.

Genius

You can also use the system Clipboard to add artwork. Simply copy the artwork to the Clipboard from your browser and then paste it in to the artwork panel. To accomplish this in the main iTunes window, right-click and choose Paste from the context menu. In the Multiple Item Information dialog box, click the artwork pane to highlight it and then press ⌘+V (Mac) or Ctrl+V (Windows) to paste in the content of the Clipboard.

3.16 Adding album artwork using the Multiple Item Information dialog box

Getting album artwork automatically

With iTunes 7, Apple recognized that many users had large libraries of content that they had added from their own CDs and other sources. Further, because the iTunes Store had such a large existing repository of music, it only made sense that the artwork for that music be made available to iTunes users to add to their own tracks. The result was a new feature in to automatically search the iTunes Store for any missing artwork on your tracks and then add it for you.

Although this feature is a very useful addition, it does have limitations, such as:

- **You must have an iTunes Store account in order to use this feature.** Album artwork is completely free, but you need to set up an iTunes Store account, as discussed in Chapter 2, because you are accessing the iTunes Store to get the artwork. This can be a serious limitation for some users because you need to use either a credit card or an iTunes Store Gift Card in order to set up an account. Note that if you are only getting album artwork, however, your credit card is not charged.

- **You can only get artwork for content that is currently available on the iTunes Store.** If the iTunes Store doesn't have the album, then, of course, it doesn't have the artwork either..

- **Your tracks must be properly tagged.** iTunes uses the album and artist name to find artwork, and although it tries to work around common naming discrepancies such as disc number suffixes on album names, the reality is that if you don't have your music tagged reasonably well, iTunes isn't going to be able to find the artwork that belongs to a given album or track.

- **Beware of generic album names.** Because the album name is used for matching artwork to your tracks, generic album names can sometimes cause problems. Common examples of this are album names like "Greatest Hits" and "Singles," which could easily apply to more than one artist.

- **You can only get album artwork for music tracks.** Other types of content such as movies, TV shows, audiobooks, and podcasts are not included, even if the iTunes Store has that content available.

- **Despite its best efforts, iTunes doesn't always get it right.** Obscure albums and tracks might be mismatched and have incorrect album artwork added to them. Note that iTunes only adds artwork to tracks that don't already have artwork, and so you don't need to be concerned about losing any existing artwork that you've added yourself. However, you may find some odd images on those obscure little single tracks that have otherwise been sitting unnoticed in your library for a while.

You can have iTunes scan your entire library for album artwork or just search for artwork for selected tracks.

How Album Artwork Is Stored

If you've used another media-management application, you may be familiar with the idea of album artwork being stored as a separate FOLDER.JPG file within your music folder structure. iTunes does not use this method, nor does it even read a FOLDER.JPG file to get album artwork. These files are ignored by iTunes completely, and if you've migrated your music library from another application, you can safely delete any JPEG files within your iTunes music folder structure.

Instead, iTunes embeds any album artwork you add manually directly into the tags within the actual file. This has the advantage of ensuring that the artwork remains with the file, regardless of where it may be located in the future — there's no corresponding FOLDER.JPG file that you have to worry about keeping around with your music. The disadvantage is that this increases the size of your files slightly because the artwork is stored in each track rather than as one file for an entire album. This size increase is generally negligible, however, compared to the overall size of your media files. Even at 128 kbps, a 5-minute MP3 file should be approximately 5MB in size. Artwork generally adds between 40K and 100K, for an increase of around 1 percent of the overall file size.

To have iTunes scan your entire iTunes library for missing artwork, follow these steps:

1. **Choose Advanced ⇨ Get Album Artwork from the iTunes menu.** iTunes begins scanning your entire library for missing artwork. The status is shown at the top of your iTunes window, similar to Figure 3.17.

3.17 The iTunes Processing Album Artwork status screen

2. **After the scan completes, iTunes displays a status message listing any tracks for which it could not find artwork, similar to Figure 3.18.**

3. **Optionally, click Save to save this listing to a text file for later review.** A standard file browser dialog box appears, requesting a name and location to save this file. This can be useful if you want a listing of tracks that you need to find artwork for manually.

4. **Click OK.**

If you want to only search for artwork for a few selected tracks, follow these steps:

1. **Select the track(s) for which you want to find artwork.**

3.18 An iTunes listing of artwork that could not be found

2. **Right-click your selection and choose Get Album Artwork from the context menu.** iTunes begins scanning for artwork for the selected tracks. Note that you must use the context menu for this. The Get Album Artwork option on the Advanced menu always searches your entire iTunes library for artwork, regardless of any tracks you may have selected. Once the scan completes, iTunes displays a status message listing any tracks for which it could not find artwork.

3. **Optionally, click Save to save this listing to a text file for later review.** A standard file browser dialog box appears, requesting a name and location to save this file. This can be useful if you want a listing of tracks that you need to find artwork for manually.

4. **Click OK.**

iTunes also searches for album artwork automatically whenever you import a CD or add tracks to your library from other sources.

Note When adding artwork automatically using iTunes, this artwork is stored in a separate cache rather than being embedded within your actual media files. Therefore, if you move your media files to another iTunes library on another computer, the artwork is not moved with them. However, because you can presumably download the artwork from iTunes again, this is normally not a serious concern.

How Do I Play My Content in iTunes?

Although many users only discover iTunes when they purchase an iPod or iPhone, you can use iTunes very effectively as your primary media player on your computer and as a hub for your digital entertainment. iTunes provides many advanced features for listening to your music, audiobooks, and podcasts, and even watching your video content.

Playing Music in iTunes

As the name implies, iTunes began as a music playback application, and despite added support for other types of content, it remains quite true to its origins. The main playback features in iTunes are still very much focused toward listening to your music, and iTunes offers a number of advanced features for getting the most enjoyment out of your listening experience.

Using iTunes DJ

Although most users just listen to their music by selecting a playlist and track, iTunes offers a more effective way of handling music playback through the iTunes DJ feature. Unlike the traditional way of playing back music in iTunes, the iTunes DJ list creates a dynamic playlist of music based on some simple criteria that you select, and allows you to queue up tracks for playback without having to resort to continuously modifying your existing playlists.

To get started with iTunes DJ, follow these steps:

1. **Select iTunes DJ from the iTunes Source list.** An iTunes DJ playlist is displayed. At the bottom of the iTunes DJ playlist, you should see options for managing your iTunes DJ selections, similar to Figure 4.1. If this is the first time you have used iTunes DJ, an introduction screen appears first; simply click Continue to bypass the introduction screen and continue to the main iTunes DJ playlist.

4.1 The iTunes DJ settings

2. **From this section, choose the playlist from which you want iTunes DJ to select its tracks.** You can select any of your iTunes playlists or the Music heading at the top to tell iTunes DJ to select from your entire music library.

3. **Click the Settings button to display the iTunes DJ settings.** The iTunes DJ Settings dialog box appears, as shown in Figure 4.2.

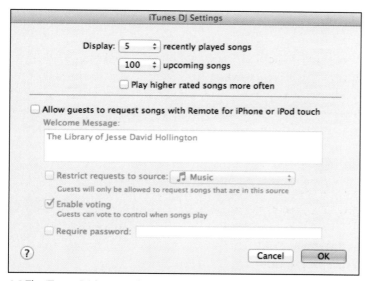

4.2 The iTunes DJ Settings dialog box

4. **In the Display section, choose the number of recently played songs and upcoming songs that you want to be shown in the iTunes DJ list.**

5. **Optionally, you may also choose to have higher-rated songs played more often in the iTunes DJ process by selecting the Play higher rated songs more often option.**

6. **Click OK to close the dialog box.**

7. **Click the Play button to begin playback of the first selected track in the iTunes DJ playlist.**

When using iTunes DJ, iTunes plays back the tracks in the order in which they are listed in the iTunes DJ listing, selecting new tracks at random from the specified playlist as needed. Unlike playing from a normal playlist, however, iTunes keeps the selection bar in the same location and refreshes the list of upcoming tracks based on the number of tracks you've selected to be displayed.

Genius With the iTunes DJ feature, you can also allow guests with Apple's Remote app for the iPhone, iPod touch, and iPad to request and vote on songs in your iTunes DJ playlist — a great idea for parties. More on the Remote app is discussed in Chapter 11.

You can remove or reorder tracks in the iTunes DJ playlist in the same way as you would for any other playlist to control which tracks are played by iTunes and in which order. You can also add new tracks to the iTunes DJ play order from anywhere in your iTunes library, regardless of whether they're in the selected playlist.

To add tracks to an iTunes DJ playlist, follow these steps:

1. **Select the track(s) that you want to add to the iTunes DJ playlist.**

2. **Right-click on the selected track(s) and choose Add to iTunes DJ to add the selected track(s) to the end of the current iTunes DJ list, or Play Next in iTunes DJ to add the selected track(s) immediately after the currently playing iTunes DJ track.** Choosing a track and selecting Play Next in iTunes DJ while the iTunes DJ list is not being played back begins the iTunes DJ playlist with the selected track. Any other music that you may be listening to from another playlist stops playing in favor of the iTunes DJ playlist.

Genius You can also add tracks to the iTunes DJ playlist simply by dragging and dropping them onto the iTunes DJ playlist as you would for any other iTunes playlist. Tracks added in this manner are queued up at the bottom of the list.

Using Sound Check

If you have collected music from a variety of sources, you may find that some albums are naturally louder in volume than others. While this is not normally a problem when listening to one album at a time, it can quickly become annoying when working with playlists or shuffling your tracks from multiple albums.

iTunes provides a solution for solving this problem through the Sound Check option. When you enable this option, iTunes analyzes the volume levels on any tracks already in your library and additional tracks that you import, and adjusts the volume to attempt to provide a balanced listening experience.

The Sound Check feature is enabled globally in your iTunes library through your iTunes preferences:

1. **Open your iTunes preferences and click the Playback tab, as shown in Figure 4.3.**

2. **Click the check box beside Sound Check.**

3. **Click OK.** The first time you enable Sound Check, iTunes scans your existing library to analyze any tracks that do not yet have Sound Check information stored in them. This may take anywhere from a few seconds to several minutes, depending on how large your iTunes library is. Any new tracks that you add to your library while Sound Check is enabled are analyzed during import to have their appropriate Sound Check information added.

4.3 The Playback tab of the iTunes preferences dialog box

Genius iTunes does not actually change the volume of each track; instead, it merely adds an adjustment value that is read by iTunes and other Apple media devices to dynamically adjust the volume during playback. Turning off Sound Check does not remove this value; rather, it merely tells iTunes to ignore it.

Note Although Apple's media devices also support Sound Check, the option must be enabled individually in the Settings on each device that you want to use it on, as well as in iTunes.

Using Crossfade

For your listening enjoyment, iTunes can also crossfade between songs when playing back music from your iTunes library. This feature has iTunes fade down at the end of the currently playing track and fade up into the next, providing a smooth transition between certain types of music.

To enable the Crossfade feature, follow these steps:

1. **Open your iTunes preferences and click the Playback tab, as shown in Figure 4.4.**

4.4 The Playback tab of the iTunes preferences dialog box

2. **Click the Crossfade Songs check box.**

3. **Drag the slider to set the crossfade interval from 1 to 12 seconds.** Longer intervals begin the fade out earlier in the first track and take longer to fade in during the second track.

4. **Click OK.**

Note

Crossfade is only supported in iTunes and on the fourth- and fifth-generation iPod nano. Other Apple media devices do not support this feature.

About gapless playback

In iTunes 7, Apple introduced a long-awaited gapless playback feature, allowing albums that had been recorded with no silence between tracks to also be played back without gaps in iTunes and on the iPod. Common examples of gapless albums include live concert recordings, certain types of mix albums, and some classical works.

Note

iPod models prior to the fifth-generation iPod do not support gapless playback.

iTunes automatically analyzes your music during import to determine gapless playback information, and no special effort is required on your part to enable gapless playback, although there are a couple of important points that should be noted about when and how gapless playback works:

- **iTunes plays tracks without gaps only if they were originally recorded that way.** Don't expect all of your music to play without gaps; also note that tracks added into iTunes from sources other than the original album CD or the iTunes Store may not match up correctly for gapless playback.

- **iTunes does not play tracks back without gaps unless they are being played in their proper order.** Gapless playback is disabled when shuffle is turned on, for example.

- **Gapless playback and crossfade playback cannot be used together on the same tracks.** If crossfade playback is enabled, then gapless tracks must be marked in iTunes to override the Crossfade feature when playing back these tracks.

You can mark individual tracks in iTunes as belonging to a gapless album to override the Crossfade feature when playing these tracks. Follow these steps:

1. **Select the track that you want to mark for gapless playback.**
2. **Choose File ⇨ Get Info from the iTunes menu.** The iTunes track properties dialog box appears.
3. **Click the Options tab from the top of the dialog box.** The track options are displayed, as shown in Figure 4.5.
4. **Click the Part of a gapless album check box.**
5. **Click OK.**

Note The Part of a gapless album setting is only to override crossfade playback and is not otherwise required for gapless playback.

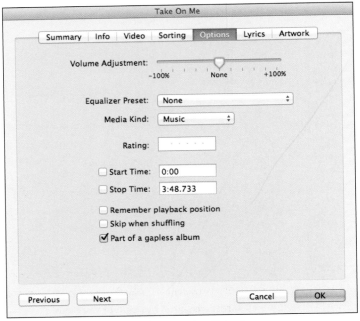

4.5 The Options tab of the track properties dialog box

To mark multiple tracks in iTunes as belonging to a gapless album, follow these steps:

1. **Select the tracks that you would like to mark for gapless playback.** As with any other application, you can use the Shift key to select a range of tracks and the ⌘ key (Mac) or Ctrl key (Windows) to select multiple noncontiguous tracks. You can also ⌘+A (Mac) or Ctrl+A (Windows) to select all of the tracks currently displayed.

2. **Choose File ⇨ Get Info from the iTunes menu.**

3. **Click the Options tab from the top of the dialog box.** The track options are displayed, as shown in Figure 4.6.

4. **From the Gapless album drop-down menu, choose Yes.**

5. **Click OK.**

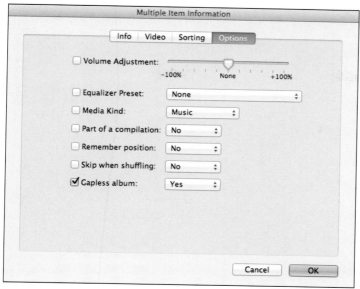

4.6 The iTunes Multiple Item Information dialog box

Using the iTunes Visualizer

If you listen to a lot of music in iTunes and have your computer in a common area where you can see it while you're listening to your music, the iTunes Visualizer can provide a very handy way to jazz up your listening experience by providing on-screen visuals to the beat of your music.

To turn on the iTunes Visualizer, simply choose View ⇨ Show Visualizer from the iTunes menu while listening to your music, and the normal iTunes track list is replaced with a visual kaleidoscope that moves to your music, similar to Figure 4.7.

In addition, you can switch to a full-screen view of the Visualizer by choosing View ⇨ Full Screen after you turn on the Visualizer. If you always want to see the Visualizer in full-screen mode, you can also easily adjust this in your iTunes preferences.

Note

iTunes 8 introduced a greatly enhanced Visualizer compared to previous versions of iTunes. It's definitely worth checking out if you haven't seen it already. If, however, you still prefer the old iTunes Classic Visualizer, you can switch back to the old one easily enough by choosing View ⇨ Visualizer ⇨ iTunes Classic Visualizer.

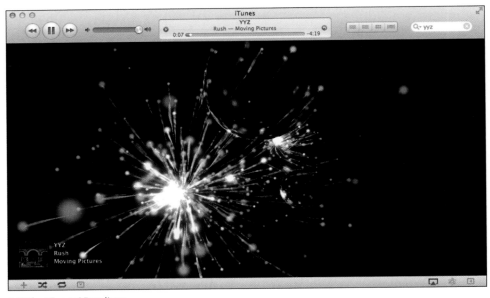

4.7 The iTunes Visualizer

1. **Open your iTunes preferences and click the Advanced tab, as shown in Figure 4.8.**

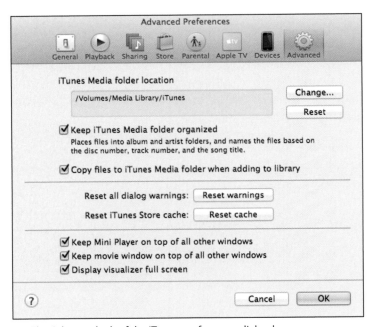

4.8 The Advanced tab of the iTunes preferences dialog box

2. **Click the Display visualizer full screen check box.**

3. **Click OK.**

Note

Third-party visualizers are available to be installed into iTunes as well. Each of these third-party visualizers has its own specific visualizer options.

Listening to Internet Radio in iTunes

In addition to playing your own imported media content, iTunes can also play streaming Internet Radio right in your iTunes player. A variety of Internet Radio sources is predefined in iTunes, and you can also open any standard MP3/M3U/PLS Internet Radio stream.

To begin listening to Internet Radio in iTunes, follow these steps:

1. **Click on the Radio category in the iTunes Source list.** A list of genres is shown in the main iTunes window, similar to Figure 4.9.

4.9 A list of iTunes radio genres

2. **Double-click the radio genre to which you want to listen.** The genre heading expands to show a list of available stations within that genre, with a bit rate and a description shown by each, as shown in Figure 4.10.

3. **Double-click a station to begin streaming audio from it.**

You may also notice that a bit rate is shown beside each individual station entry. As with audio files that you import yourself, each Internet Radio station has a bit rate at which it "broadcasts" its programming. The higher the bit rate, the higher the quality, but the more Internet bandwidth that is required. If you're on a low-speed Internet connection, such as dial-up, you should stick with streams of 48 kbps or lower.

4.10 An expanded list of iTunes radio stations

Genius

You can also add your favorite radio stations into iTunes playlists to keep track of them and play them from there. Simply drag and drop a stream from the Radio listing directly into a playlist. You can even sync this playlist to an Apple TV to get access to your favorite radio stations from there.

Streaming to remote speakers with AirPlay

If you're like many iTunes users, chances are that your computer doesn't live in the most convenient place in your home for using it as a digital jukebox. Although you can, of course, take your music with you on an iPod and play it through portable speakers, iTunes offers another option to listen to your music throughout your house.

The AirPlay feature in iTunes allows you to stream any audio playing from within iTunes to remote speakers connected to an AirPort Express base station, an Apple TV or a third-party AirPlay speaker system. Playback is still managed and controlled through iTunes in the same way you would listen to music on your computer, but the actual sound is sent over your home network to a remote device.

Genius

If you are using an Apple TV or a set of AirPlay speakers equipped with a remote, you can also control playback from the AirPlay device. Commands such as Play, Pause, Previous Track, and Next Track will be passed back from the remote device to control playback in iTunes. This option can be enabled in your iTunes Preferences on the Devices tab.

If you have AirPlay devices on your network, using them is simply a matter of telling iTunes to send audio to the remote device using the AirPlay control in the bottom-right corner of the iTunes window. Clicking this option displays a list of speakers to which you can stream your music, with the currently active set of speakers indicated by a check mark, similar to Figure 4.11. A Multiple Speakers option is also available to stream your music to more than one set of AirPlay speakers at once — a nice way to provide music to your entire household.

Caution

You need to ensure that AirPlay is also enabled on any client devices that you want to use with iTunes. AirPlay is normally enabled on the Apple TV and AirPort Express by default, and so it's unlikely to be a problem unless you specifically turned it off when you set up these devices.

Genius

If you're using an iPhone or iPod touch you can also download the free Remote application from the iTunes App Store. Doing this allows you to use your iPhone or iPod touch as a remote control for iTunes from anywhere in your house — a feature that can be very useful when combined with AirTunes.

4.11 The AirPlay speaker selection drop-down menu

Playing Videos in iTunes

In recent years, iTunes has evolved far beyond its humble roots as a simple music playback application, and now supports the storage, organization, and playback of video content as well. In addition to streaming your videos to an Apple TV, or loading them up on an iPod, iPhone, or iPad, iTunes can also act as a very capable video player in its own right.

Playing videos in a window versus full-screen

By default, iTunes plays your videos in a window, which is fine if you're just previewing the occasional video or want to play something on the side while you're working, but it's not really great for turning that 27-inch iMac into a small home entertainment system.

You can change any video while it's playing to use different screen sizes simply by selecting the appropriate option from the iTunes menu under View ⇨ Video Playback. The options are:

- **In iTunes Window.** Videos play back in the main iTunes window, occupying the full window. When a video ends, the normal iTunes window content returns.

- **In Separate Window.** Videos play back in a separate window. When a video ends, the window closes automatically.

- **In Artwork Viewer.** Videos play back in the artwork panel in the bottom-left corner of the iTunes window. The artwork viewer is automatically displayed when you begin playing a video if it is not already enabled.

- **Full Screen.** Videos play back full screen. When a video ends, you are returned to your normal screen view.

These video playback options can also be accessed by right-clicking on a video while it is playing.

Selecting high-definition or standard-definition TV shows

As discussed in Chapter 2, you can purchase high-definition (HD) TV shows and movies from the iTunes Store. These videos actually come with both an HD version that you can watch on your computer, Apple TV, iPad, or Retina Display iOS devices and a standard-definition (SD) version for viewing on older iPod or iPhone models.

By default, iTunes shows you the high-definition version of a video whenever one is available. However, if you prefer, you can choose to view the standard-definition version instead. This may be particularly useful if you're using a slower computer or video card that has problems rendering the higher-resolution HD content or if you have problems viewing copy-protected HD video on an external monitor.

When browsing your iTunes library, you can identify high-definition TV shows by a small HD-SD badge that appears next to them, as shown in Figure 4.12. From this listing, you can set an individual episode to play the standard-definition version instead of the HD version. Follow these steps:

1. **Right-click the HD episode that you would like to watch in standard definition.** A context menu appears.

2. **From the context menu, choose Version ⇨ Standard Definition (SD) as shown in Figure 4.13.** Note that no specific visual feedback is provided in the main track listing to indicate which version is presently selected, although you can confirm your selection by displaying the context menu again. The selected version is indicated with a check mark.

4.12 An iTunes HD TV show listing

4.13 The iTunes HD-SD Version context submenu

If you have a slower computer that does not meet the minimum system requirements to play back HD TV content, you may want to set iTunes to play back all of your TV shows in standard definition by default. You can adjust this globally under your iTunes playback preferences. Follow these steps:

1. **Open your iTunes preferences and click the Playback tab.**

2. **Click the Play videos using standard definition version check box, as shown in Figure 4.14.**

3. **Click OK.**

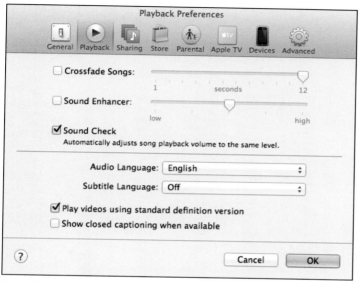

4.14 Select the Play videos using standard definition option if your computer doesn't meet HD requirements.

Using chapter markers in videos

Recent versions of iTunes have also introduced support for chapter markers within video files, similar to those found on commercial DVDs. Most of the movies that you purchase from the iTunes Store include these preset chapter markers, and you can also add them into videos that you convert yourself. For more on converting your own videos, see Chapter 9.

When playing a video in iTunes that includes chapter markers, a Chapters menu appears on the iTunes menu bar and a chapter selection icon is shown on the playback controls overlay. Clicking the Chapters menu or chapter selection icon displays a list of chapters in the currently playing video, similar to Figure 4.15.

Note that chapters may or may not include titles and thumbnails, depending on how they were encoded. Some videos offer titles or descriptions for each chapter, while others simply list text such as "Chapter 01."

4.15 The iTunes Chapter selection menu

Note   The iPhone, iPod touch, and iPad also provide chapter support. Selection of chapters works in much the same way as it does in iTunes.

Selecting alternate audio tracks

iTunes also provides support for selecting alternate audio tracks from video files that are encoded with more than a single track. This is most commonly used to provide multilanguage support for movies and TV shows from the iTunes Store, but can also be used for features such as Director's Commentaries.

If a video file has alternate audio tracks, you can select a different track while you are playing that video by choosing Controls ⇨ Audio & Subtitles from the iTunes menu. Note that this option only displays alternate audio tracks if there are any available in the currently playing track.

You can also configure which language track is selected by default when playing back a video that supports your preferred language. Follow these steps:

1. **Open your iTunes preferences and click the Playback tab.**

2. **Select your preferred audio track language from the Audio Language drop-down menu, as shown in Figure 4.16.** Video files that include the selected language use this instead of their default language track.

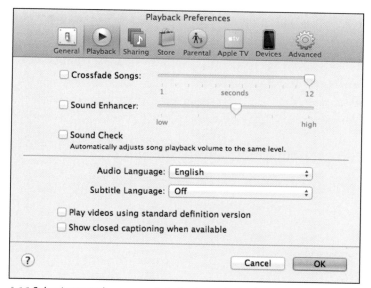

4.16 Selecting your language of choice from the Audio Language drop-down menu

3. **Click OK.** Video content that does not include your preferred language plays back in its default language.

Enabling subtitles and closed captioning

You can enable subtitles and closed captioning in your video files where available. *Closed captioning* is used to provide text for dialog and other descriptive text for hearing-impaired users. In addition to the dialog itself, closed captioning normally includes descriptive text for other audio cues within a movie or TV show. *Subtitles* are normally used to provide alternate-language translations for movies and TV shows, and therefore generally only include text for the actual dialog.

There are two types of subtitles that are used in digital video. *Soft subtitles* refer to subtitles that are stored in a separate track and can be toggled on or off. *Hard subtitles* are embedded in the main video track and cannot be turned off. iTunes does not specifically care about hard subtitles, as these are simply part of the video image displayed by iTunes.

Closed captioning and subtitles can be enabled during playback by choosing Controls ⇨ Audio & Subtitles from the iTunes menu. Note that this item only displays these options if the current track has been encoded with subtitles or closed captions.

You can choose to have iTunes display subtitles or closed captioning by default when playing videos. Follow these steps:

1. **Open your iTunes preferences and click the Playback tab.**

2. **Select your preferred subtitle language or turn the feature off from the Subtitle Language drop-down menu, as shown in Figure 4.17.** When playing videos that have subtitles in the selected language, those subtitles are automatically enabled. If subtitles are not available in the selected default language, no subtitles are shown.

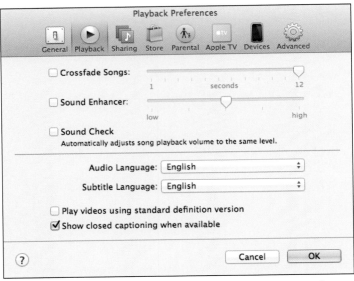

4.17 You can turn off Subtitles in the Playback tab of the iTunes preferences.

3. **Click the Show closed captioning when available check box to have iTunes automatically display closed captions for any movies that have them available.**

4. **Click OK.**

Genius

You can search for movies that include closed captioning in the iTunes Store by clicking the Power Search link from the iTunes Store page and selecting Movies.

How Can I Use Playlists to Manage My Library?

If you have even a medium-sized iTunes library, sooner or later you're going to want to find ways to make sense of it all and keep your favorite items more accessible. Like most digital media-management applications today, iTunes solves this problem by allowing you to organize your music and other media content into playlists. However, iTunes also takes it a step beyond this by providing playlists that you can manually manage, Smart Playlists that can automatically maintain themselves, and Genius playlists and mixes that automatically pick a collection of music for you.

Using Standard Playlists

For the purposes of our discussions here, a *standard playlist* is simply a normal playlist in iTunes that you create by adding and managing the content manually. Tracks only appear in standard playlists if you add them and are only removed if you remove them. For most beginning iTunes users, standard playlists are the easiest starting point, and iTunes offers a lot of features even in these seemingly basic lists.

Sorting and manually reordering tracks in playlists

You probably already know the basics about how to create and maintain your standard playlists, but what you may not realize is that you also have a number of options for sorting and reordering the content in these playlists to help further organize your music.

Basic sorting is handled in a playlist in much the same way that it is handled anywhere else in your iTunes library:

1. **Select the playlist you want to sort from the iTunes Source list.**

2. **Click the column heading that you want to sort by.** The selected column heading is highlighted with blue shading to indicate that iTunes is now using that column for its sorting, as shown in Figure 5.1.

3. **Click the same column heading again if you want to reverse the sort order.**

5.1 Sorting an iTunes playlist, here by artist

You can also manually reorder the tracks in any given playlist simply by highlighting a track and dragging it up or down within your playlist.

Sometimes you find that you cannot manually reorder a playlist. Try as you might, the tracks just don't want to move when you drag them. This is a common pitfall that many iTunes users run into, and the key is that you cannot manually reorder a playlist if you've already sorted it on another column. You must first return the playlist to its natural unsorted order:

1. **Select the playlist you want to reorder from the iTunes Source list.**

2. **At the top of the playlist, click the unnamed column heading on the left side.** This column heading is highlighted with blue shading to indicate that iTunes is now using that column for its sorting, as shown in Figure 5.2. The playlist is returned to its natural unsorted order, and you can then drag and drop the tracks up and down within the playlist to reorder them as desired.

 Note Any sort order you apply to a playlist in iTunes is also transferred to the corresponding playlist on your Apple media device.

5.2 Sorting an iTunes playlist using the unnamed column

Saving the play order

Sometimes it can be useful when reorganizing the content of your playlists to begin with a specific sort order and then reorder the tracks further from there. Although iTunes does not allow you to manually reorder tracks unless the playlist is unsorted, you can save the displayed sort order as the playlist's natural unsorted play order:

1. **Select the playlist you want to reorder from the iTunes Source list.**

2. **Sort the playlist as desired by clicking one of the column headings.**

3. **Right-click the playlist in the iTunes Source list.** A contextual menu appears, similar to Figure 5.3.

4. **Choose Copy To Play Order from the contextual menu.**

5. **Return the playlist to its natural sort order by clicking the unnamed column heading on the left.** The playlist should remain in the same order that it was previously sorted in, and you can now drag and drop the tracks into a new order as desired.

5.3 The playlist contextual menu

Genius

You can also permanently shuffle a playlist by using the same method. Simply turn on Shuffle mode in iTunes as you normally would for a given playlist, and then use the Copy To Play Order option to save the shuffled playlist order as the default for that playlist.

Finding out which playlists contain a given track

Once you set up a large number of playlists, it is often useful when browsing your library to find out which playlists contain a specific track. iTunes makes this quite simple:

1. **Highlight the track that you want to search playlists for.** You can select a track from the main iTunes library or from any of your existing iTunes playlists.

2. **Right-click the highlighted track.** iTunes displays a contextual menu.

3. **From the contextual menu, choose Show in Playlist.** iTunes displays a submenu with a list of playlists that contain the highlighted track, similar to Figure 5.4.

5.4 The Show in Playlist submenu

4. **Optionally, you can select one of the displayed playlists from the submenu to switch to that particular playlist and display the highlighted track within that playlist.**

Genius

The Add to Playlist option on the same context menu can be used as a shortcut to quickly add the selected track to an existing playlist. This can be much faster than dragging and dropping when you have a large number of playlists in your iTunes library.

Organizing playlists into folders

iTunes 7 introduced the ability to organize your playlists into folders within the iTunes library. Originally, these folders served little purpose other than as a means for organizing a large number of playlists in your iTunes library. However, with recent Apple media devices, your folder structure is now replicated on your device.

Note Apple has added folder support gradually to its media devices over the past couple of years. The iPhone and iPod touch were the last devices to add this support with the release of iOS 4 in summer 2010.

To create a playlist folder in iTunes, follow these steps:

1. **Choose File ⇨ New Playlist Folder from the iTunes menu.** A new playlist folder appears in the iTunes Source list with a default name highlighted and the insertion point ready to type a new name.
2. **Type a name for the playlist folder.**
3. **Press Enter.**

To create new playlists within your playlist folders, simply ensure that the playlist folder is high-lighted before creating a new playlist. You can also drag and drop existing playlists into playlist folders to reorganize them.

Playlist folders can also contain other playlist folders.

Using Smart Playlists to Manage Music Content

One of the more powerful features of iTunes is the Smart Playlists feature. In addition to creating standard playlists that you manage, iTunes also allows you to create Smart Playlists that automatically select content based on a set of criteria that you specify.

Think of a Smart Playlist as a saved search: You specify the criteria that you want iTunes to search for, and each time you access that playlist, it dynamically builds a list of tracks that meet those criteria. At a basic level, you could create a Smart Playlist that simply selects tracks from your favorite artist or genre; however, iTunes takes even this a step further by monitoring other information about your tracks, such as the number of times you've played each track, the date and time that you last played each track, and even the number of times and last date and time that you skipped a track. Further, you can also apply a rating to each track and to albums as a whole. All of this additional information that iTunes keeps track of makes Smart Playlists an extremely powerful and useful feature for dynamically organizing your media library.

Creating a basic Smart Playlist

At the most basic level, you can create a Smart Playlist simply to make a quick list of tracks by your favorite artist:

1. **Choose File ⇨ New Smart Playlist from the iTunes menu.** The Smart Playlist dialog box appears, as shown in Figure 5.5. Notice that the default criteria are set to Artist and contains, and the cursor is placed in the empty criteria field.

2. **Type the name of the artist you would like the Smart Playlist to match.** iTunes auto-completes the field as you type based on artists in your library to help ensure that you spell the artist's name correctly.

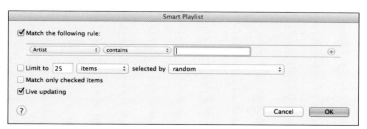

5.5 The Smart Playlist dialog box

3. **Click OK.** The Smart Playlist appears in your iTunes Source list with a default name high-lighted in editing mode.

4. **Type a new name for the Smart Playlist, if desired, or simply press Enter to accept the default name.**

When you select the Smart Playlist, you should see a listing of all tracks by the selected artist. If you later add new tracks from the same artist, they are automatically included in this Smart Playlist.

This is a very simple example of a Smart Playlist. The real power of this feature comes from your ability to specify multiple criteria within a Smart Playlist. Any of the track properties discussed in Chapter 3 can be used as criteria for your Smart Playlist, in addition to some other special proper-ties that are discussed a little bit later in this chapter.

For example, say you are throwing a party and you want to build a playlist of jazz tracks, but only those from a certain era. You can do this by creating a Smart Playlist that selects tracks based on both the genre and the year, similar to the one shown in Figure 5.6. Note that the Plus button is used to add additional criteria to a Smart Playlist.

5.6 A Smart Playlist with multiple criteria

By default, Smart Playlists match all of the specified criteria. You can create a playlist that matches any one of the specified criteria simply by changing the drop-down menu that appears in the first line of a Smart Playlist dialog box as soon as you add more than one criteria to "any" instead of "all." For example, the Smart Playlist shown in Figure 5.7 includes all classical and all jazz tracks, or more precisely, all tracks where the genre contains classical or the genre contains jazz.

5.7 A Smart Playlist with multiple criteria ("Match any")

You can also easily edit an existing Smart Playlist:

1. **Select the Smart Playlist that you want to edit from the iTunes Source list.**

2. **Choose File ⇨ Get Info from the iTunes menu.** The Smart Playlist dialog box appears with the current Smart Playlist settings displayed.

3. **Edit the Smart Playlist as desired.**

4. **Click OK.**

Smart Playlists can be built using any of the information that is stored in iTunes for your tracks, which really allows you to fine-tune your Smart Playlists, provided that your media files have been tagged properly and you therefore have this information in your database. The more information you put into your tracks, the more creative you can be with your Smart Playlists. For example, fields like Beats per Minute (BPM), if filled in, can be used to select music of a certain tempo — which can be useful for creating dynamic workout mixes, for example.

Using ratings and play counts in a Smart Playlist

So far, you have looked at creating Smart Playlists by filtering on relatively static criteria such as artist name and genre. Although this can be useful in an ever-changing library, you don't necessarily gain a huge advantage over standard playlists by doing this. After all, you can just as easily search for these tracks yourself and add them to a normal playlist.

Where the real power of Smart Playlists starts to kick in, however, is in the capability of iTunes to use your actual listening patterns as criteria to build your Smart Playlists. Under the hood, iTunes keeps track of your basic listening habits, updating information as you listen to your music (or watch your videos). iTunes monitors how many times you've listened to a given track, the date and time that you last listened to it all the way through, and even how many times you've skipped over a track without listening to the end, as well as the date and time you last did that. This all occurs regardless of whether you listen to your tracks directly in iTunes or on your iPod, iPhone, iPad, or Apple TV.

Some of the additional information that iTunes keeps track of is

- **Date Added.** This is the date that the track was added to your iTunes library.
- **Date Modified.** This is the date that the track information was last modified.
- **Plays.** This is the number of times the track has been played, either in iTunes or on any Apple media device that is synchronized with the current iTunes library. A track is considered "played" if you have listened to the very end of the track.
- **Last Played.** This is the date and time the track was last played. The same rules apply as for the Plays field.
- **Skips.** This is the number of times the track has been skipped, either in iTunes or on your Apple media device. A track is considered "skipped" if you listen to between 2 seconds and 30 seconds of the current track and skip ahead to the next track. Note that skip count tracking is only supported on newer device models with the latest firmware updates.
- **Last Skipped.** This is the date and time the track was last skipped. The same rules apply as for the Skips field.

Note Plays, last played, skips, and last skipped are only transferred from your iPod or other Apple media device to your iTunes library if you are using automatic synchronization. More on iPod synchronization is discussed in Chapter 7.

Further, iTunes gives you the ability to rate your tracks as you listen to them. Tracks begin with no rating at all, but you can assign a rating from one to five stars on a track-by-track basis, and even rate entire albums.

All of this information can be used as criteria to build very dynamic Smart Playlists that can help keep your content fresh by allowing you to select tracks based on your listening habits rather than simply using a conglomeration of artists and genres. This can be best illustrated by a few practical examples of some useful Smart Playlist ideas.

For the first example, suppose that you want to create a Smart Playlist that includes all of your rock tracks that you've listened to at least once. A Smart Playlist similar to the one shown in Figure 5.8 could be used.

5.8 This Smart Playlist selects rock tracks that you have listened to at least once.

Although such a Smart Playlist might be useful to review the tracks that you've listened to (perhaps to go back through and rate them), it is likely going to include far too many tracks to be of much use as a listening playlist. If you've been rating your tracks, why not add an additional criterion to select only those that you obviously like? Figure 5.9 shows a slight modification to your Smart Playlist to limit the criteria to only tracks with a rating higher than three stars.

This gets you a bit closer to a useful listening playlist, but it might risk becoming repetitive after a while because if you've recently listened to a given track, you may not want to hear it again right away. One other simple addition to monitor the last-played date can easily solve that problem. For example, you can exclude any tracks that have been played in the past seven days, as shown in Figure 5.10.

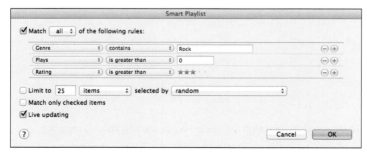

5.9 This Smart Playlist selects favorite rock tracks listened to at least once, with a rating higher than three stars.

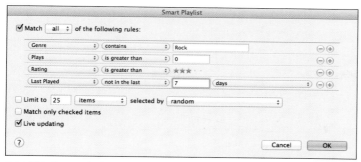

5.10 This Smart Playlist selects favorite rock tracks listened to at least once but not in the past seven days.

Now you have a truly dynamic Smart Playlist. As you listen to tracks in the playlist, they are automatically removed (because the last-played date is updated), but automatically reappear seven days later. Any new rock tracks you listen to for the first time and rate with four or five stars also automatically appear in the playlist seven days after you last listened to them.

Caution

Pay close attention when using greater-than or less-than criteria in your Smart Playlists. There is no match for greater-than or equal-to, and so you must always specify a criteria one number higher or lower than you want to include. For example, to include all tracks played at least once, you must use greater-than and type **0** in the field.

Limiting the number of tracks in a Smart Playlist

Sometimes it can be useful to limit the number of tracks that you include in a Smart Playlist. For example, if you have a lot of music in a given genre, you may not want your Smart Playlist to include the entire selection of music from that genre. This might be because of a desire to limit the amount of listening time, or to create a playlist of music that can fit on a limited-capacity iPod or iPhone.

iTunes offers the ability to easily limit the number of items selected in a Smart Playlist by either total duration (in minutes or hours) or size (in MB or GB), or simply based on a specified number of items:

1. **Choose File ⇨ New Smart Playlist from the iTunes menu.** The Smart Playlist dialog box appears.

2. **Fill in your Smart Playlist criteria as desired.**

3. **Click the check box beside Limit to.**

4. **From the first drop-down menu to the right, choose the units you want to use when limiting this Smart Playlist.** Your options are minutes, hours, MB, GB, or items.

5. **To the left of the drop-down menu, type the number of units you want to limit this Smart Playlist to, based on the unit selected in Step 4.**

6. **From the Selected By drop-down menu, choose how you want iTunes to prioritize tracks for this Smart Playlist.** Because you are limiting the number of tracks, this option is used to specify which tracks are selected first. Options include alphabetically by Album, Artist, Genre, or Name, by highest or lowest rating, by how often or how recently tracks have been played, or by how recently tracks were added to iTunes.

7. **Click OK.**

For example, if you are throwing a 1980s-themed party and want to select three hours of your favorite '80s tunes that are relatively short (in order to keep the music flowing), choosing the Smart Playlist criteria shown in Figure 5.11 could do the trick.

Limiting Smart Playlists can also be useful for controlling how much content is transferred to your iPod. This can be particularly useful for rotating the content on your iPod to keep it fresh when combined with Smart Playlists that track the last-played date. For example, if you want to keep only 4GB of jazz music on your iPod, but limit it to your favorite tracks that you have not recently listened to, the Smart Playlist criteria shown in Figure 5.12 could be used.

If you configure your iPod to only sync this particular playlist, then tracks that do not meet the criteria are removed from your iPod on the next sync with iTunes and replaced with new tracks. This allows you to effortlessly rotate the music stored on your iPod, which can be particularly useful for lower-capacity iPods. iPod synchronization is discussed further in Chapter 7.

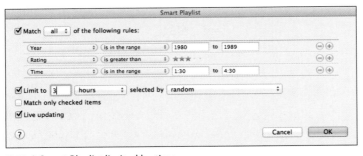

5.11 A Smart Playlist limited by time

Other criteria that can be very useful if you have a recent-model iPod are the skip count and date last skipped. When you start playing a track and suddenly decide to skip ahead to the next track, the skip count and date last skipped fields are updated. These fields can be used to filter out those tracks that you may not really feel like listening to. The example criteria shown in Figure 5.13 expand on the previous Smart Playlist examples, but also exclude all tracks that you have skipped in the past two days.

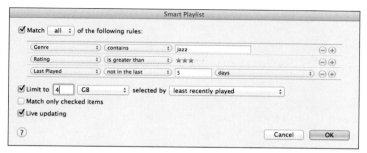

5.12 A Smart Playlist limited by size

This can be very handy to keep the same tracks from coming up repeatedly, particularly in a relatively short Smart Playlist. Skipped tracks end up being excluded in favor of other tracks that you have neither listened to nor skipped recently.

5.13 A Smart Playlist limited by size, excluding recently skipped tracks

Advanced Smart Playlists

Prior to iTunes 9, Smart Playlists could either match all of the listed criteria or any of the listed criteria, but there was no way to have a single Smart Playlist that matched all of some criteria and only some of others. Instead, users were forced to resort to nested intermediate Smart Playlists to accomplish this, cluttering up their iTunes libraries with additional playlists that served no other purpose than to combine multiple conditions. Fortunately, iTunes 9 introduces the capability to have several groups of conditions within a single Smart Playlist, eliminating the need for the cumbersome workaround of nested playlists.

For example, say that you want to create a Smart Playlist that contains all music from the Rock or Pop genres that is rated five stars and that you haven't listened to in at least three days. Prior to iTunes 9, you would have needed to create one Smart Playlist to select music from the Rock or Pop genres and then a separate Smart Playlist to select music from the first playlist that matched your rating and last-played criteria. With iTunes 9, these criteria can now be combined in a single Smart Playlist by adding a separate condition group.

1. **Choose File ➪ New Smart Playlist from the iTunes menu.** The Smart Playlist dialog box appears.

2. **Fill in the criteria for Rating and Last Played as shown in Figure 5.14.**

5.14 A Smart Playlist with Rating and Last Played criteria

3. **Hold down the Opt key (Mac) or Shift key (Windows).** The plus button to the far right of each criteria row changes to an ellipsis. Note that prior to iTunes 10.4, a separate, third ellipsis button was shown here.

4. **Click the ellipsis button to the far right of the Last Played row.** A new condition group appears, as shown in Figure 5.15.

5. **Set the criteria for the condition group to Any and fill in the criteria for the Jazz and Rock genres, as shown in Figure 5.16.**

5.15 A Smart Playlist with a new condition group

116

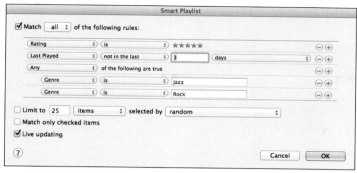

5.16 A Smart Playlist with multiple conditions

6. **Click OK to save your Smart Playlist.** The Smart Playlist appears in your iTunes Source list with a default name highlighted in editing mode.

7. **Type a new name for the Smart Playlist and press Enter.**

There is no practical limit to the number of condition groups you can have in a Smart Playlist, and you can even nest condition groups several levels deep to create very complex Smart Playlists. For example, the Smart Playlist shown in Figure 5.17 selects all Rock tracks that are rated five stars or more and have not been played in the past day and are either audio tracks between 1:30 and 4:00 long or are music videos of any length.

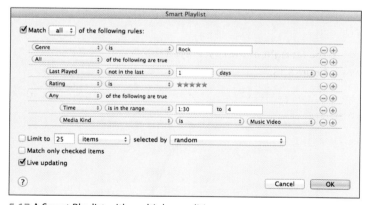

5.17 A Smart Playlist with multiple conditions

Figure 5.18 demonstrates a Smart Playlist that could be used to select different combinations of rating and played time criteria. In this case, tracks from the Rock genre are included if they are rated five stars and have not been played in the past day, or if they are rated three or four stars and have not been played in the past five days.

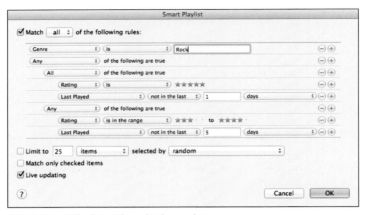

5.18 A Smart Playlist with multiple conditions

Note

Although it is no longer necessary, it is still possible to use other playlists or Smart Playlists as criteria in iTunes. This can still be useful if you have an intermediate Smart Playlist that you're using anyway, rather than merely creating one as a placeholder. Further, some users may still find it conceptually simpler to work with multiple playlists.

Removing tracks from Smart Playlists

Because Smart Playlists are dynamically generated, you cannot remove a track manually from most Smart Playlists. If a track meets the criteria for a Smart Playlist, it is always included and there's no sense in removing it because it would just reappear anyway.

The exception to this is Smart Playlists set to limit items with a random selection. In this case, you can remove an entry from a Smart Playlist as you would from any other playlist by highlighting it and pressing Delete. The selected track is removed from the playlist and replaced with another random track. This can be a useful way to refresh the content in a random Smart Playlist.

Using Genius Playlists

iTunes 8 introduced a new feature called Genius that can help you automatically build lists of songs from your iTunes library that naturally go well together in the same playlist. This is done based on analyzing your music library and tastes and comparing it to information available at the iTunes Store and from other iTunes Genius users. This produces better results than simply analyzing sound patterns in your tracks because iTunes is actually looking at a very large statistical sample of what other iTunes users are purchasing and listening to.

Enabling the Genius feature

Because the Genius feature works by analyzing your music collection against the Apple iTunes database, it requires that iTunes submit information about your music collection to Apple. Because of the privacy concerns involved with this, Apple has taken an opt-in approach where you must specifically enable and sign up for the Genius service. Note that even though your iTunes library information is stored anonymously, an iTunes Store account is required to use the Genius feature.

To enable the Genius feature, follow these steps:

1. **Select Store ➪ Turn on Genius.** An introductory screen appears as shown in Figure 5.19.

2. **Click Turn On Genius.** The iTunes Store sign-in screen appears to begin the Genius setup process, as shown in Figure 5.20.

5.19 The iTunes Genius setup screen

5.20 The iTunes Genius login screen

3. **Sign in to your iTunes Store account and click Continue.** You can also create a new iTunes Store account from this screen if you do not already have an existing account. More information on the iTunes Store can be found in Chapter 2. Once you successfully sign in to your iTunes Store account (or created a new one), iTunes presents you with the Genius terms and conditions, similar to Figure 5.21.

4. **After you review the Genius terms and conditions, click the check box indicating your acceptance and click Continue.** iTunes begins gathering information about your iTunes library and sends this information to the Apple iTunes servers for analysis. You should see a status screen similar to Figure 5.22.

Depending on the size of your iTunes library and the speed of your computer and Internet connection, the process of gathering information and sending it to Apple can take anywhere from a few minutes to a few hours. This process occurs in the background, however, and you can continue using iTunes while this is occurring. Once the process is complete, iTunes displays a screen confirming that Genius is turned on, similar to Figure 5.23.

Should you later decide that you want to turn the Genius feature off for any reason, you can do so by choosing Store ➪ Turn Off Genius from the iTunes menu.

5.21 The iTunes Genius Terms and Conditions and Apple Privacy Policy page

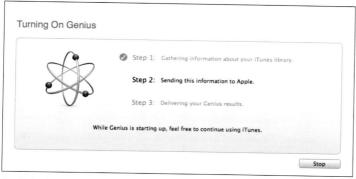

5.22 The iTunes Genius status screen

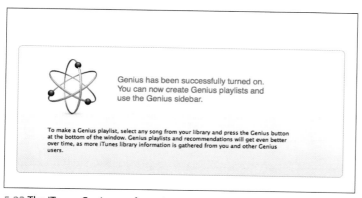

5.23 The iTunes Genius confirmation screen

Note You can also turn Genius on by selecting the Genius playlist entry above your Playlists section on the left side of the iTunes window.

Creating Genius lists

Once the Genius feature has been enabled, you are ready to begin creating Genius lists based on your music collection. To create a Genius list, follow these steps:

1. **Select a music track from your library that you want to base your Genius list on.**

2. **Click the Genius button in the bottom-right corner of the iTunes window, as shown in Figure 5.24.**

iTunes attempts to locate 24 additional tracks in your iTunes library to accompany the selected track and place them together in your Genius list, as shown in Figure 5.25.

5.24 The iTunes Genius button

5.25 A generated iTunes Genius list

By default, iTunes limits a new Genius list to 25 tracks, including the track on which the playlist is based. You can adjust this limit to 50, 75, or 100 tracks by using the Limit to drop-down menu at the top of the Genius list.

From the Genius list, you can begin playing your tracks or sort and reorder them as you would with any other playlist. You can also refresh the content to select a different group of tracks by clicking the Refresh button at the top of the Genius list.

Note

The current Genius list is only stored in iTunes — it is not transferred to other devices unless you save it as a playlist (which is covered in the next section).

The content of the most recently built Genius list remains available under the Genius entry immediately above iTunes DJ in the iTunes Source list.

If iTunes is unable to successfully build a Genius playlist, it notifies you with a dialog box similar to Figure 5.26.

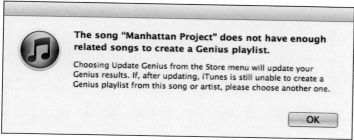

The song "Manhattan Project" does not have enough related songs to create a Genius playlist.

Choosing Update Genius from the Store menu will update your Genius results. If, after updating, iTunes is still unable to create a Genius playlist from this song or artist, please choose another one.

OK

5.26 iTunes Genius is unavailable for the selected track

This problem normally occurs because your Genius information from the iTunes Store is out of date or you simply do not have enough matching tracks in your own iTunes library. As the dialog box suggests, you can ensure your Genius results are up to date by choosing Store ▷ Update Genius from the iTunes menu. If you do this and iTunes still fails to build a Genius listing for the selected track, then the likely reason is that you simply do not have enough matching music tracks. This often occurs in very small iTunes libraries (for example, with less than 500 tracks), but can also occur even in a larger library if you're trying to build a Genius list from a more obscure track.

Saving your Genius list as a playlist

For quick Genius compilations, you can simply begin playing your music directly from the Genius listing. If you've found a particular collection that you want to keep, however, you can also easily save your Genius listing as an iTunes Genius playlist. Follow these steps:

1. **Create a Genius listing, as described in the previous section.**

2. **From the Genius listing, click the Save Playlist button at the top-right corner, as shown in Figure 5.27.**

iTunes creates a new playlist in your library with the name of the original track with which the Genius list was created. This playlist is shown with a Genius icon beside it, rather than the standard playlist icon, similar to Figure 5.28.

This Genius playlist can be renamed or moved into a folder in the same manner as any other playlist. Within the Genius playlist, you can also change the number of tracks selected or refresh the playlist content in the same way as you would for the main Genius list noted earlier. Changes made within a Genius playlist are saved automatically to that playlist.

5.28 The iTunes Genius playlist is indicated by the Genius icon

5.27 Using the iTunes Genius Save Playlist button

Genius playlists can also be synced to your iPod or other Apple media device, and even updated and managed directly on those newer devices that provide support for the Genius feature.

Using Genius recommendations

In addition to building Genius lists and playlists, iTunes also uses the Genius feature to highlight songs that you may be missing from your collection and offer recommendations for other similar music that is available on the iTunes Store. This is similar to the iTunes Mini-Store found in older versions of iTunes, but is far more accurate and flexible.

Note Older iPod models that do not have Genius support can still use Genius playlists — they are simply synced to the device as a standard playlist.

Note Hiding the Playlists section in the iTunes source list displays all Genius Playlists in the Genius section, regardless of whether they have been moved into the Playlists section or not.

Creating Genius Mixes

Once the Genius feature is enabled, iTunes 9 or later automatically creates special Genius Mix playlists in your library by genre, based on data from the Genius feature. Depending on the size of your iTunes library and the amount of similar music available, iTunes can create up to 12 Genius Mixes. Once available, Genius Mixes appear in their own category in the iTunes Source listing, as shown in Figure 5.29.

Note The Genius Mixes category won't appear at all until at least one mix has been generated. If you recently upgraded from iTunes 8, you need to ensure that your Genius data is updated from the iTunes Store. You can force this update by selecting Update Genius from the Store menu in iTunes.

5.29 Genius Mixes

Think of Genius Mixes as custom radio stations built from your own music. A Genius Mix is essentially an endless playlist of music appropriate to a given genre. You can play your Genius Mixes right from within iTunes, or sync them to any newer Apple media device that supports the Genius Mixes feature. As of iTunes 9.1, you can also reorder, rename, or remove any of the automatically generated Genius Mixes.

How Do I Manage Podcasts, Audiobooks, and iTunes U Content?

Although the majority of your iTunes media content is likely to consist of music, iTunes also provides support for three other categories of content: audiobooks, which are basically digital versions of books on tape; podcasts, which are episodic content covering a wide range of interesting topics; and iTunes U collections, which are essentially educationally focused podcasts. Although at a basic level these are all just audio or video content, some specific features are relevant for managing these types of content.

Managing Podcasts and iTunes U Collections

Podcasts and iTunes U content differ from most other audio and video tracks in that they are normally imported automatically as part of a series that you subscribe to, and you're therefore managing a series of episodes as a collection rather than on an individual track-by-track basis.

Podcasts versus iTunes U

For all intents and purposes, Podcasts and iTunes U content are managed in the same way by iTunes. In fact, iTunes U as a category was first introduced to the iTunes Store in late 2006; however, these materials were originally handled simply as podcasts. It was not until the release of iTunes 9 that iTunes U collections received their own distinct category in iTunes.

Note also that iTunes U collections are provided only through the iTunes Store, and while most iTunes U content is freely available, there may be items that are restricted only to students and faculty of particular educational institutions; the iTunes U service allows campuses to host their own internal iTunes U sites exclusively for their own students. This content is generally not visible at all to iTunes users who are not part of those institutions.

Subscribing to podcasts from outside of the iTunes Store

Most podcasts are available through the catalog maintained by the iTunes Store, but you may still find the occasional podcast that is not in the iTunes catalog for whatever reason, or you may want to subscribe to private podcasts from friends or family members.

Keep in mind that even if you find a podcast listed on another Web site, it may still be available through the iTunes Store, and many of these podcasts have a direct link somewhere on their Web page that automatically takes you to their podcast in the iTunes Store.

Further, many podcasts also have a direct iTunes link on their page that calls up your own iTunes application to automatically subscribe to the podcast.

However, if you find a podcast on the Internet that does not have an iTunes subscription link anywhere on the page, then you can subscribe to this podcast manually. Follow these steps:

1. **Find the URL for the podcast on the podcast's Web page.** If the URL isn't visible, you can sometimes find it listed as an RSS subscription link from the podcast listing.

2. **Copy this URL to your Clipboard by choosing Edit ⇨ Copy from your browser's menu.**

3. **In iTunes, choose Advanced ⇨ Subscribe to Podcast from the iTunes menu.** A URL entry dialog box appears, as shown in Figure 6.1.

4. **Paste the URL from your Clipboard into the URL dialog box by choosing Edit ⇨ > Paste from the iTunes menu.**

6.1 The Subscribe to Podcast URL entry dialog box

5. **Click OK.** You are taken to the Podcast listing in iTunes, and the newly added podcast appears and begins downloading the most recent episode or episodes.

All podcasts within iTunes are managed in the same way, regardless of how you subscribe to them.

Setting how many episodes to keep

After you subscribe to a podcast or iTunes U collection, iTunes automatically downloads new episodes as they become available. By default, however, iTunes also keeps all of the old episodes of each podcast or collection, regardless of whether you have listened to them. If you have a podcast or collection that updates on a daily basis, you can quickly accumulate a lot of episodes that may no longer be relevant yet are taking up space on your computer.

Fortunately, iTunes can perform some housekeeping for you in this regard by automatically removing old episodes. To adjust how many episodes of each podcast or iTunes U collection that iTunes keeps, follow these steps:

1. **Select Podcasts or iTunes U from the iTunes Source list.** The appropriate listing appears, as shown in Figure 6.2.

2. **Click Settings at the bottom of the listing screen.** The Settings window appears, as shown in Figure 6.3.

3. **From the Settings for drop-down menu, select the individual subscription for which you want to adjust the settings, or select Podcast or iTunes U Defaults to adjust the default settings for all podcasts or collections.**

4. **If you have selected an individual subscription, deselect the Use Default Settings option to clear it and permit you to override the default settings.** The two drop-down menus at the bottom of the dialog box become active.

6.2 The iTunes Podcasts listing screen

6.3 The iTunes Podcast Settings dialog box

5. **From the Episodes to keep drop-down menu, choose how many episodes you want iTunes to retain for each podcast or collection:**

- **All episodes.** iTunes does not automatically delete any episodes. All episodes are retained by iTunes unless you delete them manually.

- **All unplayed episodes.** iTunes automatically deletes all episodes that have been listened to at least once, based on the play count field. Episodes that you have not listened to all the way through are not deleted, regardless of age or number of episodes.

- **Most recent episode.** Only the most recent episode is retained. iTunes automatically deletes all older episodes as each new episode is downloaded.

- **Last <X> episodes.** Only the most recent 2, 3, 4, 5, or 10 episodes are retained. iTunes automatically deletes any episodes above this number as each new episode is downloaded.

6. **Click OK.**

Exempting specific episodes from automatic deletion

You can exempt specific podcast or iTunes U episodes from automatic deletion by iTunes on an individual basis. This can be useful if you have a specific favorite episode that you want to keep, but still want iTunes to automatically manage and clean up your other episodes. To exempt a specific episode from automatic deletion, follow these steps:

1. **In the iTunes podcast or iTunes U listing, right-click the individual episode that you want to exempt from automatic deletion.** A contextual menu appears.

2. **From the context menu, choose Do Not Auto Delete, as shown in Figure 6.4.** If the option Allow Auto Delete is shown instead of Do Not Auto Delete, this indicates that the podcast has already been set as exempt from automatic deletion. Clicking the Allow Auto Delete option resets the podcast to being automatically deleted according to your default podcast-retention setting in iTunes.

Note Individual podcast or iTunes U episodes that you manually download using the Get button are set to be exempted from automatic deletion by default. Because you are specifically downloading these episodes, iTunes assumes you want to keep them.

Genius You can change the automatic-deletion status for all episodes of a given podcast or iTunes U collection by right-clicking the podcast title and selecting either Allow Auto Delete or Do Not Auto Delete. Choosing either option from the context menu resets all episodes in the current podcast or collection to the selected value, overriding any individual per-episode selections.

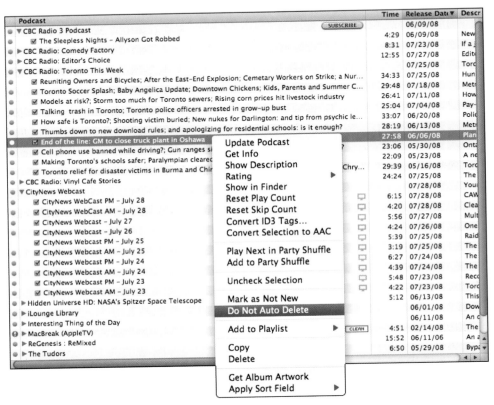

6.4 A podcast contextual menu

Managing Audiobooks

One of the first new types of content other than music to appear in iTunes were audiobooks, spoken versions of books narrated and available to be listened to through iTunes or on your iPod. Although an audiobook is really just another audio file, it differs from a music file in that it is usually quite a bit longer — sometimes several hours. Audiobooks also support bookmarking so that iTunes and your iPod can remember where you left off, and are often divided into chapters.

Converting and importing your own audiobooks

Audiobooks compatible with iTunes and the iPod and Apple's other media devices may be purchased in digital form either from the iTunes Store or from Audible.com. These come encoded in an iTunes-ready format, with chapter markers and the capability to bookmark their playback position already included. They also very nicely show up under the Books category in iTunes.

Note Audible also provides its own iOS application for downloading and listening to audiobooks from Audible.com. This application stores audiobooks separately on your iOS devices and does not interface with iTunes or your device's iPod library in any way.

You may have obtained audiobooks from other sources, however, and want to add these features to your own audiobooks. Unfortunately, if you simply import these audiobooks into your iTunes library, they are catalogued alongside your normal music files — they do not appear in the Audiobooks section, nor do they automatically remember their playback position.

An additional advantage of ensuring your audiobooks are properly categorized is that you can vary their playback speed when listening to them on your iPod, iPhone, or iPad. Normal music tracks do not provide this feature.

Although previous versions of iTunes required you to jump through some manual hoops in order to get your own files imported as audiobooks, the great news is that recent versions of iTunes now provide the ability to set any audio file as an audiobook directly. Follow these steps:

1. **Locate the file or group of files in your iTunes library that you want to set as audiobooks.**

2. **Choose File ⇨ Get Info from the iTunes menu.** The file information dialog box appears.

3. **Click the Options tab from the file information dialog box, as shown in Figure 6.5.**

4. **From the Media Kind drop-down menu, choose Audiobook.**

5. **Click OK.**

Some audiobooks that you obtain from other sources may consist of multiple files, with each chapter divided into its own MP3 file, for example. Although you can import these files individually into your iTunes library and listen to them as you would any other file, you may want to merge these tracks together and convert them into a proper audiobook for a better listening experience.

Although there are numerous tools available on the Internet that can join MP3 files together, there are some tools that also allow you to turn these files into a proper audiobook in the process.

For Mac users, I recommend checking out Audiobook Builder by Splasm Software at www.splasm. com. Windows users should look at MarkAble from iPodSoft at www.ipodsoft.com. Both of these tools provide the capability to join separate audiobook files together, convert them into an iTunes-ready audiobook format, and import them directly into your iTunes library.

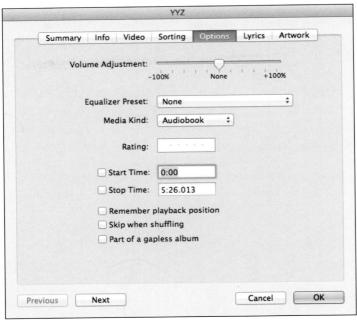

6.5 The Options tab of the iTunes file information dialog box

You can also add chapter markers to your own audiobooks with these third-party tools. Audiobook Builder for the Mac includes this capability, while MarkAble provides this feature through a companion product called Chapter Master.

Importing audiobooks from CD

Another common source of audiobooks is from CDs that may be purchased from bookstores or borrowed from your local library. Because your iPod is a far more convenient device than a portable CD player, you may want to import these audiobooks into iTunes so that you can listen to them on your iPod.

Note

When borrowing audiobook CDs from your local library, you should check your library's policies concerning the conversion of borrowed material into other formats.

Most audiobooks on CD, however, come as multiple-track CDs, and by default are imported into iTunes as separate tracks for each chapter. Although you can certainly join up these tracks later, iTunes offers a very useful built-in feature for merging tracks from a CD during import:

1. **Open your iTunes preferences and click the General tab, as shown in Figure 6.6.**

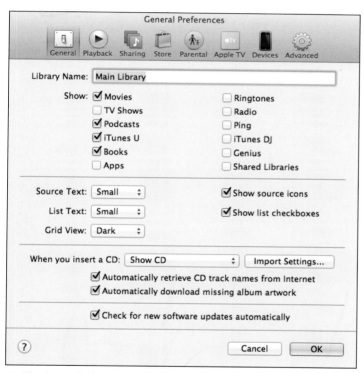

6.6 The General tab in the iTunes preferences

2. **From the When you insert a CD drop-down menu, choose Show CD.**

3. **Click OK.**

4. **Insert the CD into your computer's CD drive as you normally would.**

5. **A CD track listing appears, as shown in Figure 6.7.**

137

6.7 An iTunes CD track listing

6. **Click the first track in the CD track listing.**

7. **Choose Edit ⇨ Select All from the iTunes menu.** All tracks are selected.

8. **Choose Advanced ⇨ Join CD Tracks.** iTunes indicates that the selected tracks are going to be imported as a single track, as shown in Figure 6.8.

9. **Click Import CD in the bottom-right corner of the iTunes window.**

When the import is complete, a new single track appears in your iTunes library representing the content of the entire CD.

6.8 iTunes indicating joined tracks

Caution If the Join CD Tracks option is not available, ensure that you are not sorting your CD track listing. Only contiguous tracks may be joined together by iTunes, and the CD track listing must therefore be left unsorted.

Genius The Join CD Tracks option may be used to join any two or more contiguous tracks on a CD during import. To join only specific tracks, simply select those tracks before choosing the Join CD Tracks option.

Setting tracks to remember their playback position

One of the benefits of audiobooks is that iTunes remembers and stores the playback position in each file when you stop listening to it. This means that you can stop listening anywhere in a track and then pick up again later on, exactly where you left off. Further, this playback position is also transferred between devices, so if you listen to an audiobook on your iPod and then sync it to iTunes, this bookmark is transferred to your iTunes library, and then from there to any other device on which that file is stored, such as your Apple TV or iPad.

Audiobooks purchased from the iTunes Store or Audible.com are always set to remember their playback position by default. If you have imported your own audiobooks from other sources, however, you must specifically tell iTunes to remember the playback position in these tracks. You can set the Remember playback position option manually on any audio track in your library. Follow these steps:

1. **Select the track for which you want to remember the playback position.**
2. **Choose File ➪ Get Info from the iTunes menu.**
3. **In the iTunes track information dialog box, click the Options tab.** The track options are displayed.
4. **Select the Remember playback position option, as shown in Figure 6.9.**
5. **Click OK.**

Note If you select the track options for an audiobook purchased from the iTunes Store or Audible.com, the Remember playback position option is forced on and cannot be changed. This is normal, as this setting cannot be disabled for purchased audiobook files.

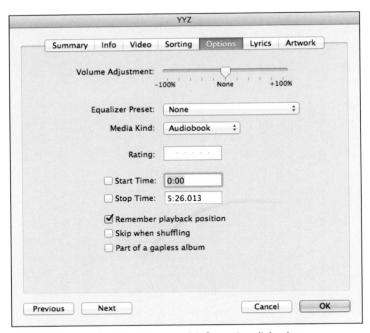

6.9 The Options tab of the iTunes track information dialog box

Setting audiobooks to be excluded from shuffled playback

Another feature common to audiobooks is that they are not included in shuffled playback because it wouldn't make much sense to start into a reading of *The Da Vinci Code* in the middle of your hip-hop party.

As with the Remember playback position option, this is a mandatory setting for audiobooks from the iTunes Store or Audible.com, but you can apply this setting to your own imported audiobooks or any other track in your library:

1. **Select the track that you want to skip when shuffling.**

2. **Choose File ⇨ Get Info from the iTunes menu.**

3. **In the iTunes track information dialog box, click the Options tab.** The track options are displayed.

4. **Select the Skip when shuffling option, as shown in Figure 6.10.**

5. **Click OK.**

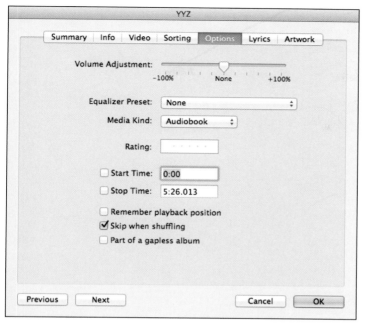

6.10 The Options tab of the iTunes track information dialog box

Note

If you select the track options for an audiobook purchased from the iTunes Store or Audible.com, the Skip when shuffling option is mandatory and cannot be changed. This is normal, as this setting cannot be disabled for audiobook files.

How Do I Manage the Content on My iPod?

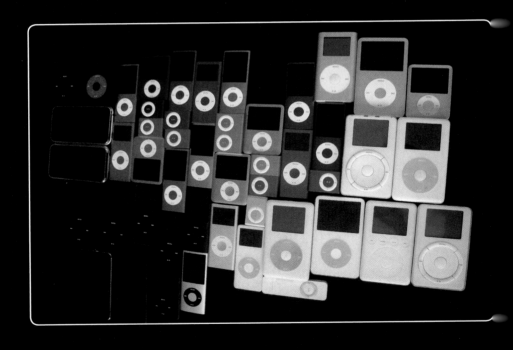

After you organize your content in iTunes, the next step is to take it with you on the go. With an iPod, iPhone, or iPad, you have a portable media device that acts as an extension of your iTunes library, allowing you to take your media content with you, including playlists and other organization within your main iTunes library. Additionally, with Apple's new iTunes Match service, you can even store your entire library in the Cloud and access it from anywhere you have an Internet connection.

Identifying Your iPod Model

The iPod was first introduced to the world back in 2001 as a 5GB audio-only media player. Since then, it has evolved dramatically from those humble beginnings, with ever-increasing capacity, support for storing and displaying photos and video content, and myriad accessory options and new features.

With a wide variety of different iPod devices now available, it's important to understand the difference among the various iPod models so that you understand what types of content and features are supported by the different models.

Current iPod models are divided into four basic categories:

- **iPod classic.** This iPod, shown in Figure 7.1, is the device that likely first comes to mind when you hear the term *iPod*. It is the direct evolution of the original iPod. Prior to 2007, this was known simply by the name iPod, and each new model was referred to using a generation designation. The original iPod that was released in 2001 is now referred to as the first-generation, or 1G, iPod, while the last model to simply bear the name iPod was the fifth-generation, or 5G, iPod. The iPod classic is considered by most to be the sixth-generation iPod. All of these models include hard drives of various sizes and have the same basic dimensions and form factors. The fourth-generation iPod was the first model to support photo playback and TV output, while the fifth-generation iPod introduced video playback. Support for iPod Games was added in a firmware update for the fifth-generation iPod, although in fall 2011 Apple quietly removed iPod Games from the iTunes Store. Today, the current iPod classic, or sixth-generation iPod, comes as a single 160GB model. Although original 80GB and 160GB models can still be found with an identical design, they do not include the latest features of the 2008 120GB and 2009 160GB models, such as Genius list support.

Note

It's worth mentioning that Apple has not updated the iPod classic since 2009, making no mention of it at all during the company's traditional 2010 and 2011 iPod events. Although the 2009 iPod classic is still being sold, Apple is clearly not developing it any further, leading many to believe that the device may eventually be discontinued in favor of the iPod touch.

- **iPod nano.** The iPod nano, shown in Figure 7.2, was introduced in 2005 as the first flash memory-based digital audio player from Apple. It was intended as a replacement for the iPod mini, which was a smaller version of the original iPod models. The transition to using flash memory instead of hard drives allowed Apple to build a much thinner iPod at the same capacities as the previous iPod mini. The iPod nano is also sometimes referred to by generation designations, and there have been six models of iPod nano as of this writing. Video playback support was added in the third-generation iPod nano and was available in both the fourth- and fifth-generation iPod nano models. The fifth-generation model that was released in 2009 also added video recording and FM radio capabilities. The sixth-generation iPod nano released in September 2010 represented a very significant change in the iPod nano lineup. This newest iPod bears almost no resemblance to prior generation models and actually removed many of the features from the previous iPod nano, including video playback and recording and support for games, trading these off for a much smaller size and a touchscreen interface instead of the traditional Click Wheel. The firmware for the sixth-generation iPod nano was updated for the fall 2011 iPod event, providing some interface changes and improvements to the built-in Nike fitness application; however, the hardware itself remains identical to the 2010 version, and users of the prior model can update their firmware to gain the same capabilities.

7.1 iPod classic

- **iPod shuffle.** In 2005, Apple also introduced a small, portable, screenless iPod known as the iPod shuffle, shown in Figure 7.3. The idea behind the iPod shuffle is that you load it up with a selection of your favorite music and just listen to it as it plays, either in a random or sequential order. The original iPod shuffle resembled a white USB flash drive. The later second-generation iPod shuffle took on a significantly different design, connecting to your computer through a special dock that plugs into the headphone port. A third-generation iPod shuffle changed the design again, moving most controls to the head-phones and connecting to your computer with a special cable through the headphone port. The fourth-generation iPod shuffle returned to the on-device control design of the second-generation. The iPod shuffle was last updated in 2010 and remains available only in a 2GB capacity.

7.2 iPod nano (with video)

● **iPod touch.** Released about three months after the debut of the Apple iPhone, the iPod touch, shown in Figure 7.4, bears more resemblance to the iPhone than it does to its iPod brethren. The iPod touch is very similar to the iPhone without the phone features, and otherwise uses the same iOS operating system and interface; current firmware includes features like a calendar, e-mail client, and even a Web browser. This makes it part personal digital assistant (PDA), part media player. There have been four models of the iPod touch released to date, with the fourth-generation iPod touch introducing a camera and high-resolution display similar to the iPhone 4 as well as support for HD video recording and playback. The fourth-generation iPod touch is available in 8GB, 32GB, and 64GB capacities. A white version was introduced at the fall 2011 Apple event, but the device remains otherwise unchanged from the 2010 model.

Copyright Jeremy Horwitz for iLounge.com

7.3 iPod shuffle

Copyright Jeremy Horwitz for iLounge.com

7.4 iPod touch

One other model of iPod that you may own or occasionally encounter is the iPod mini. This was a smaller version of the fourth-generation iPod, with 4GB and later 6GB capacities. Other than the

147

smaller form factor and lower capacity, it supported the same basic feature set as the 4G iPod. Although a very popular iPod model at the time, it was discontinued and replaced by the iPod nano in 2005.

The most important distinction between iPod models for the purposes of this book is based on the types of content that each iPod model supports and some of the restrictions on that content. For the most part, when you connect an iPod model to your computer, iTunes simply hides any options that are not available on that particular model. Therefore, if you find that certain tabs or options are missing as you read through this chapter, the most likely reason is that your particular iPod does not support those features.

Note Apple's other two mainstream portable media devices, the iPhone and iPad, behave much like the iPod touch relative to iTunes and the playback and synchronization of media content.

Further, there is normally a correlation between features added to new versions of iTunes and the iPods released around the same time. For example, the new Genius Mixes featured in iTunes 9 (discussed in Chapter 5) was also added to the fall 2009 iPod models. With the exception of the iPhone, iPod touch, and iPad, Apple rarely provides firmware updates to bring these features to older iPod models.

Note For the sake of simplicity, I use the term *iPod* in this chapter to refer to all of Apple's portable media devices, including the iPhone and iPad unless specifically noted otherwise. The term *iOS devices* collectively refers to Apple's touchscreen devices — the iPod touch, iPhone, and iPad.

Managing Music and Video Content on Your iPod

Although today's iPods have evolved into more than just media players, the ability to play back music and video content remains the primary purpose of the iPod for most users. Unlike many other portable media players on the market, the iPod is designed to work hand-in-hand with the iTunes application on your desktop computer, based on the concept that you manage your music content in the form of a main library on your computer and then carry around some or all of it on your portable device by synchronizing your iPod with your iTunes library.

Synchronizing your content to your iPod automatically

By design, iTunes is intended to manage all of the content on your iPod through automatic synchronization. In this default mode, you simply connect your device to your computer and iTunes detects it and mirrors the state of your computer's library onto your iPod. Any tracks you have added to iTunes since the last synchronization are transferred onto your device, and any tracks you have removed from your iTunes library are removed from your device.

Further, during automatic synchronization, certain data is transferred back from your iPod into your iTunes library. This includes information, such as the play count, last played date, and rating for any tracks you've listened to and/or rated on your device.

If you are using an iPod that is large enough to store your entire iTunes media library, there is rarely any need to be concerned about your automatic synchronization settings. iTunes handles this automatically for you, and your device simply mirrors your entire iTunes library.

However, if your library is larger than the capacity of your iPod, you may want to adjust some settings to choose which content from your library is synchronized with your device. If iTunes detects that you are trying to synchronize a library larger than your iPod's capacity, it notifies you of this with a dialog box similar to Figure 7.5 and automatically syncs a selection of music from your iTunes library.

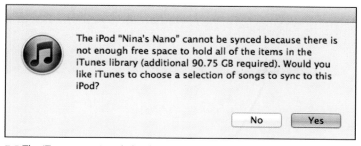

The iPod "Nina's Nano" cannot be synced because there is not enough free space to hold all of the items in the iTunes library (additional 90.75 GB required). Would you like iTunes to choose a selection of songs to sync to this iPod?

No   Yes

7.5 The iTunes warning dialog box when syncing a library larger than the iPod's capacity

Generally, iTunes's choices for this are somewhat random and are not likely to reflect your own preferences. Rather than relying on iTunes to simply build a random playlist of music from your library, you can build your own playlists and simply select those playlists for synchronization to your device:

1. **Create a playlist or series of playlists containing the content you want to synchronize to your device.** Smart Playlists that limit content by MB or GB sizes are ideal for this purpose, as discussed in Chapter 5.

2. **Connect your device to your computer.**

3. **Select your device from the iTunes Devices list on the left side of the iTunes window.** You see a Summary screen for your iPod, similar to Figure 7.6.

4. **From the tabs that appear at the top of the Summary screen, click the Music tab.** The screen switches to your music sync settings, similar to Figure 7.7.

5. **Click the check box beside Sync Music if it is not already checked.**

6. **Select the Selected playlists, artists, and genres option to choose to synchronize only selected content to your device.**

7. **From the list of playlists, click the check box beside each playlist that you created in step 1 that you want to sync to your device.**

7.6 iPod Summary screen

8. **Optionally, from the list of genres, click the check box to indicate any genres that you want to sync to your device.** This selects all music from selected genres in addition to the other playlists and artists that you have selected.

9. **Optionally, from the list of albums, click the check box to indicate any albums that you want to sync to your device.** This selects all music from selected albums in addition to the other playlists, artists, and genres that you have selected.

10. **Optionally, select the Include music videos check box if your playlists contain music videos that you want to transfer to your device.** This option is only displayed if your iPod model supports video playback.

11. **Optionally, click the Automatically fill free space with songs check box if you want iTunes to select additional content at random to fill any remaining space on your device.**

12. **Click Apply.** iTunes saves the settings for your device and begins synchronizing the selected content.

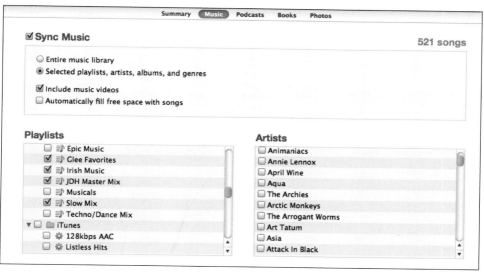

7.7 iPod music sync settings

Genius

When building playlists for synchronization to your iPod, you can confirm the size of the content in each playlist by looking at the bottom of the iTunes window. The size is shown in number of songs, total playing time, and capacity.

Genius

The search field in the top-right corner of the iTunes window can be used to filter the list of artist, genre, and album names on the Music sync settings screen.

Note that first- and second-generation iPod shuffles behave a bit differently from all other iPod models. Instead of providing automatic synchronization of your entire library or only selected playlists, you select one playlist from which the iPod shuffle automatically fills its content. When you connect the iPod shuffle to your computer, it simply transfers as many tracks from this playlist as possible onto the device. To configure your iPod shuffle, follow these steps:

1. **Connect your iPod shuffle to your computer.**

2. **Select your iPod shuffle from the iTunes Devices list on the left side of the iTunes window.** You see a Settings screen for your iPod shuffle, similar to Figure 7.8.

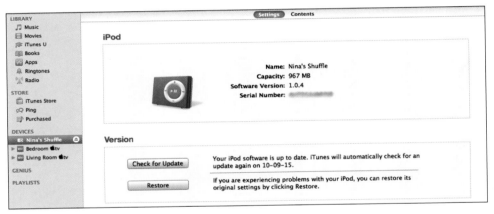

7.8 iPod shuffle Settings screen

3. **From the tabs that appear at the top of the iPod shuffle Settings screen, click the Contents tab.** The screen switches to your iPod shuffle content settings, similar to Figure 7.9.

4. **In the Autofill From drop-down menu, located at the bottom of the Contents screen, choose the playlist from which you want to fill your iPod shuffle.** You may also choose Music to simply autofill your iPod shuffle using your main iTunes library, rather than limiting the content to a specified playlist.

5. **Optionally, click Settings to choose additional options.** Other options you can decide to use include:

- **Replace all items when Autofilling.** Click this check box to enable iTunes to replace any existing content on the iPod shuffle with content from the selected playlist. If this option is not selected, iTunes adds the content of the selected playlist to the content already on the iPod shuffle.

- **Choose items randomly.** Click this check box if you want iTunes to determine if it fills the iPod shuffle with the playlist content in its original playlist order or randomly.

- **Choose higher rated items more often.** Click this check box if you want iTunes to give preference to higher-rated items when filling the iPod shuffle.

6. **Click Autofill to begin filling the iPod shuffle.**

	Name	Time	Artist	Album	Genre	Rating
1	Rule the World	4:57	Take That	Stardust (Music fro...	Soundtrack	★★★
2	Love Theme from the Godfather	2:45	Nino Rota	The Godfather – Tri...	Soundtrack	
3 ⊘	The Rose	3:34	Bette Midler	Hit Singles 1980–1...	Rock	
4	I'll Stand By You	3:59	The Pretenders	Last of the Indepen...	Rock	★★★
5 ⊘	Viva la Vida	4:01	Coldplay	Viva la Vida	Alternative	
6 ⊘	Objects in the Rear View Mirror M...	10:15	Meat Loaf	Bat Out of Hell II: B...	Rock/Pop	★★★
7	Don't Stop Believin'	4:09	Journey	Escape	Pop	★★★
8 ⊘	Hold Onto the Nights	5:14	Richard Marx	Richard Marx: Grea...	Rock	★★★
9 ⊘	Yesterday	2:03	The Beatles	Help!	Rock/Pop	
10	Making Love Out Of Nothing At All	5:43	Air Supply	Air Supply: Greates...	Rock/Pop	★★★
11 ⊘	I Don't Want to Miss a Thing	4:28	Aerosmith	Devil's Got a New D...	Rock	
12 ⊘	Right Here Waiting	4:23	Richard Marx	Richard Marx: Grea...	Rock	★★★
13 ⊘	Where the Streets Have No Name ...	4:38	U2	The Complete U2 –...	Rock/Pop	
14 ⊘	Hey There Delilah	3:52	Plain White T's	Hey There Delilah –...	Alternative	
15 ⊘	I Want to Hold Your Hand	2:46	T.V. Carpio	Across the Univers...	Soundtrack	
16 ⊘	February Song	5:12	Josh Groban	Awake	Vocal	
17 ⊘	I've Got You Under My Skin	3:40	Michael Bublé	It's Time	Easy Listen...	
18	Dream Come True	4:18	Frozen Ghost	Nice Place to Visit	Rock/Pop	★★★
19 ⊘	In Too Deep	4:59	Genesis	Genesis: Platinum ...	Rock/Pop	★★★
20 ⊘	Falling Into You	4:18	Celine Dion	Falling Into You	Rock/Pop	★★★
21 ⊘	Hold On	4:11	Sarah McLachlan	iTunes Originals – ...	Rock/Pop	★★★
22 ⊘	This Is The Time	5:01	Billy Joel	Billy Joel's Greatest ...	Rock/Pop	
23 ⊘	Fields of Gold	3:39	Sting	The Very Best of Sti...	Rock/Pop	
24 ⊘	No Son of Mine	6:39	Genesis	Genesis: Platinum ...	Rock/Pop	★★★
25	Price Of Love	4:48	Bad English	Bad English	Rock/Pop	★★★
26	I Know You're Out There Somewh...	6:39	The Moody Blues	The Best Of The Mo...	Rock/Pop	★★★

Settings | Contents

Autofill From: ♪ Slow Mix   Settings...   Autofill

7.9 iPod shuffle Contents screen

iTunes Phones

Prior to the introduction of the iPhone, Apple established a partnership with Motorola to add iPod-like functionality to Motorola's cellular phones.

The first of these to be introduced was the Motorola ROKR E1 in mid-2005, followed later by the Motorola RAZR V3i — an iTunes version of Motorola's very popular RAZR V3 series phones. These devices operated like normal Motorola phones, but instead of the generic MP3 player that other Motorola phones included, these phones had an iTunes application, providing iPod-like functionality.

Synchronization of an iTunes Phone was handled over the phone's USB v1.1 interface, and iTunes basically treated the phone in the same way as the iPod shuffle. However, these phones had an artificial limit of 100 tracks, regardless of the size of memory card used in the phone.

The iTunes Phones were never hugely popular, mostly because of their slow USB interface, 100-track limitation, and proprietary headphone connectors. However, they did represent the first foray by Apple into an iTunes-integrated phone solution and were not a bad companion solution for those iPod users who simply wanted to carry around a few music tracks on their phone.

Genius

iTunes 9 introduced a new option on the Summary tab for all iPod devices: Convert higher bit rate songs to 128kbps AAC. Previously limited to the iPod shuffle, this option automatically converts any larger tracks down to a lower bit rate during sync in order to fit more music onto your device. Only the copies transferred to the iPod are converted; the original files remain untouched.

Managing content on your iPod manually

When using automatic synchronization, iTunes takes the approach that your iPod is simply an extension of your main iTunes library — a portable device that you carry your content around on when away from your desktop computer. As a function of this iTunes-iPod relationship, your iPod becomes associated with your main iTunes library. Connecting your iPod to a different iTunes library yields a warning that your iPod is associated with a different iTunes library and informs you that you must erase all of the current content on your iPod in order to sync with this second library, similar to the message shown in Figure 7.10.

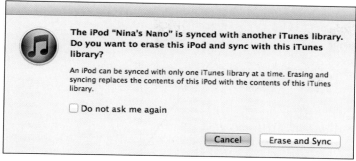

The iPod "Nina's Nano" is synced with another iTunes library. Do you want to erase this iPod and sync with this iTunes library?

An iPod can be synced with only one iTunes library at a time. Erasing and syncing replaces the contents of this iPod with the contents of this iTunes library.

☐ Do not ask me again

Cancel   Erase and Sync

7.10 iPod synchronization warning

This is necessary because an iPod in automatic synchronization mirrors the content in a single iTunes library. You therefore cannot synchronize the same device to a second iTunes library without mirroring that library instead, thereby removing all of the content from the first iTunes library and replacing it with the content from the second library.

Fortunately, for users who want to load content onto their device from more than one computer, iTunes offers the ability to manage the audio and video content on the iPod manually, rather than using automatic synchronization. In this mode, instead of the device acting as an extension of your main iTunes library, it acts as its own separate library that you manage directly from iTunes.

In a manual configuration, it is not even necessary to maintain an actual iTunes library on your computer — iTunes merely becomes the conduit by which you transfer your audio and video content onto the iPod, and once transferred, this content does not need to remain in your iTunes library.

Caution Although you can use manual management to store your music and video content exclusively on your iPod, this is not recommended. The iPod is a portable device that can be lost, stolen, or damaged, and is therefore not a good place to store the only copy of your music. If you're not going to keep your music on your computer, at least ensure that it's backed up somewhere else.

To set your iPod to manage the audio and video content on it manually, follow these steps:

1. **Connect your iPod to your computer.** If you are connecting your iPod to a new iTunes library, you are prompted with the warning dialog shown in Figure 7.10.

2. **If a warning dialog box appears, simply click Cancel.** Your iPod remains connected to your iTunes library, but no automatic synchronization occurs.

3. **Select your iPod from the iTunes Devices list on the left side of the iTunes window.** You see a Summary screen for your iPod.

4. **Click the Manually manage music and videos check box, as shown in Figure 7.11.** If you're using an older iPod model that does not support video, this simply reads Manually manage music instead.

5. **Click Apply.**

Note

When an iPod is in Manual mode, changes made on the iPod, such as rating, play count, and last-played information, are not transferred back to your iTunes library. This information is stored only on the iPod.

7.11 iPod Summary screen with Manually manage music and videos selected

Note

First- and second-generation iPod shuffles always behave as if they are in Manual mode for the purposes of content management. There is no Manual mode setting for these iPod shuffles, as you can drag and drop content to them at any time.

After your device has been set to Manual mode, it no longer automatically syncs with any iTunes library unless you disable this setting. Even if you connect the device to another iTunes library, it remains in Manual mode. Any content that was synchronized to your iPod manually remains on your device, including any playlists, but the device is treated as a completely separate library while in Manual mode.

To add content to your iPod manually, simply drag and drop that content directly onto your iPod icon in the iTunes Devices list on the left side of your iTunes window. You can also transfer playlists from your iTunes library onto your iPod by simply dragging and dropping them onto the iPod icon in the same way you do for music and video content.

To modify or remove content from a manually managed iPod, first expand the iPod to show its content by clicking the small triangle to the left of your iPod icon, as shown in Figure 7.12.

You can then select content directly on the iPod from within iTunes as you would for your main library. Most of the same iTunes library-management functions are available while managing an iPod's content manually, including the ability to update track information and delete tracks.

Keep in mind that not all content is managed manually on an iPod. The manual-management option only applies to audio and video content. Individual podcast episodes can be added to your iPod manually, or you can still choose to synchronize whole podcast subscriptions automatically while still managing the rest of your iPod content manually. Other types of content, such as photos, apps, contacts, and calendars, are always synchronized automatically if enabled.

7.12 Managing content of an iPod (here called iPod classic) manually

157

Note You can only manage the content on an iPhone manually from a single computer. The iPhone does not appear in Manual mode when you connect it to another iTunes library, and you cannot enable Manual mode on a second library without erasing your iPhone content.

Genius In iTunes 10 or later you can add content manually to an iPod that is configured for automatic synchronization. To do this, simply drag and drop the content onto the iPod as if it were in Manual mode. Manually added content appears in a separate list at the bottom of the Music sync settings screen for your device.

Synchronizing checked items

You can also control which items are synchronized to your iPod through the use of the check boxes that appear beside your items in your iTunes library. By default, iTunes synchronizes all items to your iPod, regardless of whether they are checked in your iTunes library. You can easily change this on a per-device basis, however.

To set your device to transfer only checked items, follow these steps:

1. **Connect your iPod to your computer.**

2. **Select your iPod from the iTunes Devices list on the left side of the iTunes window.** You see a Summary screen for your iPod.

3. **Click the Sync only checked songs and videos check box, as shown in Figure 7.13.** For older iPod models that do not support video, this simply reads Sync only checked songs.

4. **Click Apply.**

When you select this option, any items on your device that are not checked in your iTunes library are removed from the device during the sync operation that occurs immediately after clicking Apply.

Note Unchecked songs do not play back in iTunes, either, unless you specifically select them by double-clicking them. This method of iPod management can therefore be useful to exclude items that you do not want to listen to anyway, such as seasonal or holiday music. However, using specified playlists is the recommended option for syncing an iPod that is smaller than your iTunes library.

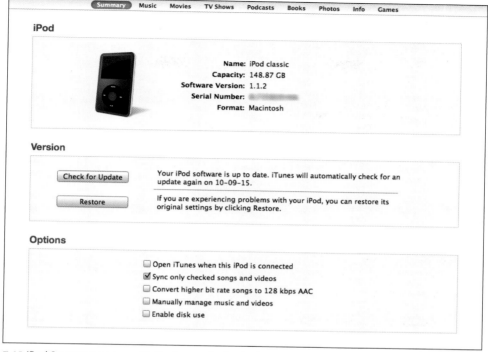

Summary	Music	Movies	TV Shows	Podcasts	Books	Photos	Info	Games

iPod

Name: iPod classic
Capacity: 148.87 GB
Software Version: 1.1.2
Serial Number: ▇▇▇▇▇▇▇
Format: Macintosh

Version

Check for Update — Your iPod software is up to date. iTunes will automatically check for an update again on 10-09-15.

Restore — If you are experiencing problems with your iPod, you can restore its original settings by clicking Restore.

Options

☐ Open iTunes when this iPod is connected
☑ Sync only checked songs and videos
☐ Convert higher bit rate songs to 128 kbps AAC
☐ Manually manage music and videos
☐ Enable disk use

7.13 iPod Summary screen with the Sync only checked songs and videos option selected

Synchronizing movies

If you are using a video-capable iPod model, you can also control which movies and TV shows are transferred to your iPod in a similar manner. In this case, however, you can either build playlists as you would for music, or you can simply select specific movies and TV shows directly.

To select which movies you want to synchronize to your device, follow these steps:

1. **Connect your iPod to your computer.**

2. **Select your iPod from the iTunes Devices list on the left side of the iTunes window.**

3. **Click the Movies tab.** The screen switches to your movie sync settings, similar to Figure 7.14.

4. **Click the Sync Movies check box if it is not already selected.**

7.14 iPod movie sync settings

5. **Click the Automatically include check box if you want to simply sync all of your movies or automatically sync recent movies to your device.** You can then choose all movies or a specified number of recent or unwatched movies from the drop-down menu. If you choose not to synchronize all movies automatically, a movie and playlist selection appears, similar to Figure 7.15.

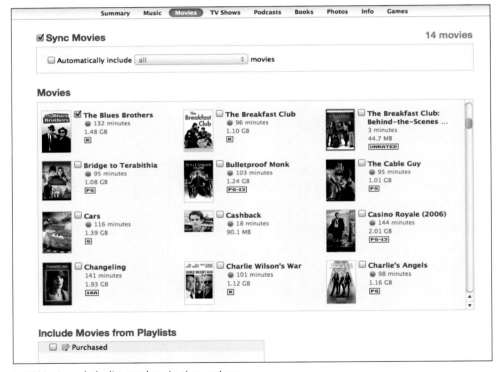

7.15 Movie and playlist synchronization options

6. **Click the check boxes beside the movies or playlists that you want to synchronize to your device.** Movies you have not yet viewed are displayed with a blue dot next to the movie title, and movies that you have viewed partially are shown with a half-filled blue dot. You can also use the search box that appears in the top-right corner to search for specific movie titles. Also note that the playlists section only appears if there are playlists in your library containing movies, and only playlists containing movies are displayed here.

7. **Click Apply.** iTunes saves the settings for your device and begins synchronizing the selected content.

Genius

The search field in the top-right corner of the iTunes window can be used to filter the list of movies on the Movie sync settings screen.

Synchronizing TV shows

The process for selecting specific TV shows is quite similar, although in this case, you are selecting shows by series and episode and for automatic synchronization simply by choosing the number of episodes of each selected show that you want to sync. To select which TV shows you want to synchronize to your device, follow these steps:

1. **Connect your device to your computer.**

2. **Select your device from the iTunes Devices list on the left side of the iTunes window.**

3. **Click the TV Shows tab.** The screen switches to your TV Shows sync settings, similar to Figure 7.16.

4. **Click the Sync TV Shows check box if it is not already selected.**

5. **Click the Automatically include check box if you want iTunes to automatically select TV shows for synchronization to your device.** From the two drop-down menus you can choose to synchronize all unwatched TV shows, or a specified number of recent or unwatched episodes and choose to include all shows or only selected shows.

6. **If you have chosen selected shows, click the check boxes beside the TV shows that you want to synchronize to your device.**

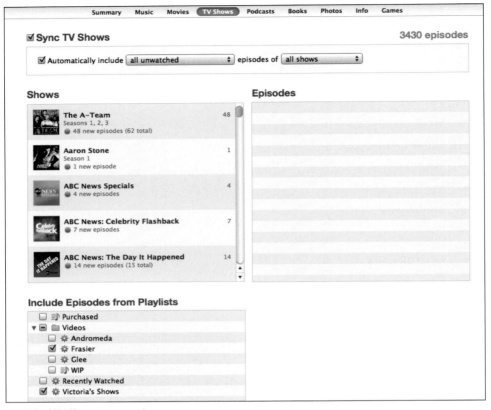

7.16 iPod TV Shows sync settings

7. **Optionally, if you want to choose specific episodes of a show to transfer to your device, select the title of the show from the Shows listing on the left.** A list of episodes appears on the right allowing you to choose them individually for synchronization, similar to Figure 7.17. Episodes included in the automatic synchronization settings are automatically selected.

8. **Optionally, click the check box beside selected playlists in the Include Episodes from Playlists panel at the bottom.** This section only appears if there are playlists in your library containing TV shows, and only playlists containing TV shows are displayed here.

9. **Click Apply.** iTunes saves the settings for your device and begins synchronizing the selected content.

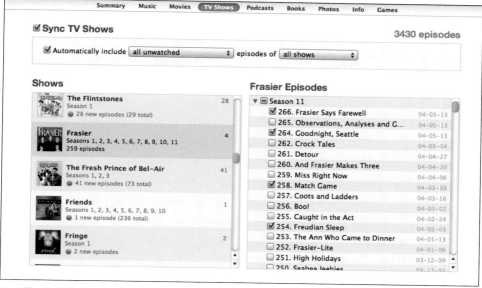

7.17 iTunes TV Shows selected for sync by episode

Genius

The automatic TV Show synchronization settings in iTunes apply to all episodes of each selected show, and therefore may not provide the level of control that you want. The use of Smart Playlists with criteria for play count and limits based on date added can be a much more flexible way to control the synchronization of TV shows. Smart Playlists are discussed in Chapter 5.

Transferring rented movies

Introduced to the iTunes Store in January 2008, movie rentals are a special case because of the time-based restrictions that are placed on them by iTunes.

The first point you should keep in mind is that only the more recent models of iPod support the playback of rented movies. This includes the iPod classic, video-capable iPod nano models, iPod touch, iPhone, and iPad. All of these devices must also be running firmware released after January 2008 to provide rental playback support. Most notably, however, the fifth-generation iPod, which introduced video playback into the iPod family, does not support the playback of rented content, regardless of the firmware version. If you are using an unsupported iPod model, the rental options simply do not appear in your synchronization settings.

Note

Apple briefly tried out TV show rentals with the release of the second-generation Apple TV in the fall of 2010. The idea never caught on with customers or TV studios, and TV show rentals were discontinued in August 2011 and replaced with the ability to redownload and stream purchased TV Shows from iTunes in the Cloud.

The main area in which managing rented content on an iPod differs from other types of content is that it can only reside in a single place at a time. When you transfer rented content from your iTunes library onto your iPod, it is moved rather than copied. If you want to transfer your rented content to another device, you must move it back from whatever device it is on, and then move it to the new device.

To transfer rented content to and from your device, follow these steps:

1. **Connect your device to your computer.**

2. **Select your device from the iTunes Devices list on the left side of the iTunes window.**

3. **Click the Movies tab.** The screen switches to your movie sync settings. If you have any rented content in your iTunes library or on the currently selected device, it appears at the top of this section, similar to Figure 7.18.

7.18 iPod movie rental transfers

4. **In the In your iTunes library column on the left side, click the Move button beside the movies that you want to transfer to your iPod.** The titles move to the iPod column, indicating that they are selected for transfer to your device.

5. **Optionally, in the On Device column, click the Move button beside any movies that you want to transfer back to your iTunes library.** The titles move to the iTunes column, indicating that they are selected for transfer back to iTunes.

6. **Optionally, you may also click the Delete button beside any movies on your device that you would simply like to delete without transferring back to your iTunes library.** The titles disappear, indicating that they are selected for deletion.

7. **Click Apply.** iTunes transfers the selected movies to and from your iPod and removes any movies you've marked for deletion.

No transfers or deletions occur until you actually click Apply. If you make a mistake and do not want to commit your changes, simply click Cancel instead.

Note You must be connected to the Internet and logged in to the iTunes Store with the account that was used to purchase the movies that you are transferring. iTunes updates the authorization keys each time a movie is transferred to a new device to ensure that the rental time restrictions can be properly enforced.

You can also now rent movies directly on Apple's iOS devices using the iTunes Store app. Movies can be rented directly on older iPhone or iPod touch models in standard-definition only and can be transferred back to iTunes in the same manner as any other rental. Movies can be rented on an iPad, iPhone 4/4S, fourth-generation iPod touch, or Apple TV in either standard or high definition but cannot be transferred back to your iTunes library — they must be watched directly on the device used to rent them.

Managing Podcasts on Your iPod

Although podcasts are actually just audio and video files like any other track, the subscription nature of podcasts makes them a special case for synchronization to your iPod. Unlike most of your media content, podcasts tend to show up automatically in your iTunes library, and you most likely want to ensure that you have your latest podcasts ready to take with you on your iPod.

As a result, podcast synchronization has more in common with synchronizing TV shows. You choose which podcasts you want stored on your iPod and how many episodes of each that you want to keep:

1. **Connect your device to your computer.**

2. **Select your device from the iTunes Devices list on the left side of the iTunes window.**

3. **Click the Podcasts tab.** The screen switches to your Podcasts sync settings, as shown in Figure 7.19.

7.19 iTunes Podcast sync settings

4. **Click the Sync Podcasts check box if it is not already selected.**

5. **Click the Automatically include check box if you want iTunes to automatically select Podcasts for synchronization to your device.** From the two drop-down menus, you can choose to synchronize all unplayed podcast episodes, or a specified number of recent or unplayed episodes and choose to include all podcasts or only selected podcasts.

6. **If you choose Selected podcasts, click the check boxes beside the specific podcasts that you want to synchronize to your device.**

7. **Optionally, if you want to choose specific episodes of a podcast to transfer to your device, select the title of the podcast from the Podcasts listing on the left.** A list of episodes appears on the right allowing you to choose them individually for synchronization, similar to Figure 7.20. Episodes included in the automatic synchronization settings are automatically selected.

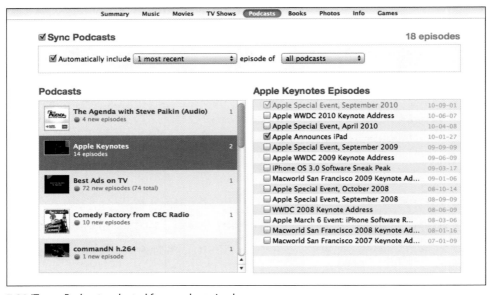

7.20 iTunes Podcasts selected for sync by episode

8. **Optionally, click the check box beside each selected playlist in the Include Episodes from Playlists panel at the bottom.** This section only appears if there are playlists in your library containing podcast episodes, and only playlists containing podcast episodes are displayed here.

9. **Click Apply.** iTunes saves the settings for your iPod and begins synchronizing the selected content.

Note The settings on the Podcasts tab are not affected by manual-management mode. This means that you can still sync your podcasts onto your device automatically while managing the rest of your audio and video content manually. Alternatively, individual podcast episodes can still be transferred to your device using manual mode.

Syncing Photos to Your iPod

Support for photos was introduced to the iPod family in late 2004 when Apple debuted its first iPod with a color screen: the iPod photo. This was basically a fourth-generation iPod with a color screen and added photo support. Every Apple media device released since that time has included support for displaying photos.

Synchronization of photos to your device is one of the more offbeat features of iTunes because iTunes does not provide any way to actually manage or even display photos. Rather, iTunes acts simply as a conduit to transfer photos onto your device from another application such as iPhoto or simply from a folder of photos on your computer.

Specifically, iTunes recognizes the photo album structure from either iPhoto or Aperture on your Mac, or from Adobe Photoshop Album or Photoshop Elements on your Windows PC. If you are not using any of these applications, you can still point iTunes to a folder on your computer, and it uses the first level of subfolders to represent your photo albums on your iPod.

To configure photo synchronization for your device, follow these steps:

1. **Connect your device to your computer.**

2. **Select your device from the iTunes Devices list on the left side of the iTunes window.**

3. **Click the Photos tab.** The screen switches to your Photos sync settings.

4. **Click the Sync Photos from check box if it is not already checked.**

5. **From the drop-down menu beside the Sync Photos from option, choose where you want to sync your photos from.** Compatible applications such as iPhoto (as shown in Figure 7.21) or Adobe Photoshop Elements are listed if these are installed on your computer. Alternatively, you may select a predefined folder such as Pictures (Mac) or My Pictures (Windows) to sync from, or select the Choose Folder option to specify your own folder anywhere on your computer.

6. **Click either All items or Selected items to choose which photos you want synchronized to your device.** If you are syncing from a photo-management application, the albums from that application appear here. If you are syncing from a folder, each of the first-level subfolder names appear as albums. Note that iTunes provides a count of the number of photos that are selected for synchronization.

7. **If you have chosen Selected items, click the check box beside the selected photo albums or folders that you want to synchronize to your device.** The number beside each album or folder shows the number of photos that it contains. Deselecting previously selected albums tells iTunes to remove these from your device on the next sync. If you are using iPhoto '09 or Aperture 3.0 or later, additional options appear here allowing you to also choose specific Events and Faces (iPhoto) or Projects and Faces (Aperture). You can also choose to automatically include recent events or projects from these applications.

8. **If you are using an iPod classic or iPod nano, you can click the Include full-resolution photos check box to place a copy of the original photo on the iPod as well during synchronization.** Photos transferred to the iPod are resized by iTunes during transfer into an iPod-optimized format, which is usually much smaller than the original photo size. This option places a copy of the original photo onto the iPod that can be accessed from the iPod in disk use mode.

9. **If you are using a fifth-generation iPod nano or an iOS device, you can click the Include videos check box to also transfer any compatible videos contained within your photo albums or folders.**

10. **Click Apply.** iTunes saves the settings for your device and begins synchronizing the selected content.

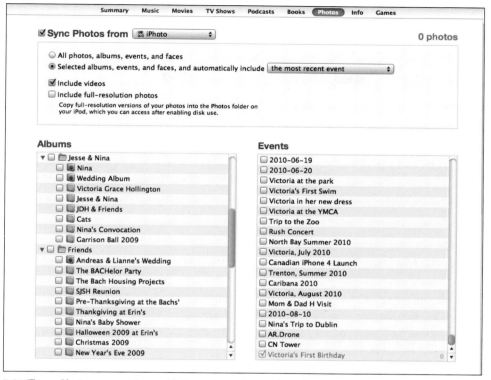

7.21 iTunes Photos sync settings with Sync photos from selected and iPhoto selected as the sync location

Note that there is no manual-management option for photos — they are always automatically synced with your iPod. The key point to remember about photo synchronization is that this is a synchronization process, rather than simply a transfer. Each time you connect to your device, iTunes checks your photo application or photo folders, and any photos or albums that are no longer available are removed from your device. You must therefore leave the photos on your computer in order for them to remain on your device.

Although you can turn off synchronization and leave the photos on the device, you must reenable synchronization to add additional photos, and of course, if you reenable synchronization, any photos that are no longer on your computer are removed from your iPod.

The iPod Photo Cache

Whenever iTunes synchronizes photos to your iPod, it goes through an optimization process to convert these photos into resolutions appropriate for display on the device. In fact, several sizes of each photo are stored on an iPod, optimized for each of the possible display modes — thumbnail view, on the device's screen, on the TV output, and so forth. In some situations, this may actually mean that a photo can take up more space when transferred to an iPod than the original photo did on your computer.

In fact, the average size of a single photo on the iPod classic is approximately 900K. This is in addition to any space taken up by the full-resolution version of the image (if you choose to sync that as well).

More importantly, however, iTunes also creates an iPod Photo Cache to store these optimized versions on your computer, so that if you ever need to transfer them back onto your iPod, or onto another similar iPod model, it can save the time of having to go through the optimization process again. The problem is that for a large photo library, this iPod Photo Cache folder can grow very large, taking up needless space on your computer. At 900K per photo, you can see how even 1,000 photos selected for synchronization to your iPod would consume close to 1GB of storage space.

Further, because different iPod models and other devices store different resolutions of the photos, the iPod Photo Cache can grow even larger if you're syncing the same photos to multiple devices.

Unfortunately, there's not much you can do about this folder while still syncing photos. If you delete it, iTunes simply re-creates it the next time you sync your device. About the only option if you're critically low on disk space is to disable photo synchronization to your iPod entirely. In this case, you can still leave any existing photos on your iPod, but they become static content — iTunes does not synchronize them with anything on your computer. After photo sync is disabled, you can delete the iPod Photo Cache folder with impunity. The catch? If you ever want to add any additional photos to your iPod, you'll have to turn sync back on and allow the cache folder to be re-created and wait through the time-consuming photo-optimization stage as well.

Enabling Disk Use on Your Click Wheel iPod

Many users of higher-capacity iPods find that they have much more space available on their iPods than their actual media content requires. Rather than letting that space go to waste, the traditional Click Wheel iPod models support a Disk Use feature that allows you to access your iPod simply as an external hard drive. In this mode, you can save other files on it and basically use the iPod as a portable storage device. Note that this mode is not supported on iOS devices, as these devices use a different synchronization protocol that does not rely on disk use.

To enable disk use on your iPod, follow these steps:

1. **Connect your iPod to your computer.**

2. **Select your iPod from the iTunes Devices list on the left side of the iTunes window.**
   You see a Summary screen for your iPod, similar to Figure 7.22.

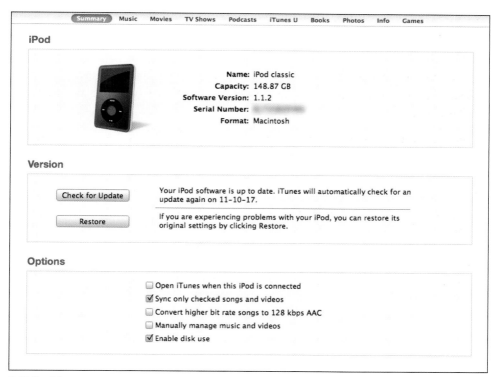

7.22 iPod Summary screen with Enable disk use selected

171

3. **Click the Enable disk use check box.** Note that if the Manually manage music and videos option is selected, disk use is forced on and the check box is unavailable.

4. **Click Apply.**

Caution Enabling disk use on your iPod requires that you manually eject it from your computer before you physically unplug it. This is done by clicking the small Eject symbol that appears next to the iPod in your iTunes Devices list. Failing to eject the iPod properly may cause corruption of your media and other content.

In reality, the traditional iPod models always present themselves as an external USB mass storage device. In fact, this is how iTunes updates information on the iPod as well. What the Enable disk use option actually does is to simply tell iTunes to not automatically eject the iPod following an automatic sync operation. Instead, the iPod remains connected so that you can continue to access it as an external storage device, and then simply eject it yourself when you are done with it. However, you can connect your iPod to any computer that is not running iTunes, and it always appears as an external storage device because iTunes is not present to automatically eject it.

Note If you have a Mac-formatted iPod, you cannot access it from a Windows PC because Windows is not able to read the Mac HFS+ file system without additional software. If you really need to access a Mac-formatted iPod in Windows, MacDrive from MediaFour (www.mediafour.com) is a $50 software application that allows Windows PCs to read Mac-formatted disks, including the iPod.

Syncing Calendars and Contacts to Your Click Wheel iPod

In addition to its use as a media player, you can also use your Click Wheel iPod for viewing your calendar and contacts on the go.

The traditional iPod models (iPod classic and iPod nano) provide read-only support for this information. You can store and view your contacts and calendars on the iPod, but you cannot change or modify them, nor does iTunes sync any of this information back to your computer — it's strictly a one-way relationship.

The iPhone, iPod touch, and iPad, on the other hand, allow full editing of your contacts and calendars on the device itself, and full two-way synchronization with iTunes. I discuss these devices later in this chapter.

You can synchronize your contacts onto your iPod either from Address Book in Mac OS X or from Windows Address Book or Outlook 2003 or later in Windows. Calendars can be synchronized from iCal on the Mac or from Outlook 2003 or later in Windows.

Contact and calendar synchronization is configured in your iPod sync settings in iTunes. Follow these steps:

1. **Connect your iPod to your computer.**

2. **Select your iPod from the iTunes Devices list on the left side of the iTunes window.**

3. **Click the Contacts tab.** The screen switches to your Contacts/Calendars sync settings, similar to Figure 7.23.

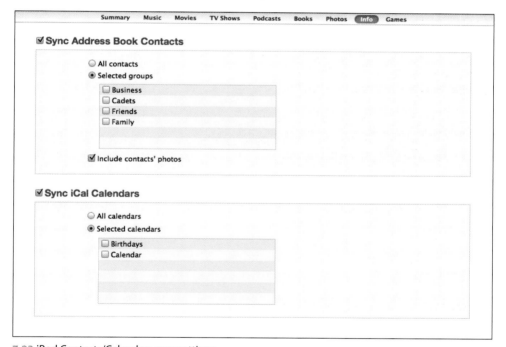

7.23 iPod Contacts/Calendars sync settings

4. **Click the Sync Address Book Contacts check box if it is not already selected.** Windows users must also choose the application to sync their contacts from the drop-down list beside the Sync option. Only those applications installed on your computer are shown.

5. **Select either the All contacts option or the Selected groups option to choose which contacts you want synchronized to your iPod.**

6. **If you have chosen Selected groups, click the check box beside each of the groups that you want to synchronize to your iPod.**

7. **Click the Include contacts' photos check box if you want to include your contact photos on your iPod.** This option is not available for all models of iPod or all contact applications.

8. **Click the Sync iCal Calendars check box if it is not already selected.** Windows users must have Outlook 2003 or later installed for this option to be available.

9. **Select either the All calendars option or the Selected calendars option to choose which calendars you want synchronized to your iPod.**

Manually Copying Contacts and Calendars

Contact and calendar information is stored on the iPod in the open standard vCard and vCal formats. If you are using an application that is not supported by iTunes, or simply want to do a quick one-time transfer of contact information, you can easily do this by accessing the appropriate folders on the iPod in disk use mode:

1. **Enable disk use on your iPod.**

2. **Export your contact information into a vCard format (VCF file) or your calendar information to a vCal/iCal format (VCS or ICS file).**

3. **Open your iPod in Finder (Mac) or Windows Explorer (Windows).**

4. **Locate the Contacts folder and copy your VCF file from step 2 into this folder.**

5. **Locate the Calendars folder and copy your VCS or ICS file from step 2 into this folder.**

6. **Eject the iPod from your computer.**

Note that the information does not need to be combined into a single VCF/VCS/ICS file. The iPod reads all of the VCF files from the Contacts folder or all of the VCS/ICS files from the Calendars folder and combines them to display as a single contact or calendar list. Therefore, you can even drop VCF files that you receive as Contact Cards directly onto the iPod's Contacts folder to take them with you.

10. **If you have chosen Selected calendars, click the check box beside each of the calendars that you want to synchronize to your iPod.**

11. **Click Apply.** iTunes saves the settings for your iPod and begins synchronizing the selected content.

Storing Notes on Your Click Wheel iPod

Click Wheel iPods also provide support for rudimentary notes that can be displayed on the go. However, iTunes does not provide any way of updating, syncing, or managing these. You must add them directly to the iPod's Notes folder in disk use mode.

The notes themselves are simple text files, and may be up to 4K in length per file. The iPod also supports a basic HTML-style tagging system within notes that can be used to build rudimentary menus, link notes together, and even link to media content on your iPod.

More information on how to build complex notes can be found in the Apple iPod Notes Feature Guide, which you can download from http://developer.apple.com/ipod.

Syncing Contacts, Calendars, and Bookmarks with an iOS Device

As discussed earlier, traditional Click Wheel iPod models allow you to synchronize your contact and calendar information to your device. On these devices, however, this has always been a one-way trip — information is simply copied from your desktop address book or calendar application for viewing on your iPod.

iOS devices on the other hand — the iPhone, iPod touch, and iPad — include full contact and calendar applications that allow you to not only view your information but also add new contacts and appointments and make changes to existing ones. As a result, iTunes has to handle two-way synchronization of this information between your device and your desktop applications.

Syncing contacts

As with the traditional iPod models, you can synchronize your contacts with the Mac OS X Address Book or with Microsoft Outlook or Windows Address Book. For iOS devices, however, iTunes provides full two-way synchronization with not only these desktop apps, but can also sync your Yahoo! or Google address books.

To configure contact synchronization for your iPhone, iPod touch, or iPad, follow these steps:

1. **Connect your device to your computer.**

2. **Select your device in the iTunes Devices list.**

3. **In the main window, click the Info tab.** The Info sync settings appear, as shown in Figure 7.24.

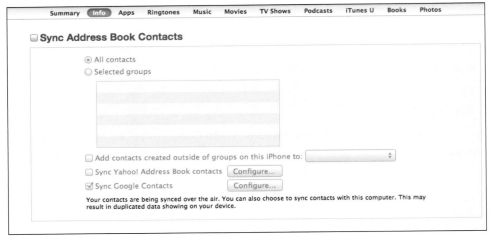

7.24 The iPhone Address Book Contacts sync preferences

4. **Click the Sync Address Book Contacts check box.**

5. **Select the All contacts option or the Selected groups option.** The Selected groups option is only available if you have groups in your Address Book application.

6. **If you have chosen Selected groups, click the check box beside each group that you want to sync with your device.**

7. **Optionally, if you want to have all contacts created on your device placed in a specific Address Book group, click the Add contacts created outside of groups check box and choose a group from the drop-down menu.**

8. **Optionally, if you want to synchronize with your Yahoo! Address Book, click the Sync Yahoo! Address Book contacts check box and then type your Yahoo! ID and password.**

9. **Optionally, if you want to synchronize with your Google contacts, click the Sync Google Contacts check box and then type your Google ID and password.**

10. **Click Apply to save your settings and sync your contact information with your device.**

For Windows users, the preceding process differs slightly in that you can only synchronize to a single contacts application. Outlook, Windows Address Book, Google Contacts, and Yahoo! Address Book are all supported for this, but you must select which one you want to use. Further, the Contact Groups feature is only available if you are synchronizing with an application that supports groups.

Note If you have setup a free iCloud account, you can sync your contacts over the air using iCloud in addition to syncing through iTunes. In this case, the Contacts sync settings in iTunes include a note that you are also using iCloud.

Syncing calendars

Like contacts, calendars can also be synchronized to older iPod models in a view-only mode; however, the iPhone, iPod touch, and iPad provide a two-way synchronization of your calendar information with iCal in Mac OS X, or Microsoft Outlook 2003 or later in Windows.

Note Unlike Mac OS X, Windows XP does not include a built-in calendar application, and Windows Calendar in Windows Vista and Windows 7 is not supported by iTunes. If you do not have Microsoft Outlook 2003 or later installed, you cannot sync your calendar through iTunes.

To configure calendar synchronization for your iPhone or iPod touch, follow these steps:

1. **Connect your device to your computer.**

2. **Select your device in the iTunes Devices list.**

3. **In the main window, click the Info tab.** The Info sync settings appear, similar to Figure 7.25.

4. **Under Calendars, click the Sync iCal Calendars check box.** In Windows, this option is Sync calendars with Outlook.

5. **Select either the All calendars option or the Selected calendars option.** The Selected calendars option is only available if you have more than one calendar in your calendar application.

Summary	Info	Apps	Ringtones	Music	Movies	TV Shows	Podcasts	iTunes U	Books	Photos

☐ **Sync iCal Calendars**

○ All calendars
◉ Selected calendars

☐ Personal
☐ Work
☐ Family
☐ School
☐ Vacation
☐ Community

☑ Do not sync events older than [30] days

Your calendars are being synced over the air. You can also choose to sync calendars with this computer. This may result in duplicated data showing on your device.

7.25 The iPhone calendar sync preferences

6. **If you have chosen Selected calendars, click the check box beside each calendar that you want to sync with your device.**

7. **If you want to limit the amount of calendar data that is synchronized with your device, click the Do not sync events older than check box and type a number of days of calendar information that you want to sync with your device.**

8. **Click Apply to save your settings and sync your calendar information with your device.**

If you have selected multiple calendars for synchronization, each calendar appears individually in the Calendar application on your device, and you can select in which calendar you want new items to be created by default from your device settings.

Note

If you're an iCloud user, you can sync your Calendar directly via iCloud over the air in addition to syncing through iTunes. In this case, the Calendar sync settings in iTunes include a note that you are also using iCloud. If you're a Google Calendar user, you can synchronize your Google calendar to your device indirectly by first synchronizing it with iCal or Microsoft Outlook. Mac users can connect newer versions of iCal directly to Google Calendar via CalDAV or check out either BusySync (www.busy-mac.com) or Spanning Sync (www.spanningsync.com). For Microsoft Outlook users, Google provides its own Google Calendar Sync application. Alternatively, you can also bypass iTunes and set up calendar synchronization wirelessly via CalDAV directly on your device.

Synchronizing bookmarks

iOS devices include a mobile version of the Safari browser, and iTunes, therefore, also provides the ability to synchronize your Internet bookmarks from your computer to your device, and vice versa. In Mac OS X, bookmarks are synced from your Safari browser. Windows users can choose to sync bookmarks with either Internet Explorer or Safari for Windows. Other browsers, such as Firefox, Internet Explorer, and Google Chrome are not supported.

To configure bookmark synchronization, follow these steps:

1. **Connect your device to your computer.**

2. **Select your device in the iTunes Devices list.**

3. **In the main window, click the Info tab.**

4. **Scroll down on the Info tab to see the Other section, as shown in Figure 7.26.**

| Summary | Apps | Music | Movies | TV Shows | Podcasts | iTunes U | Books | Photos | Info |

Other

☑ Sync Safari bookmarks
☐ Sync notes

7.26 The iPhone bookmark sync preferences

5. **Click the Sync Safari bookmarks check box (Mac) or Sync bookmarks with check box (Windows).** If you're using Windows, choose a browser in the drop-down menu with which to sync your bookmarks.

6. **Click Apply to save your settings and sync your bookmark information with your device.**

Note iCloud users can sync bookmarks directly over the air rather than going through iTunes. In this case, the Bookmark sync settings in iTunes are disabled with a note that you are using iCloud instead.

Synchronizing and Managing Apps on an iOS Device

The iPhone, iPod touch, and iPad are unique from traditional iPods in their capability to run third-party applications. These apps can be purchased directly on an iOS device or purchased from the iTunes App Store using iTunes on your computer and then synced to your device in much the same way as media content. Purchasing content from the iTunes Store is discussed in Chapter 2.

Any apps stored in your iTunes library are available for synchronization to any compatible iOS device, and in the same way as music and video content, you can sync apps to more than one device. Keep in mind, however, that some apps are written specifically for a particular type of device, such as the iPhone or iPad and will not run on other devices.

iTunes 9 also introduced the ability to manage your iOS device home screen layout from within iTunes as well, making it easy to move icons around and place them where you want when installing apps on your device. To manage applications on your device, follow these steps:

1. **Connect your device to your computer.**

2. **Select your device in the iTunes Devices list.**

3. **In the main window, click the Apps tab.** A list of applications should appear, similar to Figure 7.27. A list of all apps in your iTunes library is shown on the left, with checkmarks beside those apps already installed on your device. A view of your device's home screen is shown on the right.

7.27 Apps sync settings

4. **From the list of apps, click the check box beside any new apps that you want to install on your device or deselect the check box from any existing apps to remove them.** You can also drag and drop apps directly from the left-hand list to the home screen on the right in order to place them in a specific position on your home screen.

5. **Optionally, you can rearrange the home screen layout by dragging and dropping apps on the existing screen or to any of the pages on the far right to assign them to different home screens.** If you are using an iOS 4 device, you can also create and manage home screen folders from here in much the same way as you would on the device itself.

6. **When done selecting and deselecting apps, click Apply.** iTunes commits your changes and begins synchronizing to install and remove the designated apps.

Genius

By default, all new apps that you download into iTunes are automatically transferred to any iOS device syncing with your library. You can disable this for an individual device by deselecting the Automatically sync new apps option that appears on the Apps sync tab.

Syncing Books and PDF Files with an iOS Device

The debut of the App Store brought several third-party electronic book readers to the iOS platform; however, it wasn't until the release of the iPad that Apple ventured into the e-book space itself through the release of its own iBooks app. With the release of iBooks and the iPad came the capability for iTunes to import and manage e-books for transferring to your iOS device.

Although Apple runs its own online iBookstore, at this time books can only be purchased directly on an iOS device using the iBooks app. Books purchased on the device, however, are automatically transferred to iTunes. You can also import your own books in the popular ePub format for transferring to iBooks on your iOS device.

Note

On iOS devices you can also delete Apps and iBooks directly from your device. Syncing with iTunes after deleting items on your device automatically updates the sync selections in iTunes so that the items won't be automatically readded, however, they remain in the iTunes library.

iBooks was initially released as an iPad-only application and was later upgraded to include iPhone and iPod touch support with the release of iOS 4 in June 2010. The iBooks update also introduced support for PDF files.

Books and PDF files are synchronized to your iOS device in much the same way as other types of content. Follow these steps:

1. **Connect your device to your computer.**

2. **Select your device in the iTunes Devices list.**

3. **In the main window, click the Books tab.** The screen switches to the Books sync settings, similar to Figure 7.28.

4. **Click the Sync Books check box if it is not already selected.**

5. **Select the All books option if you want to synchronize all books and PDF files in your iTunes library, or select the Selected books option if you want to select specific titles to transfer.**

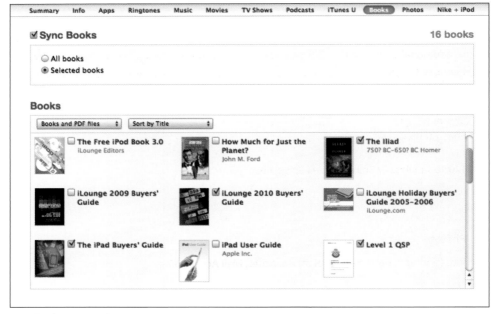

7.28 Books sync settings

6. **If you have chosen Selected books, click the check box beside specific books or PDF files you want to transfer.** You can use the search box in the top-right corner to search by specific title or the drop-down list in the top-left corner to sort by title or author.

7. **Click Apply.** iTunes begins syncing and transfers the selected books onto your device.

You can add PDFs and ePub format books to your iTunes library in the same manner as any other media file by using the File ⇨ Add to Library option on the iTunes menu or simply dragging-and-dropping the content into the iTunes application.

Note

Audiobooks are also transferred from the Books tab as well in a similar manner to e-books. In older versions of iTunes, Audiobooks were synced as part of the Music sync settings, rather than having their own settings.

Syncing Content from Multiple iTunes Libraries

Although you can only automatically sync a single type of content (such as Music) with one iTunes library at a time, it is possible to synchronize different categories of content from different iTunes libraries. To do this, simply configure the settings for the category of content that you want to sync on the additional computer(s), being sure to leave the other settings alone. For example, you could choose to sync music with your Mac at home while loading apps from a Windows PC at work. You could even choose to sync podcasts form a third computer.

For automatic synchronization purposes, content is grouped according to the following list. Content within a given group must all be synced from the same computer.

- Music, Movies, TV Shows, Books, Ringtones
- Apps
- Podcasts and iTunes U
- Photos
- Info (Contacts, Calendars, Bookmarks, Notes, Mail Accounts)

Using Multiple Apple Media Devices on One Computer

Many iPod users start out with a single iPod and iTunes library, and before they know it, everybody in the family has one. Or perhaps they're simply adding an iPhone or iPad to their existing iPod collection. A common question as a result of using multiple Apple media devices is how to use more than one device on a single computer. Many users become very concerned about having to set up an alternate iTunes library or how to figure out which content goes onto which device, and so forth.

Note

If you plan to use multiple iPods or other Apple media devices on one computer but do not want to share a single music library, be sure to check out Chapter 12 for information on how you can create multiple iTunes libraries on a single computer.

However, the answer is really as simple as "plug it in." iTunes knows the difference between your devices. Each iPod, iPhone or iPad you connect gets its own independent synchronization settings and is treated completely as its own device. Settings that you configure on one device are specific to that device and do not affect any of your other devices. In fact, given enough USB ports or USB hubs, you can even connect multiple devices at once. Figure 7.29 illustrates a single iTunes library with one iPad, four iPhones, an iPod classic, five iPod nanos, two iPod shuffles, an iPod touch and two first-generation Apple TVs all synchronizing to the same iTunes library simultaneously.

I'm not quite sure what the upper limit is of the number of devices that can be synced with a single iTunes library simultaneously, but I suspect you would run out of USB connections before you reach it.

Enabling Wi-Fi Synchronization

iTunes 10.5 and iOS 5 introduced the ability to cut the cable between iTunes and iOS devices, allowing users to wirelessly sync their iPhone, iPod touch, or iPad to an iTunes library located on the same Wi-Fi network. Wi-Fi Sync works

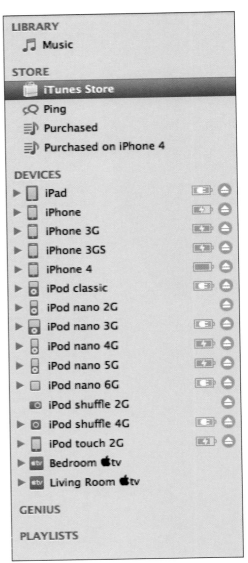

7.29 Synchronizing multiple devices

more or less in the same manner as USB synchronization and all of the same settings and options already discussed apply in the same manner when using Wi-Fi to sync; only the lack of a physical connection to the computer is different.

Wi-Fi Sync is disabled by default; you must connect your device to iTunes through USB to enable it for the first time:

1. **Connect your iOS device to your computer.**

2. **Select your device in the iTunes Devices list.** You should see the Summary screen for your device, similar to Figure 7.30.

7.30 iPhone Summary screen

3. **Click the Sync with this (device) over Wi-Fi check box, as shown in Figure 7.31.**

4. **Click Apply.**

Options

☑ Open iTunes when this iPhone is connected
☑ Sync with this iPhone over Wi-Fi
☑ Sync only checked songs and videos
☐ Prefer standard definition videos
☐ Convert higher bit rate songs to 128 kbps AAC
☐ Manually manage music and videos

Configure Universal Access...

7.31 iPhone Summary screen with Wi-Fi Sync enabled

After you have enabled Wi-Fi Sync and disconnected your iOS device from your computer it remains listed in your iTunes Device list as if it were still connected over USB— only the battery status icon disappears as battery level is not tracked over Wi-Fi. With Wi-Fi Sync enabled you can

configure and perform almost all of the same tasks that you could over a USB connection with the exception of restoring or updating the operating system, which must still be done via a direct USB connection.

iTunes Wi-Fi Sync occurs automatically whenever the device is connected to a power source, as long as iTunes is running and both the device and your iTunes library are on the same Wi-Fi network. You can also initiate a sync manually at any time regardless of whether the iOS device is plugged in or not. From iTunes this is done in the same way as for a USB-connected device, but you can also initiate a sync from the iOS device:

1. **Tap Settings ⇨ General ⇨ iTunes Wi-Fi Sync.** An iTunes Wi-Fi Sync summary screen should appear similar to Figure 7.32.

7.32 iTunes Wi-Fi Sync screen on iPhone

2. **Tap Sync Now.** Your device attempts to locate the iTunes library via Wi-Fi and initiate a sync.

You can also cancel a sync operation from the same screen; the Sync Now button changes to Cancel Sync whenever a sync is in progress.

As with USB synchronization, iTunes Wi-FI Sync allows you to sync different types of content with different iTunes libraries — for example, you could sync your music with your home iTunes library and your podcasts with a library at the office. To configure this, simply repeat the previous steps to enable Wi-Fi sync on each iTunes library. Once configured, the iTunes Wi-Fi Sync settings on the iOS device display an extra screen allowing you to see the sync settings and last synced time for each library, similar to Figure 7.33.

When syncing with multiple libraries over Wi-Fi, the device will attempt to sync in sequence with each library that it can find on the current Wi-Fi network, skipping those that are not available.

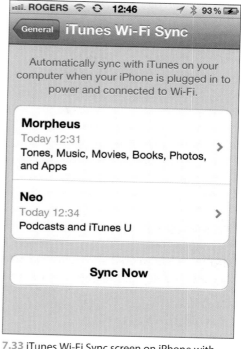

7.33 iTunes Wi-Fi Sync screen on iPhone with multiple libraries configured

Subscribing to iTunes Match

With the introduction of iCloud and iOS 5 in fall 2011, Apple also debuted iTunes Match. It is a new online service that effectively allows you to sync your entire iTunes music library up to the cloud and have it available on all of your iOS devices and other computers.

iTunes Match accomplishes this by analyzing all of the music in your iTunes library and matching your songs with those available on the iTunes Store, regardless of whether they were originally purchased from the iTunes Store or not. Songs in your library that can't be found on the iTunes Store are simply uploaded directly from your library to the iTunes Match servers. Playlists and other metadata are also transferred via the iTunes Match service.

Genius

Because iTunes Match uses the iTunes Store catalog, it provides you with unprotected 256kbps AAC versions of all of the tracks that it matches from your iTunes library, regardless of the original source format. iTunes Match can therefore effectively provide you with a free iTunes Plus upgrade for any older DRM-protected music that is still in your library.

iTunes Match is a subscription service, and as of this writing it costs $24.99 per year and is only available in the United States. Apple has indicated plans to expand the service internationally after the required music licensing agreements can be worked out.

To subscribe to and enable iTunes Match

1. **From the Store menu in iTunes, choose Turn on iTunes Match.** An iTunes Match signup screen appears, similar to Figure 7.34.

7.34 iTunes Match signup screen

2. **Click Subscribe for $24.99 from the iTunes Match signup screen.**

3. **(Optional) If prompted, enter the Apple ID and password for your iTunes Store account.** This step may not appear if you have recently signed into the iTunes Store from this computer.

4. **Click Agree to the iTunes Match Terms and Conditions page.** iTunes Match begins analyzing your library as shown in Figure 7.35.

As illustrated in Figure 7.35, the iTunes Match setup process occurs in three stages: gathering information about your iTunes Library, matching your music with songs in the iTunes Store, and then uploading the remaining songs and artwork. The process of enabling iTunes Match may take anywhere from a few hours to a couple of days depending on the size of your library, how much content can be matched with the iTunes Store, and what your upload bandwidth is for unmatched content.

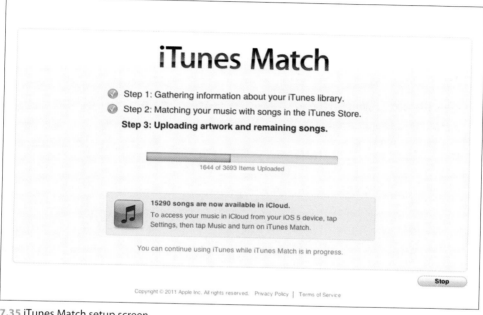

7.35 iTunes Match setup screen

You can continue using iTunes normally while this process is under way and check back on your progress at any time by selecting the iTunes Match entry from the Store section on the left of your iTunes window. Once iTunes Match has completed, you are presented with a screen similar to Figure 7.36 notifying you that your iTunes library is now available in iCloud and providing information on how to enable iTunes Match on your iOS devices. Using iTunes Match on iOS is discussed in the next chapter.

Note iTunes Match currently only handles music. You still need to synchronize other types of content, such as audiobooks, movies, TV shows, and podcasts to your iOS device in the traditional manner.

You can also enable iTunes Match within iTunes on any of your additional computers, even in a brand new iTunes library. All of your music and playlists from iTunes Match appear in the additional library and can be played in the same manner as any other track or downloaded to the new library by clicking on the download button to the right of each track name, as shown in Figure 7.37.

7.36 iTunes Match setup complete

7.37 iTunes Match content appearing in a second iTunes library

How Do I Get the Most Out of My iPod?

After your media content is organized in your iTunes library and transferred onto your iPod, iPhone, or iPad, you're ready to enjoy listening to your music and audiobooks and watching videos while on the go. Apple's media devices are pretty intuitive, thus basic operation isn't likely to be a problem, but there are some hidden inner workings and tricks that you may not be aware of.

How Content Is Organized on the iPod

The first important thing to understand is that content is organized on the iPod based on the information contained within each track. The iPod doesn't care about things like filenames or folders any more than iTunes does, and so when you browse the content on your iPod, you are accessing it based on the information contained within the headers, or tags, and not based on what you may have named the file before you imported it into iTunes.

Internally, the iPod uses a database to keep track of where your media files are stored on the device and to catalog them by information such as artist, album, name, and genre. For the most part, this database is only read by the iPod — the information contained in it is written by iTunes when you sync your content to the iPod.

This is also the reason why you cannot just connect the iPod to any computer and copy files directly onto it in disk use mode: The iPod doesn't know about files that aren't listed in its database, and you need iTunes to update that database and tell it where those files are.

Organizing your content in iTunes is discussed more in Chapter 3.

Rating Content on the Go

One of the more useful organizational features on the iPod is the ability to rate your audio content while you listen to it. Your media files begin their lives in iTunes and on your iPod with no rating at all — it's up to you to set one, and whatever rating you give your tracks is synchronized between your iTunes library and your device in both directions. This means that any ratings you set on the iPod are transferred back to your iTunes library the next time you sync your iPod.

Note

Although video tracks have a rating field, this field is not accessible from the device. You must adjust video ratings in iTunes.

You can only rate tracks on the iPod while you actually listen to those specific tracks. The method for doing this differs slightly, depending on your iPod model. To rate tracks on an iPod classic or Click Wheel iPod nano, follow these steps:

1. **Ensure the track that you want to rate is currently playing.**

2. **From the Now Playing screen on the iPod, press the center SELECT button twice.** The second press displays the rating screen for the current track, similar to Figure 8.1.

3. **Scroll using the iPod Click Wheel to adjust the number of stars from one to five.**

8.1 iPod classic rating screen

4. **Press the center SELECT button to return to the normal Now Playing screen.** Note that you may also simply leave the iPod at the rating screen — it times out and returns to the Now Playing screen after a few seconds of inactivity.

You can also adjust the rating on the iPod touch and iPhone, although the method is slightly different. Follow these steps:

1. **Ensure the track that you want to rate is currently playing.**

2. **On the Now Playing screen, locate the album button in the top-right corner, as shown in Figure 8.2.**

3. **Tap the album button.** The album cover art flips over and is replaced by a track listing, as shown in Figure 8.3.

4. **Tap the position representing the number of stars you want to assign to the current track.**

5. **Tap the album button in the top-right corner again to return to the Now Playing screen.**

Note

Older iPod models support adjusting the rating in much the same way as the iPod classic, although the number of times you press the center SELECT button to access the rating screen varies on different iPod models, and in some cases depends on whether you have album artwork assigned. In these cases, simply press the center SELECT button on the iPod until you see the rating screen appear.

8.2 iPhone Now Playing screen

8.3 iPhone album track listing and rating screen

Note

On the sixth-generation iPod nano the track rating screen is accessed by tapping the small Info button that appears in the bottom-right corner of the album artwork.

Caution

If you are managing the content on your device manually, ratings do not transfer back to your master library. In this case, your ratings exist only on the device. Further, switching back to automatic sync may result in these ratings being lost. Some third-party tools are available to transfer these ratings to your library in manual mode. These are discussed in Chapter 10.

Ratings assigned on the device take effect immediately, making this a useful way to select tracks through the use of Smart Playlists based on their ratings. These ratings transfer back to iTunes during the next sync operation.

Using Shuffle Settings Effectively

Listening to all of your albums and playlists in sequential order can get a bit dull, but fortunately, iPod supports a few different shuffle modes to mix things up a bit.

You may have noticed that your iPod classic or Click Wheel iPod nano has a Shuffle Songs option right on the main menu. Selecting this menu option starts playing back the entire content of your iPod at random, with the exception of those tracks such as audiobooks and podcasts that have been specifically excluded from shuffled playback. On a device like the iPod nano, which is loaded only with your favorite tracks, this can be a very handy option, but it loses a lot of its practicality when you're dealing with a 160GB iPod classic with a wide variety of music because there's no way to specify any one genre or type of music to play back. If you have a wide variety of content, you probably won't find much use for this option unless you really do enjoy mixing it up with reggae, rock, jazz, and classical all together.

Configuring shuffle settings on the iPod classic and Click Wheel iPod nano

Fortunately, the iPod offers more shuffle options, and so if you don't need the Shuffle Songs option on the main menu, then you can easily remove it. Follow these steps:

1. **From your main iPod menu, select the Settings option.** The settings menu is displayed.

2. **From the Settings menu, select the Main Menu option.** A listing of menu items is displayed. On an iPod classic or recent Click Wheel iPod nano, a series of check marks appears beside those options that are presently shown on the main menu. On older iPods, this is instead represented by the words ON and OFF, where ON indicates that an item is displayed on the main menu, and OFF indicates that it is not.

3. **Using the Click Wheel, scroll down until you see Shuffle Songs.** This appears near the bottom of the menu listing, as shown in Figure 8.4.

4. **Press the center SELECT button to toggle the Shuffle Songs option off.** The checkmark disappears, or the word ON toggles to OFF, depending on the iPod model you are using.

8.4 iPod classic main menu settings

197

5. **Press the MENU button on the iPod several times until the main menu reappears.**
The Shuffle Songs option is no longer shown.

Instead of going for the global shuffle option, you may prefer to shuffle your music a bit more selectively. This is done by turning on the iPod's general Shuffle setting, at which point any set of tracks you select, be it a playlist, album, artist, or genre, is played back randomly. To enable Shuffle mode, follow these steps:

1. **From your main iPod menu, select the Settings option.** The Settings menu is displayed.

2. **From the Settings menu, scroll to the Shuffle option, as shown in Figure 8.5.**

3. **Press the center SELECT button to toggle among the three available shuffle modes, as follows:**

   - **Off.** Tracks are played in the order they appear in the selected playlist or other play sequence.

8.5 iPod classic shuffle setting

   - **Songs.** Tracks are played in a random order, starting with the first track selected.

   - **Albums.** Tracks are played sequentially within a given album, and the next album is selected randomly from the available albums. Note that this option only plays those tracks that are in the current selection, and so if you are playing from a playlist that only includes three tracks from a given album, only those three tracks are played in the order they appear on the album, and then the next set of tracks is selected randomly. Naturally, this option only has an effect if your playlist contains tracks from more than one album.

4. **Press the MENU button to return to the main menu.**

Note

If you have tracks that have been marked as Skip when shuffling in iTunes, these are excluded from any shuffle mode on the iPod classic, iPod nano, or 5G iPod using firmware v1.2 or later, whether they are in the current playlist or not. Older iPod models only excluded these tracks when the main menu Shuffle Songs option was selected.

Genius

On the iPod classic and third-, fourth- or fifth-generation iPod nano, Shuffle mode can be enabled directly from the Now Playing screen. Simply press the center SELECT button three times to display the Shuffle options, and then use the Click Wheel to select the appropriate Shuffle mode. On the sixth-generation iPod nano, the Shuffle option is found by swiping to the left from the playback controls screen. Note that this option is only available when listening to music tracks.

Configuring shuffle settings on the iPhone and iPod touch

On the iPhone and iPod touch, the process for shuffling songs is slightly different. Each track listing includes a Shuffle option at the very top that can begin playing that entire set of tracks in Shuffle mode, similar to Figure 8.6.

Further, you can toggle Shuffle on and off while playing a given set of tracks. Follow these steps:

1. **On the Now Playing screen, tap the album artwork image.** A track position indicator appears beneath the track title, as shown in Figure 8.7.

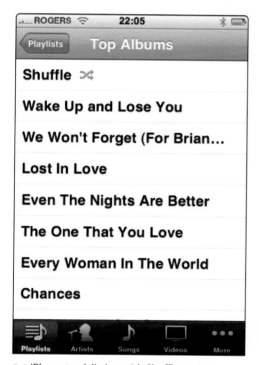

8.6 iPhone track listing with Shuffle option

8.7 iPhone Now Playing screen

Using Shake-to-Shuffle

The iPhone, iPod touch, and recent iPod nano models include an accelerometer that can be used to detect when the device is being moved or shaken. With the addition of this new hardware, Apple has also added a feature that allows users to initiate Shuffle mode simply by shaking the device. This is enabled by default on those devices that support it, and on the iPod nano it can be used to either start shuffled playback, similar to the Shuffle Songs menu option, or to switch to a new song while listening to a playlist. Shake-to-Shuffle on the iPod nano is disabled along with the other controls when the device lock switch is enabled or when the screen is off, in the case of the sixth-generation iPod nano.

On the iPhone and iPod touch, the Shake-to-Shuffle option is only active during playback when either in the Music application or when the playback controls are displayed on the screen.

The Shake-to-Shuffle feature can be turned off in your device's settings if you find that the feature is more annoying than helpful.

Although the iPad includes an accelerometer, Shake-to-Shuffle is not available on this device, likely because of its larger size.

2. **In the top-right corner of the screen, tap the shuffle icon.** The icon changes color to indicate the current shuffle mode status, with blue being ON and white being OFF.

3. **Tap the album artwork image again to return to the normal Now Playing screen.**

The iPod touch, iPhone, and iPad do not presently support an album Shuffle mode.

Note

Viewing Lyrics on the Go

Recent-model iPods have introduced the ability to view lyrics while listening to your music, provided that these lyrics have been previously added to the tracks in iTunes. At this time, no purchased music from the iTunes Store includes lyrics, and so you're going to have to add these yourself. Chapter 3 discusses more about how to add lyrics to your tracks within iTunes.

Note that there is no specific option for lyric display on the iPod. In fact, the capability of the iPod to display lyrics at all remains hidden away unless you're actually playing a track that includes lyrics within the track.

If you're playing a track that includes lyrics on your fifth-generation iPod, iPod classic, or Click Wheel iPod nano, simply press the center SELECT button a few times to scroll through the different Now Playing screens until you see the lyrics appear. On the sixth-generation iPod nano, the lyrics can be found by swiping right to a third screen, past the shuffle and repeat controls.

If the track you are playing does not include lyrics, the iPod skips the lyrics screen entirely.

On the iPod touch or iPhone, displaying lyrics is even simpler: Just tap the album artwork from the Now Playing screen, and the lyrics overlay the album artwork.

Again, if the track you are playing does not include lyrics, no lyrics overlay is shown — only the track position and repeat and shuffle icons.

Note If you have recently added lyrics to your tracks and these are not appearing on your iPod, ensure that you have synchronized your changes from iTunes properly. Note that if you are using manual management for your iPod, you must recopy the tracks onto your iPod after adding lyrics, as you are not synchronizing changes from your main iTunes library in this case.

Note As of iOS 4 the display of on-screen lyrics can now be toggled off in the Music Settings. Be sure to double-check this setting if you're not seeing lyrics where you think they should be appearing.

Improving Your Podcast Experience

Listening to podcasts on the iPod can be a different experience from music playback, largely because of the episodic nature of these programs. Generally, most podcast listeners prefer to listen to new podcasts on a regular basis and sometimes prefer to listen to several podcasts in sequence.

Although the iPod has supported podcasts since the fourth-generation models, there have been some changes and discrepancies to how podcasts are handled among different iPod models and firmware versions that you may find confusing, particularly if you recently upgraded to a newer iPod.

continued

continued

The first thing that trips up most podcast enthusiasts is the change to Skip when Shuffling behavior in the recent iPod models. Podcasts downloaded by iTunes always have Skip when Shuffling enabled by default, and although you can change this for individual podcast episodes that you have already downloaded, you cannot change this default behavior for new episodes.

The problem comes into play when listening to podcasts with Shuffle mode enabled on the iPod. In this case, the iPod plays a single podcast episode and then stops because all of the remaining podcast episodes are flagged to be skipped during shuffled playback. This has been the default behavior since the version 1.2 firmware update for the fifth-generation iPod and continues on to the iPod classic and iPod nano.

In this case, if you want to listen to an entire series of podcast episodes, you must ensure that you disable shuffle on the iPod before you begin listening to the first podcast episode; otherwise, you can only play a single episode at a time. Even in this case, however, there are certain limitations:

- When playing podcasts from the Podcasts menu on the fourth-generation iPod nano, only the selected episode is played, after which the iPod stops, regardless of the shuffle settings.
- When playing podcasts from the Podcasts menu on the iPod classic and iPod nano, podcast episodes are listed in reverse-chronological order with the newest episode at the top, which is the order they are played in.

In light of these limitations, you may want to consider using Smart Playlists to organize your podcasts, and then listening to them directly from your playlist rather than the podcasts section. This can be particularly useful if you subscribe to several different podcasts that you catch up on regularly.

Adjusting Audiobook Playback Speed

One of the unique features of audiobooks on the iPod is that you can adjust their playback speed without affecting their overall sound quality. This feature is only available on tracks that have been properly tagged as audiobooks, as described in Chapter 6.

To adjust audio playback speed on the iPod classic and Click Wheel iPod nano, follow these steps:

1. **From your main iPod menu, select the Settings option.** The Settings menu is displayed.

2. **From the Settings menu, scroll to and select the Audiobooks option.** The iPod Audiobooks speed setting screen is displayed, as shown in Figure 8.8.

3. **Use the Click Wheel to select your preferred audiobook playback speed, and press the center SELECT button.**

4. **Press the MENU button to return to the main menu.**

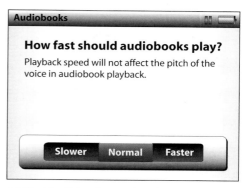

8.8 iPod Audiobooks speed setting screen

You can also adjust audiobook playback speed on the iPod touch and iPhone during playback. Follow these steps:

1. **On the Now Playing screen, tap the audiobook artwork image.** A track position indicator appears beneath the track title with additional controls, as shown in Figure 8.9.

2. **In the top-right corner of the screen, tap the 1X icon.** The icon changes to a blue color and shows a 2X to indicate a faster playback speed is being used.

3. **To slow down playback, tap the icon a second time.** The icon changes to show 1/2X to indicate that a slower playback speed is being used. You can tap the icon again to return to the normal 1X playback speed.

4. **After you select your preferred playback speed, tap the audiobook artwork image again to return to the normal Now Playing screen.**

8.9 iPhone Now Playing screen with Audiobook speed controls

On the iPhone and iPod touch, the same method can be used to adjust the playback speed for audio podcasts.

Listening to Music Videos

All of the iPod models that support video playback also support the storage and playback of music videos in addition to the other types of video content. However, music videos are normally treated as just another type of music content, and are organized alongside normal music tracks by the same artists.

Although you can play your music videos directly from the Videos menu on an iPod classic or iPod nano, you can also access these same music videos from the Music section. When playing a music video from the Music menu, only the audio portion of the video is played back, with the normal Now Playing screen displayed as for any other audio track. This allows you to listen to your music videos mixed into your playlists alongside your normal tracks without having to actually display the video content on your iPod screen.

Note Playing music videos in audio-only mode saves on the battery because the iPod screen is not used while these are being played. However, the iPod must still load the entire video file, and with hard drive-based iPod models, this larger file results in more frequent hard drive access, which can still adversely affect battery life.

The iPod touch and iPhone play the video portion of music videos regardless of where they are selected from. Music videos played from a normal playlist or track listing can be played in either portrait or landscape orientation and can continue playing with the iPhone or iPod touchscreen off.

Genius Although the sixth-generation iPod nano no longer provides the ability to watch videos, you can still sync your music videos onto the iPod nano to listen to them.

Using the On-The-Go Playlist on Click Wheel iPods

Normally, you build and manage your playlists in iTunes and then transfer them onto your iPod; however, the iPod also supports one special type of playlist known as the On-The-Go playlist. This allows you to queue up a list of tracks from your iPod into a temporary playlist. You can add and remove tracks from the On-The-Go playlist.

When you sync your device with iTunes, the On-The-Go playlist is transferred back to iTunes, where you can rename it, reorganize it, or simply delete it.

The On-The-Go playlist can be found at the bottom of your Playlists menu. By default, this playlist is empty, and selecting it provides basic instructions on how to add tracks to this playlist, as shown in Figure 8.10.

To add tracks to the On-The-Go playlist on an iPod classic or Click Wheel iPod nano, follow these steps:

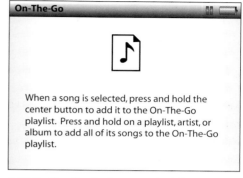

When a song is selected, press and hold the center button to add it to the On-The-Go playlist. Press and hold on a playlist, artist, or album to add all of its songs to the On-The-Go playlist.

1. **Locate the track that you want to add by browsing through the iPod Music window.**

8.10 On-The-Go playlist on an iPod classic

2. **Press and hold the center SELECT button for about 1 second until the highlight bar flashes.**

Note You can also add entire albums, artists, genres, or even other playlists; simply hold the center SELECT button on the appropriate menu entry rather than the individual track.

Removing items from the On-The-Go playlist is done in much the same way: Highlight the item that you want to remove and hold the center SELECT button on the iPod.

Note On the 2008 and later iPod classic models and the fourth- and fifth-generation iPod nano, holding down the center SELECT button presents an options menu instead of simply adding the current track to the On-The-Go playlist. With these models, simply select Add to On-The-Go from this pop-up menu when it appears.

During the next sync, your On-The-Go playlist is transferred to your iTunes library as a new playlist, and the current On-The-Go playlist on the device is cleared. The new playlist created in iTunes may be renamed, edited, or deleted as with any other standard playlist.

Note

Creating and Editing Playlists on an iPhone or iPod touch

Although the iPhone and iPod touch originally provided an On-The-Go playlist, iOS 4 added the capability to create and edit standard playlists on your device. The iPad also introduced similar capabilities in iOS 3.2.

Note

The original iPhone and first-generation iPod touch cannot be upgraded to iOS 4 and therefore still use the older On-The-Go playlist system. The instructions for adding and removing tracks are similar to iOS 4, except that you cannot give the playlist a custom name nor can you edit existing playlists.

To create a new playlist on your iPhone or iPod touch, follow these steps:

1. **Open the Music app on your device and choose the Playlists option.** A list of playlists should appear, similar to Figure 8.11.

2. **From the top of the Playlists menu, tap Add Playlist.** A dialog box appears prompting you to enter a name for the new playlist, similar to Figure 8.12.

3. **Type a name for your new playlist and tap OK.** A list of all available songs appears, similar to Figure 8.13.

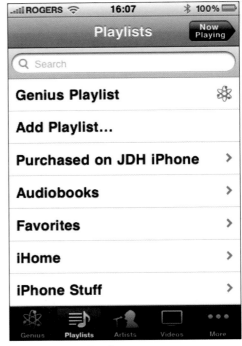

8.11 iPhone Playlists listing

8.12 iPhone New Playlist dialog box

8.13 Adding tracks to a new playlist

4. **Scroll to locate the song you want to add, and tap it to add it to your new playlist.**
   You may also tap Add All Songs to add all of your songs to your playlist, or use the other menu buttons at the bottom of the screen to browse by other categories, such as Playlists, Artists, or Albums.

5. **Continue selecting songs to add to your new playlist by browsing and tapping on those songs you want to add.**

6. **Tap Done.** Your new playlist is displayed.

Note

Prior to iOS 5, the iPhone used an app named "iPod" to access music and video content and the iPad used the same-named application for audio content only, with a separate Videos app for movies, TV shows, and music videos. iOS 5 unifies these apps across all device models, with specific Music and Videos apps in the same way the iPod touch has always been organized.

The iPhone and iPod touch also enable you to edit any playlist directly on the device, including adding new tracks, removing tracks, or changing the order of tracks in the playlist. Playlists can be edited on the device regardless of whether they were originally created on the device or synced from iTunes, and any changes you make on the device are automatically transferred back to iTunes during the next sync if you are using automatic synchronization with iTunes. To edit a playlist on the iPod touch or iPhone, follow these steps:

1. **Select the playlist you want to edit.** You are shown the current list of tracks in the selected playlist.

2. **Tap the Edit button at the top of the playlist.** The playlist switches to edit mode, similar to Figure 8.14.

3. **You can make a few different edits from here:**

   - To move a track up or down in the playlist, tap and hold the icon to the right of the track name and drag your finger up or down.

   - To remove a track from the playlist, tap the red delete icon at the left side of the track name.

   - To add more tracks, tap the Plus button at the top-left corner of the screen.

4. **Tap Done when you finish editing.**

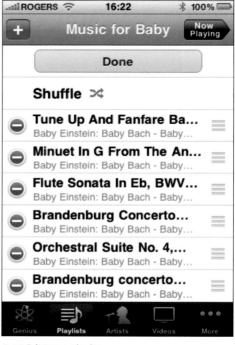

8.14 Editing a playlist

You can also clear the content of a playlist or delete it entirely from your device by tapping the Clear or Delete buttons shown at the top of a playlist. As with changes made within playlists, any playlists you delete from your device are also removed from iTunes during the next sync if you are using automatic synchronization.

Note

Smart Playlists cannot be created, modified, or deleted on the device. These must be changed in iTunes and transferred back onto your device from there.

Creating and Using Genius Playlists

With the addition of the Genius feature in iTunes 8, recent iPod and iOS devices also include direct support for creating and saving Genius playlists directly on your device. Support for this feature is also available on the Apple TV.

Note

> After you enable Genius in your iTunes library, you must sync your device with iTunes at least once before the Genius feature works on the device.

The on-device Genius support allows your Genius playlists from iTunes to be recognized as Genius playlists and modified on the device. Further, Genius playlists may be created directly on your device and are automatically transferred back to iTunes during the next sync.

To create a Genius playlist on the iPod classic or fourth- or fifth-generation iPod nano, follow these steps:

1. **Locate a song that you want to use as the basis for your Genius list.** You can either find a song on the iPod track listing or use the currently playing track.

2. **Press and hold the center SELECT button for about 1 second until a menu appears, similar to Figure 8.15.**

3. **From the menu, select Start Genius.** The current track is used to create a Genius playlist of 25 tracks, and the resulting list is displayed, similar to Figure 8.16.

From the Genius listing, you can simply begin playing back the content of your Genius playlist, refresh the content to select different tracks, or save the Genius listing as a separate playlist.

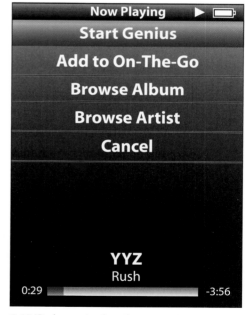

8.15 iPod nano track options menu

Note Genius playlists created directly on your device are always limited to 25 tracks. You can, however, save them and sync them back to iTunes, where you can select a larger number of tracks.

Selecting Save Playlist saves your Genius listing as a playlist named after the main track. This playlist is transferred back into iTunes the next time you synchronize your iPod.

Note that if you do not have sufficient tracks on your iPod to create a Genius listing, an error message appears similar to Figure 8.17, indicating that Genius is not available.

8.16 iPod nano Genius listing

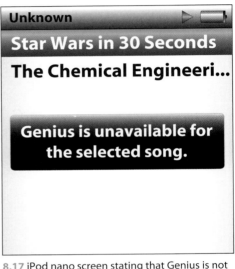

8.17 iPod nano screen stating that Genius is not available

Note The sixth-generation iPod nano uses a touchscreen interface and handles Genius playlists in a manner more similar to the iPod touch than its Click Wheel predecessors.

This message usually means that there are not enough tracks loaded onto your device to build a Genius listing. You may, however, still be able to create a Genius listing in iTunes, save it as a playlist, and then sync it with your device from iTunes. Additional tracks are copied from iTunes to your device as they would be for any other playlist.

Genius

You can also refresh existing Genius playlists on your iPod, regardless of where they were created. Refreshed playlists are updated in iTunes when you sync your iPod.

On the iPhone and iPod touch, the concept behind creating a Genius playlist is the same, but the actual process differs slightly. To create a Genius playlist from the main Playlists menu, follow these steps:

1. **From the Playlists menu, select the Genius option, as shown in Figure 8.18.**

2. **Browse for a song to use to create your Genius listing.** A Genius playlist is created and the selected song begins playing.

3. **To view your Genius listing, tap the left arrow button shown at the top-left corner of the Now Playing screen.** The Genius track listing appears, as shown in Figure 8.19.

4. **Tap the Save button to save the Genius listing as a new playlist.**

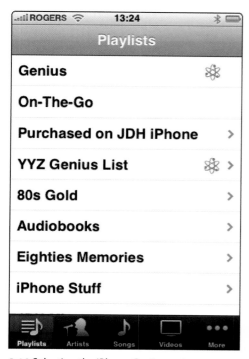

8.18 Selecting the iPhone Genius option

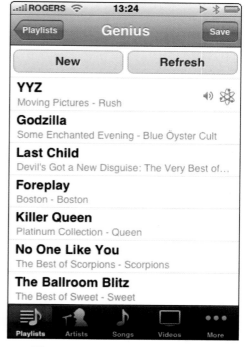

8.19 iPhone Genius track listing

You may also refresh your Genius listing with new tracks prior to saving it by tapping the Refresh button, or start over with a new Genius listing by tapping the New button.

Genius

You can also create a Genius listing directly from the Now Playing screen on your iPhone or iPod touch by tapping the screen and then tapping the Genius icon that appears at the center near the top of the screen.

As with the other iPod models, Genius playlists saved on your device are transferred back to iTunes during the next sync, and Genius playlists created from iTunes can be edited and refreshed on the device.

Note

The iPad also supports Genius Playlists in a manner similar to the iPhone and iPod touch, with a slightly different user interface tailored for the larger screen.

Caution

While you can play your tracks directly from the main Genius listing, this queue is not saved back to iTunes when you sync your iPhone or iPod, and is actually cleared after you sync. Always ensure that you save your Genius listings as Genius playlists before syncing if you want to keep them.

Genius Mixes

iTunes 9 introduced a new automated form of Genius playlist known as a Genius Mix. At the same time, newer Click Wheel iPod models and iOS devices were updated to provide support for syncing and playing Genius mixes on the device. Genius Mixes in iTunes are created automatically and are discussed in more detail in Chapter 5.

Genius Mixes can be synced to a supported iPod or iOS device in the same way as a playlist — they are simply listed in your playlist sync settings and can be selected from there. Once you have transferred at least one Genius Mix onto your device, a new Genius Mixes section appears on the menu allowing you to access and play these mixes. In all other respects they function simply as another form of a playlist.

Purchasing and Downloading Content on iOS Devices

iOS Devices such as the iPod touch, iPhone, and iPad include the capability to purchase and download new iTunes Store content directly on the device. Two built-in apps are included for this purpose: The iTunes app provides access to media content on the iTunes Store while the App Store app provides on-device access to the App Store. The use of these applications is relatively straightforward, although there are a few points worth noting:

- By default, your device uses the same iTunes Store account that you are logged into on your desktop computer when you sync. You can choose to switch to a different iTunes Store account on the device itself.

- Both stores can be used over either a Wi-Fi or 3G cellular data connection; however, when using a Wi-Fi connection you cannot download any single item larger than 20MB.

- Purchases made on the device are automatically transferred back to iTunes during the next sync, provided your computer is authorized for the account that was used to purchase the items. Special purchased playlists are created for each device that you have purchased content with.

- You can download individual podcast episodes using the iTunes app on your iOS device; however, you cannot actually subscribe to podcasts from the device or have new episodes downloaded automatically. New podcast episodes are transferred back to iTunes in the same way as any other content, and a Subscribe button appears in the podcast listing for any episodes that you're not already subscribed to in iTunes.

- You can stream podcast episodes directly through the iTunes app rather than downloading them. The 20MB cellular data limit does not apply to streamed podcast episodes.

- If an album purchase includes extra content, such as a digital booklet or iTunes LP, only the music is downloaded on the device. Additional content is queued up to be downloaded by iTunes.

- Only the iPad, iPhone 4/4S, and fourth-generation iPod touch support HD movies and TV shows. When purchasing a high-definition movie or TV show on older iPhone or iPod touch devices, only the standard-definition version is downloaded to the device. The HD version is queued up to be downloaded by iTunes.

- You can rent movies on your device, subject to the limitations of your specific device model. The iPad, iPhone 4/4S, and fourth-generation iPod touch support both standard- and high-definition movies, while only standard-definition content is available for rent on older iPod touch and iPhone models.

● Movies rented on the iPhone and iPod touch are not automatically transferred to iTunes — they must be moved manually in the same way as any other rented movie. Movies rented on the iPad, iPhone 4/4S, or fourth-generation iPod touch cannot be transferred back to iTunes at all — they must be watched on the device on which they were rented.

Downloading Purchased Content from iTunes in the Cloud

In June 2011, Apple debuted its new iCloud online service, which introduced iTunes in the Cloud: The capability to automatically download newly purchased content and access and redownload any of your previously purchased content from any iOS device or computer running iTunes. This particular feature was released as a public beta for iOS 4.3.3 and iTunes 10.3 in June, followed by a general release in October 2011 with iOS 5 and iTunes 10.5.

Redownloading previously purchased content

Depending on which country you're in, iTunes in the Cloud allows you to redownload any of the music, books, or TV shows that you've purchased from the iTunes Store. The iTunes and App Store apps on your iOS device include a Purchased section that lists the content in your purchase history, similar to Figure 8.20. A search field is available to help locate previously purchased content and you can also choose to see only content that is not already on your device.

Content can be redownloaded from the iTunes or App Store applications in much the same way as purchasing new content. Note that the same limitations noted in the previous section also apply to redownloading content.

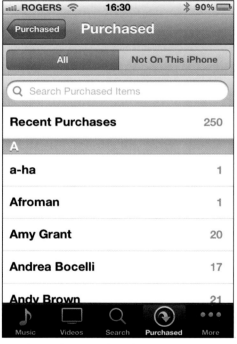

8.20 iTunes Store purchase history

Automatic downloading of new purchased content

One of the features of iTunes in the Cloud is the capability to automatically download content that was purchased on a different device with the same iTunes Store account. For example, you could have new music tracks purchased in iTunes on your computer automatically downloaded to your iPod touch and iPad, or have new apps purchased on your iPhone automatically downloaded to your iTunes library. This option is disabled by default on iOS devices but can easily be enabled:

Note Although U.S. users can redownload TV shows from iTunes in the Cloud, this content is not currently available for automatic downloading.

1. **On your iOS device, choose Settings ⇨ Store.**

2. **If you are not already signed into the iTunes Store on your device, tap the Sign in button and enter your iTunes Store Apple ID and password.** A screen similar to Figure 8.21 appears.

3. **Select the categories of purchased content you wish to have automatically downloaded to your device.** Currently, Music, Apps, and Books are available in the U.S.; not all options may be available in other countries.

4. **Select Use Cellular Data if you want automatic downloads to occur over the cellular data network.** If this option is off, new content will only be downloaded when your device is connected to a Wi-Fi network.

8.21 iTunes in the Cloud Settings on iOS 5

Caution   After you enable iTunes in the Cloud on an iTunes Store account either by turning on automatic downloads or by redownloading a past purchase your device becomes locked to that account and cannot be associated with a different account for 90 days. Note that this limitation does not apply to downloading apps.

Using iTunes Match

As discussed in Chapter 7, iTunes Match is a subscription-based service that allows you to upload your entire iTunes music library to iCloud and access it from any of your iOS devices. You must subscribe to and enable iTunes Match from iTunes before you are able to use it on your device — you cannot match or upload music from an iOS device.

Enabling iTunes Match

Enabling iTunes Match completely replaces the music library on your device with the iCloud version, giving you access to all of your music anywhere that a data connection is available. Any song can be played directly from iCloud, and you can also specifically download individual songs, albums, and playlists to your device for offline listening.

To enable iTunes Match, follow the steps below:

1. **On your iOS device, select Settings ➪ Music.** A screen similar to Figure 8.22 appears.

2. **Tap the on/off switch beside iTunes Match.** A warning message appears reminding you that activating iTunes Match will replace the music library on this device, as shown in Figure 8.23. If you have not yet subscribed to iTunes Match from your iTunes library, a warning message appears here instead advising you of this requirement.

3. **Tap Enable to confirm the warning and activate iTunes Match.**

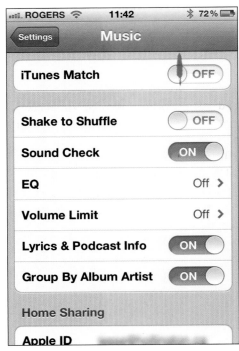

8.22 Music Settings on an iOS 5 device

After iTunes Match is enabled, a second option appears allowing you to choose whether you want your Music app to display all of the tracks from your iTunes Match library or only those tracks that have been downloaded to the device. Because you must specifically download any tracks you want stored on your device, you should leave this option off until you've done so.

Using iTunes Match

Once enabled, iTunes Match effectively becomes your iOS device's music library, replacing all of the content synced from iTunes. Your entire iTunes Match library appears in the iOS Music app and can be played in much the same way as content synced directly from iTunes. You can even create and edit playlists directly on your device and these changes will be automatically synced back to your iTunes library via iCloud.

8.23 Enabling iTunes Match on an iOS 5 device

When you begin playing a track or playlist in iTunes Match, playback begins within a few seconds while the track simultaneously downloads in the background. Each track you play from iTunes Match is cached on your device. You can also download complete albums and playlists manually for offline listening by tapping on the Download All button that appears at the bottom of a playlist, as shown in Figure 8.24.

iTunes Match also includes your purchased music videos, which can be found in the Videos app on iOS 5. Other types of content, such as movies, TV shows, podcasts, and audiobooks, must still be synced directly from iTunes.

Connecting Your iPod, iPhone, or iPad to a TV

With the exception of the sixth-generation iPod nano and the obvious exception of the iPod shuffle, all of the recent iPod models now have the capability to display video, in addition to, of course, the iPhone and iPad, but if you're tired of squinting at your device's screen, you'll be happy to know that you can also view your video content on a normal television screen with the appropriate cables.

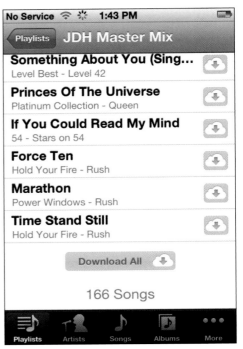

8.24 Downloading a complete Playlist from iTunes Match

However, the question of which cables are appropriate for your device can be a bit complicated. Apple first brought video capabilities to the iPod with the fifth-generation iPod, released in 2005, and for two years this was the only video-capable iPod. This model supported video output through the iPod headphone jack with a simple minijack-to-RCA cable, such as the one shown in Figure 8.25. Further, you could output video through the iPod Dock Connector with a variety of third-party cables and accessories, none of which required any more technology than the capability to take the video signal from the Dock Connector pins and push it out through a standard RCA video connection.

Genius

If you have a fifth-generation iPod, you can use just about any camcorder minijack-to-RCA video cable with your iPod. Simply reverse the yellow and red leads when connecting it to your TV.

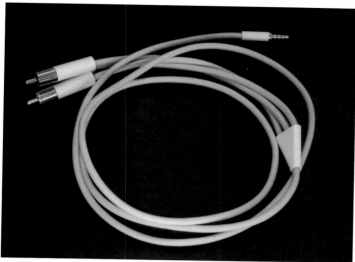

Copyright Jeremy Horwitz for iLounge.com

8.25 iPod AV cable

Unfortunately, when Apple released the 2007 iPod models — the iPod classic, iPod nano (with video), and iPod touch — it removed the capability to output video through the headphone port, rendering the first category of iPod video cables obsolete. More importantly, however, it also chose to restrict video output through the Dock Connector port to those accessories that were approved by Apple through the use of an authentication chip. It was no longer enough to build a video cable that took the video from the Dock Connector — rather, the accessory had to include an authentication chip supplied by Apple to unlock the video output capabilities. Without the presence of this chip, the iPod would simply refuse to output video through the accessory.

Note Unlike earlier iPod nano generations, the sixth-generation iPod nano that was released in September 2010 does not support video playback at all. However, the TV output feature is still available with this model to display photo slideshows.

This had the unfortunate impact of rendering all video accessories manufactured for the fifth-generation iPod completely incompatible with the iPod classic. Users upgrading from the 5G iPod to the iPod classic (or iPod nano, iPod touch, or iPhone) had to buy new video accessory cables certified for these devices, and for the first six months, the only cables available were Apple's own Composite AV or Component AV cables, shown in Figure 8.26, which were a bit on the expensive side compared to the fifth-generation AV cables.

The bottom line is that when purchasing a video cable or other video-related accessory for your iPod, ensure that you check the packaging carefully to confirm that the cable or accessory is, in fact, compatible with your particular model of iPod (for example, the iPod classic, iPod nano, and/ or iPod touch). With the fifth-generation iPod on the market for more than two years, many video accessories were manufactured for that model and simply listed as iPod-compatible and can still be found in stores even now, four years later. If in doubt, always do some online research before spending money on a cable. Sites like iLounge.com provide reviews of a wide range of iPod accessories, including AV cables.

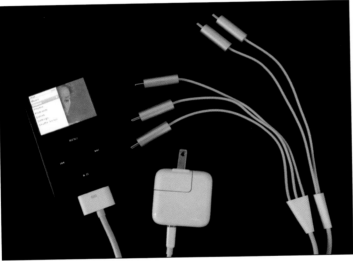

8.26 Apple Composite AV cable

Caution Beware of cables from unknown manufacturers that claim compatibility with the iPhone or newer iPod models. Building a video cable for the newer iPods requires a licensed authentication chip from Apple, and so only Apple Made-for-iPod-certified partners can manufacture these cables. Further, the licensing costs involved mean that these cables generally cost at least $30.

Once you have the appropriate cable and it's connected to your iPod and your TV, the next step is to enable TV output on the iPod. On the iPod classic or video-capable iPod nano, follow these steps:

1. **From the iPod main menu, select Videos.** The Videos menu appears.
2. **From the Videos menu, select Settings.** The Settings menu appears.

3. **Select TV Out, as shown in Figure 8.27, and press the center SELECT button.** The TV Out setting toggles among the following three options:

- **Off.** Video is displayed on the iPod screen.

- **Ask.** Whenever you start a video, the iPod asks whether you want to use the screen or TV output.

- **On.** Video is displayed using the TV output connection.

4. **Press MENU twice to return to the main menu.**

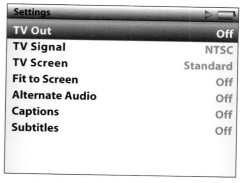

8.27 iPod video Settings menu

If no compatible video cable is detected, the iPod classic and iPod nano display a message asking you to connect a video accessory, similar to Figure 8.28. If you see this message, check to ensure that your video cable is connected directly to your iPod and that you are in fact using a compatible video cable.

8.28 Connect Video Accessory warning

On the iPod touch, iPhone, and iPad, the process is somewhat simpler: Just ensure that the video cable is connected before starting video playback, and you are prompted as to whether you want to use the TV output, similar to Figure 8.29. Note that some AV cables trigger the video output on the iOS devices automatically without prompting.

If this prompt does not appear and your video still plays directly on your device's screen, then ensure that your video cable is connected directly to your device rather than through a dock or extension cable, and that you do, in fact, have a compatible video cable.

Genius

A variety of video output accessories are available for the iPod, ranging from portable video displays to wearable video glasses. Despite the name, all video accessories connect to the iPod using the TV Out functionality. The same cautions apply with regard to video accessory compatibility; however, always ensure that the device you're thinking of purchasing is compatible with your particular iPod model.

8.29 Display on TV prompt on an iPhone

Types of TV connections supported

All current iPod and iOS devices support standard-definition TV output formats and resolutions through the use of either the component or composite cables described earlier. Composite cables provide a 480i output signal while the component cables can provide a slightly better 480p signal.

Apple now also sells both a Dock Connector-to-VGA Adapter cable that allows the iPad to be connected to a standard VGA-capable computer monitor or TV and a Digital AV Adapter that provides a connection to an HDTV via HDMI. These cables are compatible only with the iPad, iPhone 4/4S, and fourth-generation iPod touch and can output video in high-definition 720p or 1080p resolutions.

Unfortunately, not all video content purchased from the iTunes Store will play using the VGA adapter cable. Because of copyright protections, purchased HD TV shows and all purchased movies can only be played using either the Apple Digital AV Adapter, which provides an HDCP-protected HDMI connection or the lower-quality component and composite cables, providing standard-definition output only. Even with the Apple Digital AV Adapter, however, if you're looking to watch a lot of HD content that you've purchased from the iTunes Store, you'll probably want to get an Apple TV instead of using your iOS device anyway.

Adjusting Your Device's Video Settings for Optimal Display

When displaying video content on your device, you may find that the display is less than ideal, depending on the source content. Further, you may also need to adjust your settings for TV output, depending on what type of television you are connecting your device to.

These discrepancies exist primarily because some TV shows and movies use a different aspect ratio from the device's screen. To put it simply, most movies today are released in a widescreen format, while the iPod classic and even the iPad still use the traditional 4:3 aspect ratio from standard televisions, and the iPhone and iPod touch use a 3:2 aspect ratio that also falls short of the standard widescreen format. See Chapter 9 for more information on aspect ratios.

Although the iPod and iPad screens fit traditional TV content with no problems, when watching widescreen movies, the content does not fit perfectly on the screen. Instead, your movies are either displayed in a letterbox format with black bars at the top and bottom, or they are displayed to fill the entire screen with the left and right edges cropped.

For Click Wheel iPods, you can choose which playback mode you prefer by going into your iPod video settings. Follow these steps:

1. **From the iPod main menu, select Videos.** The Videos menu appears.

2. **From the Videos menu, select Settings.** The Settings menu appears, similar to Figure 8.30.

3. **Select Fit to Screen and press the center SELECT button.** The Fit to Screen option toggles between ON and OFF each time you press the SELECT button. OFF presents your widescreen content in a letterbox format, while ON zooms in on the screen, cropping the sides to fit the image to the screen.

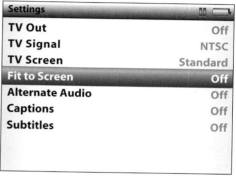

8.30 iPod video Settings menu

4. **Press MENU twice to return to the main menu.**

When displaying your iPod content on a TV, you must also specify whether you are using a standard 4:3 TV set or a widescreen 16:9 TV set so that your iPod knows how to present the TV output in the proper aspect ratio. Follow these steps:

1. **From the iPod main menu, select Videos.** The Videos menu appears.

2. **From the Videos menu, select Settings.** The Settings menu appears, similar to Figure 8.31.

3. **Select TV Screen and press the center SELECT button.** The TV Screen option toggles between Standard and Widescreen.

4. **Press MENU twice to return to the main menu.**

On the iOS devices, the aspect ratio issue on-screen is handled a bit differently. The iPod touch and iPhone each use an aspect ratio midway between standard TV and widescreen, meaning that they can handle both aspect ratios reasonably well, with either minimal letterboxing or minimal cropping. Sadly, the iPad still uses a 4:3 aspect ratio, making it poorly suited for many of the high-aspect-ratio Cinemascope movies. Instead of a Fit to Screen setting, the iOS devices zoom in and out simply by double-tapping the screen while a video plays.

Settings	
TV Out	Off
TV Signal	NTSC
TV Screen	**Standard**
Fit to Screen	Off
Alternate Audio	Off
Captions	Off
Subtitles	Off

8.31 iPod video Settings menu

For TV output from an iOS device, you must still select your appropriate TV type, however. Follow these steps:

1. **Connect the Apple Composite AV Cable or Apple Component AV Cable to your iOS device.** The TV Out option is hidden until the appropriate cable is connected and do not apply to the VGA or HDMI adapters.

2. **From your home screen, tap the Settings icon.** The Settings menu is displayed.

3. **From the Settings menu, scroll to and tap the General option.**

4. **Tap the TV Out option, as shown in Figure 8.32.** Note that this option only appears if you have the appropriate cable connected. The TV Out settings screen appears, similar to Figure 8.33.

5. **Tap the button beside Widescreen to toggle the setting on or off, depending on the TV that you are connecting your device to.**

6. **Press the HOME button to return to the home screen.**

Note Prior to iOS 5, the TV Out settings were located under the Video settings on the iPod touch and iPad and under the iPod settings on the iPhone.

Note

If your videos look distorted when playing them back on your TV, chances are that the TV Screen setting is incorrect. Try changing this setting to see if this resolves the problem. If not, then there may be an encoding problem with the video file, particularly if this is a video that was encoded from a source other than the iTunes Store. See Chapter 9 for more information on encoding your own videos.

8.32 iOS General Settings with TV Out option displayed

8.33 iOS TV Out Settings

225

How Do I Get My Own Movies onto My iPod?

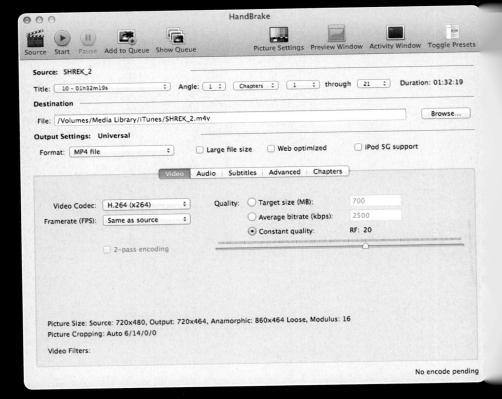

The iTunes Store is a great source of video content for your iPod, but it is not the only option available. Further, you might not even live in a country where video content is available on the iTunes Store. Fortunately, you can also encode your own movies and other videos into an iPod-ready format through the use of a variety of third-party tools.

About Converting Video for the iPod

Unlike the world of digital audio formats, where the MP3 format is the reigning standard, the world of digital video formats can be much more confusing. At this point, there is no single standard video format, and therefore you are going to find a wide variety of formats on the Internet and a wide variety of conversion tools to support these different formats. Further, even videos that you record yourself are unlikely to be in an iPod-ready format and will also require conversion for viewing on your iPod.

The most important point to keep in mind when converting video for the iPod and Apple's other media devices is that these devices actually support a very limited set of video formats and display resolutions, so you must specifically convert your videos into the proper format. To add to the confusion, iTunes supports a much wider range of video formats than the iPod, iPhone, or iPod touch, so being able to watch a video in iTunes is not an indication that it can be played on your device.

Note

Newer iOS devices and the fifth-generation iPod nano support video recording and naturally store their videos in a format that is already compatible with Apple's media devices. These videos can be imported into iTunes directly to be synced as movies, or they can be synced to supported devices as part of your photo library. See Chapter 7 for more information.

Video formats supported by the iPod

The iPod and other Apple media devices support video formats based on the MPEG-4 standard, subject to certain limitations, which are discussed shortly. Specifically, these devices support the MPEG-4 standard and the H.264 standard, which is an evolution of the MPEG-4 standard optimized for portable devices with smaller file sizes at the same quality level.

The original fifth-generation iPod introduced video playback into the iPod family at a very limited 320×240 resolution. Because this resolution is still the size of the iPod classic screen today, this may not have seemed like a serious problem until you consider that the iPod supported TV output capabilities, and even the most basic television can display a 640×480 image. The result was that the videos played back from the original fifth-generation iPod on a television generally looked somewhat blurry.

Fortunately, Apple chose to increase this maximum resolution to 640 × 480 in subsequent firmware updates. Today, all iPod models, including the iPod touch and iPhone, support this 640 × 480 resolution for their video content, a resolution suitable for display on any standard television set. The iPad and recent iPhone and iPod touch models expand this even further by supporting video in on-screen resolutions up to 1024 × 768 on the iPad and 960 × 640 on the iPhone and iPod touch Retina Displays. These newer devices also support high-definition 720p video formats for television output using the appropriate HDMI or VGA adapter cables.

Note The iPad 2 supports 1080p output using the Apple Digital AV Adapter for display mirroring and third-party apps, however, the maximum resolution for iTunes video content is still only 720p.

In addition to these maximum resolutions, the iPod and other Apple media devices are also limited to certain maximum bit rates for video content. The published specifications indicate a maximum bit rate of 1500 kbps for H.264 files and 2500 kbps for MPEG-4 files, although in my experience you can get away with pushing these slightly higher, depending on your source video.

Keep in mind that iTunes supports any video format that can be played by QuickTime. As a result, just because your video can be imported into iTunes does not mean that it can play on your iPod. This is especially true if you have installed additional QuickTime extensions on your Mac or PC.

Recommended video conversion settings

For most video content, the recommended conversion format is H.264 in a 640 × 480 resolution at 1500 kbps (or 1.5 Mbps). The H.264 format provides equivalent quality at a lower bit rate, and therefore a smaller file size and more efficient battery life. These settings provide maximum compatibility with all of Apple's media devices, from the first video-capable iPod to the iPhone and iPad.

In principle, video bit rates work in much the same way as audio bit rates do. Put simply, a lower bit rate produces a smaller file size while sacrificing quality, because there is less data available to store the actual video content. With video files, however, there is a direct correlation between the resolution of a video and its bit rate. Because higher-resolution videos contain more data (more pixels on the screen), a higher bit rate is needed to produce an acceptable quality. The iPod's standard limit of 1500 kbps at 640 × 480 is typical of the generally acceptable bit rates for the H.264 codec, and produces approximately standard TV-quality video, depending largely on the source material.

Note

When choosing your bit rate, keep in mind that the way digital video compression works. The optimal bit rate is based on the amount of motion in the video. Compressed digital video formats work by encoding the differences and motion between frames, so a video of a newscaster talking is going to require less data to effectively reproduce than an action movie.

When converting video content, it is also important to keep in mind the intended playback methods to be used. If you are converting video solely for playback on your iPod or older iPhone screen, for example, and never intend to play this video back on a TV screen, you can get away with much smaller files by encoding at 320×240 (the size of the iPod's screen) or 480×320 (the resolution of the pre-Retina Display iPhone and iPod touch), and therefore also use a lower bit rate of approximately 750-900 kbps to produce an acceptable-quality video file. Keep in mind, however, that the encoding process for your own videos takes a while, so it's always a good idea to plan for the future rather than having to go back and reconvert your videos into a higher-quality format later.

Aspect Ratio

One other concern when dealing with video conversion is the aspect ratio. The aspect ratio of a video refers to the ratio between the width of the image and the height of the image, and can also be thought of as how square or rectangular the image is. Three common aspect ratios are in use today:

- 4:3 (or 1.33:1) is used for some older movies and most standard-definition TV content. Standard TV screens use this aspect ratio, and this is also the aspect ratio used by the fifth-generation iPod, iPod classic, third-generation iPod nano, and the iPad.

- 16:9 (or 1.78:1) is the standard widescreen format used by some movies and almost all high-definition TV content. Widescreen and HDTV screens use this aspect ratio and this is the native aspect ratio of the Apple TV and the approximate aspect ratio of the fifth-generation iPod nano.

- 2.35:1, also known as Cinemascope, is an extremely widescreen presentation used by many theatrical movies. There are very few home-based devices available that use this aspect ratio — it is normally only seen in movie theaters.

Knowing which aspect ratio your source material uses is often useful for ensuring the best-quality conversion. The aspect ratio of a video can be computed simply by dividing the width of the video by the height. For example, for a 640×480 video, you would divide 640 by 480, yielding an amount of 1.33, making the aspect ratio of a 640×480 video 1.33:1.

Note The Apple TV, iPad, and newer iPhone and iPod touch permit much higher resolutions and bit rates for your videos: up to 1280×720 (720p HD) resolution at bit rates of up to 4000 kbps (4 Mbps). However, videos encoded in these higher resolutions cannot be played on older iPod or iPhone models.

Note The iPhone and iPod touch use a 1.5:1 aspect ratio — more or less halfway between the standard definition 4:3 (1.33:1) and widescreen 16:9 (1.78:1) aspect ratios. This ratio provides the best compromise for watching content in either of the most common aspect ratios.

Converting DVDs

In the same way that many iPod and iTunes users begin with an established library of music on CDs, you may also have a collection of existing DVDs that you want to be able to play on your iPod. Unfortunately, while iTunes makes importing CDs extremely easy, DVD conversion is a more complicated process, both because of the video formats involved and the legal issues around the conversion of copy-protected DVDs. Put simply, Apple cannot legally include DVD-importing technology within iTunes, at least not for copy-protected content.

However, in many other countries the copyright laws do not prohibit you from converting content you already own into another format, regardless of whether or not it is copy protected. If you live in one of these countries, there are a number of ways that you can do this with third-party software.

Caution The legality of copying commercial DVDs varies in different countries. For example, in the United States, the Digital Millennium Copyright Act effectively makes it illegal to copy a commercial DVD's content for any reason because of digital copy protection. Always be sure to check the laws in your particular jurisdiction.

Using Handbrake for one-step DVD conversion

The most popular software application for converting your DVDs into an iPod-ready format is Handbrake (www.handbrake.fr). This free, open-source application can handle the entire process for you, including extracting the content from the DVD and converting it into an iPod-ready format.

The Handbrake application provides a wide range of options for advanced users, while also being perfect for users who want a simple way to convert their DVDs for their iPod or other Apple media devices. Handbrake provides several standard presets that creates H.264 video files in a 640×480 resolution at 1500 kbps and preserves the original aspect ratio of the source video.

Note The popularity of video conversion for the iPod and other Apple media devices has spawned a plethora of aggressively marketed video conversion tools that are available online. Most of these cost money and few are worth it, particularly considering that Handbrake is both free and much more frequently updated to support the newest Apple devices and features.

To convert a DVD using Handbrake, follow these steps:

1. **Insert the DVD into your computer's DVD drive.**

2. **Start Handbrake.** On initial startup, Handbrake prompts you to select a video source with a standard file open dialog box, as shown in Figure 9.1. If this does not appear, click the Source button in the top-left corner to open the file selection dialog box.

9.1 The Handbrake file open dialog box

3. **Choose your DVD from the file open dialog box and click Open.** Handbrake scans the DVD content and displays the main Handbrake window, similar to Figure 9.2.

4. **From the Title drop-down menu, choose the title for the main video feature.** Most DVDs have multiple titles for additional content, previews, special features, and so forth. The length of each title is shown beside the title number. For a DVD movie, the main title is usually the longest one.

Note

Handbrake is available for both Mac OS X and Windows, although neither version includes the capability to decrypt copy-protected DVDs natively. Handbrake on OS X automatically uses the appropriate libraries from the free, open-source VLC Media Player if it is installed on the same computer. Windows users need to use a separate tool, such as DVD43, which can present a copy-protected DVD to Handbrake as if it were unprotected. However, you should always consult the laws in your particular jurisdiction before using a tool like this.

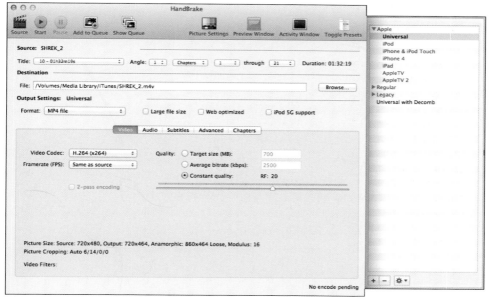

9.2 The Handbrake main window

5. **Click the Browse button under Destination to choose a destination file and folder for the converted DVD file.**

6. **From the presets list on the right, choose Universal to load the Handbrake Universal preset.** Click the Toggle Presets button in the top-right corner if the presets list does not appear. The Universal preset provides the best experience on all of Apple's current media devices, although it excludes compatibility with the fifth-generation iPod. If converting for a fifth-generation iPod, use the iPod Legacy preset instead.

7. **Click Start to begin conversion.**

233

Genius

Handbrake provides a number of more advanced settings that can be used to include and label chapter markers, subtitles, and alternate audio tracks such as additional languages or director's commentaries. Handbrake also provides support for including Dolby Digital audio, which can be used on the Apple TV.

Handbrake begins converting the selected title from the DVD into an H.264 file. This process can take anywhere from 2 to 10 hours for an average movie depending on the speed of your computer. When the process is complete, the resulting MP4 file can be imported directly into your iTunes library.

Anamorphic Encoding

Standard DVDs store their video files in a 720×480 resolution, which works out to a 1.5:1 aspect ratio. It may occur to you that this doesn't match either of the standard TV or widescreen aspect ratios. This is because DVDs actually use a process known as anamorphic encoding to either stretch or compress the video image, depending on the required aspect ratio.

What is happening in this case is that the video is actually stored on the DVD in a 1.5:1 aspect ratio, and the DVD player or playback application is advised to either stretch the video to 854×480 for widescreen (16:9) presentation or compress it to 640×480 for standard TV (4:3) presentation, depending on the content. DVD players also add letterboxing (black bars above and below the image) or pillarboxing (black bars to the sides of the image) as necessary to present the full-screen image, regardless of the aspect ratio of your TV set. This is done by setting a Pixel Aspect Ratio (PAR) flag, which renders the pixels as rectangular instead of square.

This comes into play for your own video conversion as Apple media devices also support the PAR flag, which means you can use anamorphic encoding for your own videos with an application that supports it, such as Handbrake. This is especially useful with widescreen content because a 16:9 movie without anamorphic encoding can only be a maximum of 640×352 resolution on older iPod and iPhone models, whereas anamorphic encoding can take a 640×480 video and stretch it to 854×480, pushing the vertical resolution to the full 480 lines used by standard television sets and producing much better on-TV output quality. Even on newer HD-capable Apple media devices, using anamorphic encoding is more efficient because it produces smaller files — there's nothing gained except wasted space by artificially increasing a 720×480 video to a full 854×480 resolution.

Genius

If you want to convert multiple titles from the same DVD in one session, click the Add to Queue button instead of the Start button. Handbrake adds the currently selected title to the queue, and you can then select another title from the same DVD. When you are finished adding to the queue, click the Start button to begin conversion.

Importing digital copies from DVD

In January 2008, several movie studios began including iPod-compatible digital copies with some of their DVD releases. This provides a simple and legal means to import these DVDs directly into iTunes while still preserving the copy protection of the original DVD.

Digital copies are normally included on an extra disc, separate from the standard DVD that you would play back in your DVD player. This additional disc is encoded in a format that is specifically designed to be imported into iTunes when inserted into your computer. Digital copies also normally come with an insert containing an unlock code that you must type during import.

Keep in mind that you must have an iTunes Store account to use a digital copy, as the digital copy remains copy protected and tied to your iTunes Store account in the same way as any item purchased from the iTunes Store.

To import a digital copy into your iTunes library, follow these steps:

1. **Check to ensure that you are using iTunes 7.6 or later.** Previous versions of iTunes do not support digital copy technology.

2. **Insert the digital copy disc into your computer.** iTunes should detect the digital copy disc and display it in the iTunes Source list in the same way that an audio CD would appear.

3. **Select the entry for the digital copy disc from your iTunes Source list.** An information and import screen should appear, similar to Figure 9.3.

4. **Type the code that came with your DVD and click Redeem.**

iTunes begins importing the digital copy into your iTunes movie library. This process occurs in the same manner as when a movie is downloaded from the iTunes Store, and, in fact, the import even appears in the normal download queue. In this case, however, the download is actually occurring from the DVD to your iTunes library, rather than over the Internet.

235

Once imported, the digital copy is stored as a copy-protected movie in your iTunes library in the same way as any other movie purchased from the iTunes Store, with the same usage restrictions applied to it. The code contained within the DVD packaging is essentially an activation code that ties the digital copy to your iTunes Store account as a zero-dollar purchase. In fact, you even receive an e-mail receipt from the iTunes Store. You may use the same code from the DVD packaging to reimport the digital copy as often as you like using the same iTunes Store account, but you cannot use this code with any other iTunes Store account.

9.3 An iTunes digital copy import screen

Converting unprotected DVD VOB files

If you are working with noncopy-protected DVDs, or you've already extracted the DVDs into an unprotected format using another DVD extraction tool, you have a few more options for conversion.

The video files on DVDs use a VOB extension, but in reality these are just MPEG-2 format files, and you can therefore view or convert them with any number of tools that can read the MPEG-2 format. The only problem is that if you're reading the VOB files directly from the DVD, there is rarely a one-to-one match between VOB files and DVD content, so it may be difficult to find or stitch together the exact files you're looking for.

Handbrake can still read an unprotected DVD, of course, but another tool that is worth looking at for this purpose, particularly if your conversion needs are more complex, is MPEG Streamclip, available for free from www.squared5.com. This is a tool designed for the express purpose of working with various flavors of MPEG video content, and it provides editing capabilities in addition to the capability to convert these files into an iPod-ready format.

Converting Video Files

In addition to converting your own DVDs, you may find various video files from other sources on the Internet that you want to copy onto your iPod. There are a considerable number of tools available today to convert just about any unprotected video format into the H.264 format used by the iPod.

Note Video files that you download from the Internet come in a wide variety of formats and resolutions. One important thing to keep in mind is to adjust your output settings to match the source file. Nothing is gained by converting a 160 × 120 video clip to 640 × 480, except wasted space.

Converting video files with QuickTime and iTunes

The first and simplest tool, if not the fastest, is iTunes. Although the iPod's supported formats are quite limited, iTunes can import and play any video supported by QuickTime.

If you can import your video and play it in iTunes, then you can convert it directly within iTunes without the need for any other third-party software:

1. **Import your original video into iTunes.** Your video appears in the Movies section by default.

2. **Select Movies in the Source list, and locate and select the video that you just imported.**

3. **From the iTunes Advanced menu, choose Create iPod or iPhone Version to create a version that can be played on your iPod, iPhone, iPad, or Apple TV, or Create iPad or Apple TV Version to create a version using the higher-quality settings.** iTunes begins converting the video, with its progress displayed in the status panel at the top of the iTunes window, as shown in Figure 9.4.

4. **When conversion is complete, a second copy of the movie appears in your iTunes library ready to be synced to the appropriate Apple media devices.**

9.4 The video conversion status panel

Note iPod or iPhone videos can also be played on the Apple TV and iPad, so the Create iPad or Apple TV Version option is only useful when you are converting higher-quality source material such as HD TV programming that can take advantage of the higher resolutions and bit rates offered by the Apple TV and are not concerned about iPod or older iPhone compatibility.

Caution

iTunes and QuickTime Pro can also convert MPEG-2 video files with the QuickTime MPEG-2 plug-in available from Apple. However, QuickTime does not support multiplexed MPEG video files. This usually results in the video being properly encoded, but having no audio track, and is a frequent source of confusion for many new users to iPod video conversion.

This method of conversion has the advantage of being built in to iTunes so that no additional software is required; however, it does not support all formats and provides absolutely no conversion options. Further, QuickTime conversion to H.264 is presently the slowest of all of the tools that are available.

Converting video files with third-party tools

If you are looking for either faster video conversion or support for more formats than QuickTime provides, there are a number of additional software tools that can assist you with this.

As of version 0.93, Handbrake now supports converting almost any stand-alone video file format into the H.264 format in much the same way as it does for DVDs discussed earlier in this chapter. Converting video files with Handbrake is handled in the same manner as converting DVDs — simply choose a file from the Source browser rather than a DVD.

To convert a video file using Handbrake, follow these steps:

1. **Start Handbrake.** On initial startup, Handbrake prompts you to select a video source with a standard file open dialog box. If this does not appear, click the Source button in the top-left corner to open the file selection dialog box.

2. **Choose your source file from the file open dialog box and click Open.**

3. **Click Browse under Destination to choose a destination file and folder for the converted file.**

4. **From the presets list on the right, choose Universal to load the Handbrake Universal preset.** Click the Toggle Presets button in the top-right corner if the presets list does not appear. The Universal preset provides settings to provide the best experience on all of Apple's current media devices, although it excludes compatibility with the

fifth-generation iPod. If converting for a fifth-generation iPod you will need to use the iPod Legacy preset instead.

5. **Click Start to begin conversion.**

Although Handbrake is available in both Mac and Windows versions, there are numerous other tools available for Windows users. The landscape of these video conversion applications for Windows users is much more varied and can be a bit confusing, although for basic video conversion, most of these tools perform similarly. One of the first iPod video conversion tools that still remains a popular choice today and continues to be regularly updated is Videora, a free conversion application that can be downloaded from www.videora.com.

Genius

If you're converting a lot of video and are looking for a faster option, be sure to check out turbo.264 HD from Elgato Systems if you're a Mac user or Instant Video to Go from ADS Technologies for Windows users. These hardware devices connect to your computer and can dramatically accelerate the video conversion process, particularly on older computers.

Converting Home Movies

Another type of content that you may be interested in converting for display on your iPod is your own home movies. Depending on how and when these were recorded, they may be in a range of different formats, but they are otherwise converted in much the same way as any other digital video file.

Types of digital home video formats

Digital video cameras normally record in one of four possible formats:

- **DV.** Short for digital video, this is the standard format used by the first digital camcorders and uses a minimally compressed video stream recorded onto a digital videotape. DV is normally transferred from the camcorder to your computer through a FireWire connection, although some cameras also provide USB transfer capabilities.

- **MPEG-2.** Similar to the format used by the DVD standard, some newer hard drive- and DVD-R-based camcorders have adopted the MPEG-2 format. Most camcorders that use the MPEG-2 format save recorded videos into a file system on either an internal hard drive or a recordable DVD. These files are then transferred either through USB or directly from the DVD onto the computer.

- **MPEG-4.** Some newer camcorders and most digital cameras and cell phones that provide video-recording capabilities record directly in different variations of the MPEG-4 format. Despite this format being directly supported by the iPod, not all cameras necessarily use a resolution or bit rate that is iPod compatible, and so these files may still require conversion. Recorded videos are usually stored on internal flash memory and transferred to your computer through a USB connection.

- **AVCHD.** This is a high-definition video format based on the H.264 codec to provide a high level of compression. As this is a high-definition format, however, videos are likely to be in a much higher resolution or bit-rate than is supported by the iPod, and therefore still require conversion into an iPod-ready format. Even Apple's HD-capable devices such as the iPad and Apple TV do not provide direct AVCHD support.

Converting standard digital video

Standard digital video (DV) is usually transferred from your camcorder to your computer through a FireWire connection using an application such as iMovie or Windows Movie Maker. Because these videos must first be preprocessed by an actual video authoring application, the usual method of converting these files into an iPod-ready format is to export them directly from these applications.

In fact, most recent versions of iMovie provide a direct iPod or Apple TV export option that uses the underlying QuickTime engine to generate an optimized iPod- or Apple TV compatible file that is transferred directly into your iTunes library.

Windows users may find this a bit more challenging, however, as the included Windows Movie Maker application does not provide any direct support for MPEG-4 or H.264 video output. In fact, almost all of its output formats are based on the Windows Media Video (WMV) codec. This makes it necessary to use another tool such as Handbrake or Videora to convert the resulting file into an iPod-compatible format.

Genius

When exporting videos from Windows Movie Maker for iPod conversion, use the DV-AVI output setting for the best results. DV-AVI provides the lowest amount of video compression and is therefore less likely to suffer from additional quality loss that normally results from converting between lossy video formats.

Converting MPEG-2 or MPEG-4 home video

If you are using a camcorder or digital camera that already encodes your videos into MPEG-2 or MPEG-4 formats, these are normally saved as files on your device and transferred to your computer through USB. These video files can be converted into an iPod-ready format using the same tools as for any other digital video file discussed earlier in this chapter. Further, because Apple's media devices natively support the MPEG-4 format, some standard-definition MPEG-4 videos can be transferred directly into iTunes and from there onto your media device with no conversion required.

Converting VHS recordings

If you have old home movies on VHS videotapes, you can also convert these for viewing on your iPod, but the process is a bit more complicated and requires additional hardware.

The first and most important requirement for accomplishing this is a video capture card that you can use to connect your VCR to your computer because you're essentially going to be recording your videotapes manually into your computer. Most capture cards available on the market today also include software to handle the recording aspects and save your recordings to a digital video file.

If your particular capture card and software support MPEG-4 or H.264 in the appropriate bit rates and resolutions for the iPod, then this can make the conversion process much simpler. If not, you must save your captured videos into an intermediate format and then use one of the tools discussed earlier in this chapter to perform the actual conversion for the iPod.

For Mac users, one very useful application for performing video capture and iPod conversion is the EyeTV software from Elgato. This software is normally included with video capture and TV tuner devices from Elgato, as well as several other manufacturers.

In addition to acting as a TV tuner/recorder, EyeTV provides a VHS Assistant feature (shown in Figure 9.5) that guides you step by step through the process of connecting your VCR and capturing your VHS tapes and then converting them into an iPod-ready format.

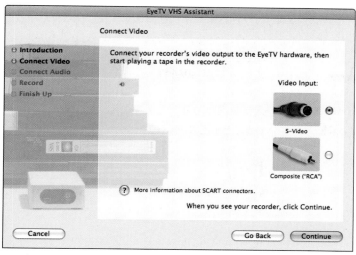

9.5 The Elgato EyeTV VHS Assistant window

How Do I Get Content from My iPod Back to My Computer?

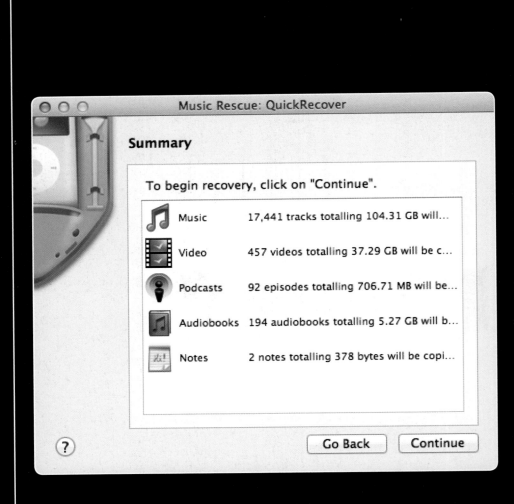

No matter how well you manage your content in your iTunes library, sooner or later you're going to come across the situation where you need to copy some or all of the content from your iPod back onto your computer. Unfortunately, iTunes has traditionally been a one-way conduit for your content — it flows from your computer out to your iPod, but seldom in the other direction. However, as with most things in the world of technology, where there is a will, there is a way, and many enterprising software developers have stepped in to fill the void.

Transferring Purchased Content

For years, iTunes provided no means for getting back any content that was stored on your iPod. Content was synced from your computer to iTunes, but other than ratings and play counts, nothing was ever transferred back in the other direction. iTunes 7 changed this slightly, however, by introducing the capability to transfer any content you have purchased from the iTunes Store back onto any of your authorized computers. This seemed like a reasonable-enough compromise from the point of view of Apple because although your iTunes purchases were potentially vulnerable to loss, presumably any music or other content that you had not purchased from the iTunes Store would be available on physical media in your CD collection.

The process for transferring purchases is intended for mass transfers of your purchased content to another library or recovery of purchased content in the event that you have lost your main iTunes library. This feature is an all-or-nothing deal in that there is no way to selectively transfer specific content from your iPod back to your computer; every purchased item on your iPod that the connected computer is authorized to play and that does not already exist in your iTunes library is copied back from your iPod.

To transfer purchases from your iPod back to your iTunes library, follow these steps:

1. **Ensure that the computer is authorized for the iTunes Store account that corresponds to the content that you are transferring.** More information on authorizing your computer can be found in Chapter 2.

2. **Connect your iPod to your computer.**

3. **Right-click your iPod in the iTunes Devices list.** A context menu appears, similar to Figure 10.1.

4. **From the context menu, choose Transfer Purchases.** iTunes scans through your iPod to locate any purchased content the current computer is authorized to play and that does not already exist in the current library. These items are transferred back to your iTunes library.

10.1 An iPod context menu.

The Transfer Purchases feature includes all types of purchased items that are found on your iPod, including not only music and video content, but also iPod or iPhone games and applications. Because of this, no separate tools are necessary to transfer these from your iPod back into iTunes. The Transfer Purchases feature also transfers back any games from your Click Wheel iPod or applications stored on your iPhone, iPod touch, or iPad, if your host iTunes computer is authorized for the iTunes Store account that was originally used to purchase them.

Note   If you have content on your iPod that was purchased with different iTunes Store accounts, simply ensure that all of your accounts are authorized on your computer before using the Transfer Purchases feature. iTunes copies purchased content that is authorized by any account in the current iTunes library.

The Transfer Purchases feature works whether you are using automatic synchronization or managing your iPod content manually, and it can be used with any iTunes library that is authorized for your iTunes Store account. In fact, if you are using automatic synchronization and connect your iPod to a different iTunes library, you are given the option to transfer purchases in the standard warning dialog box that indicates that your iPod is linked to another iTunes library, as shown in Figure 10.2.

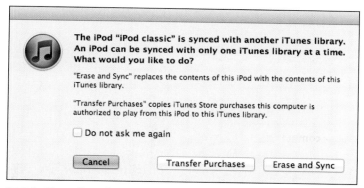

10.2 An iTunes Transfer Purchases warning dialog box

A similar dialog box, shown in Figure 10.3, also appears when you connect your iPod to your primary library if iTunes detects purchased content on the iPod that does not also exist in iTunes.

In this case, if you had recently deleted purchased items from your iTunes library intentionally, you would probably want to click Don't Transfer to remove these purchased items from your iPod as well.

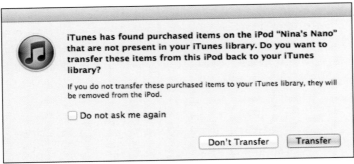

iTunes has found purchased items on the iPod "Nina's Nano" that are not present in your iTunes library. Do you want to transfer these items from this iPod back to your iTunes library?

If you do not transfer these purchased items to your iTunes library, they will be removed from the iPod.

☐ Do not ask me again

Don't Transfer   Transfer

10.3 An iTunes Transfer Purchases warning dialog box

Caution   If you have deleted nonpurchased items from your iTunes library that are still on your iPod, these are not transferred back by iTunes, and they are lost if you allow your iPod to automatically sync with your computer. With a different iTunes library, you are warned that your iPod is linked to a different library, but if you're syncing to the same library, iTunes removes any content from your iPod that is no longer in your iTunes library.

Transferring Content Manually

The iTunes built-in capability for transferring your purchased content is a useful feature for moving iTunes purchases between libraries, but it is not a practical solution for recovering your entire library. This is because very few users have iTunes libraries that consist exclusively of purchased content.

Fortunately, if you're using a Click Wheel iPod model such as the iPod classic or iPod nano, there is actually a fairly straightforward way to copy all of the content from your iPod back to your computer en masse. The secret is that a traditional iPod model simply appears to your computer as an external USB mass storage device in the same way as any other external USB hard drive or memory key does. In fact, this is how iTunes communicates with your iPod, by simply copying your media files to it in the same way that Windows Explorer or the Mac Finder does, and updating the iPod's database directly. As a result of this, you can quite easily retrieve your music and video content from your iPod by copying it back in the other direction. All of your content is sitting on your iPod as files on a hard drive — you just have to know where to look for it.

However, there are some difficulties in actually getting at your media content on your iPod. If you're trying to recover your content into a new iTunes library, the first problem is that iTunes is going to try to sync your iPod to the new, blank library, which could result in it erasing all of the content on your iPod. Many users are afraid to connect their iPod to a new computer for fear that they will lose the content on it by iTunes synchronizing it with a blank library. However, this is only a concern in the rare case that you have specifically deleted items from within your existing iTunes library database so that they're not even listed anymore. Even if you have lost the actual media files from your computer, iTunes does not remove anything from your iPod as long as it remains listed in your iTunes library.

Note The iPhone, iPod touch, and iPad use a completely different synchronization method from traditional iPod models and do not appear as external hard drives. As a result, manually copying your content off is not possible on these devices. If you're using one of these devices skip ahead to the next section and use a third-party application instead.

However, if you're looking to recover all of the content from your iPod, chances are that you're starting over with a brand-new library database, either because you have formatted your computer and reinstalled your OS, or because you're using a new computer entirely. When you're using a new library, iTunes recognizes that your iPod has been automatically synchronized with a different library, notifies you of this, and asks you what you want to do, as shown in Figure 10.4.

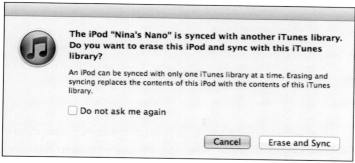

10.4 An iTunes sync warning dialog box

Simply click Cancel in this dialog box to prevent iTunes from performing an automatic sync. Your iPod remains connected and visible in iTunes, so you can adjust any other settings, but no synchronization occurs.

Genius If you're recovering your iPod to a brand-new computer or you have restored your computer from scratch, then the simplest method is to connect the iPod and copy the content off before you install iTunes or allow it to launch for the first time. In this case, the iPod simply shows up as an external drive and you don't need to worry about avoiding interference from iTunes in the process.

249

Note

If you're trying to migrate your iTunes library to a new computer, it is far better to simply copy the original iTunes library and content directly from the old computer rather than from your iPod. The full iTunes library database contains additional information and settings that cannot be recovered from your iPod. Transferring your iTunes library to a new computer is discussed in Chapter 12.

In addition to iTunes trying to sync your iPod to a new library, the second problem is that iTunes does not normally leave your iPod connected long enough for you to see it appear as an external drive unless you have your iPod set to either manage the content on it manually or you have enabled disk use in iTunes. Basically, you have to tell iTunes that you want to access your iPod as an external hard drive; otherwise, it simply assumes that it no longer needs to remain connected after syncing.

1. **With your iPod connected to your computer, select it from the iTunes Devices list at the left side of your iTunes window.** A Summary screen appears, similar to Figure 10.5.

10.5 The iPod Summary screen

2. **From the Summary screen, select the Enable disk use check box.**

3. **Click Apply to save this setting.** You may see a dialog box advising you that you now need to manually eject your iPod after use. If this dialog box appears, simply click OK to acknowledge it. Your iPod now appears as an external drive in Windows Explorer or the Mac Finder.

Genius

There's nothing particularly magical about the Enable disk use option in iTunes. Your iPod always appears to your computer as an external hard drive, regardless of whether this option is set. Enabling this option merely tells iTunes not to automatically eject your iPod when it's finished syncing.

Once you are able to access your iPod as an external drive through Windows Explorer or the Mac Finder, you then need to actually locate your media content on your iPod. The next problem is that the folder containing your content is actually hidden from normal view, and so you need to configure Windows Explorer or the Mac Finder to display hidden folders.

If you're using Windows, this setting can be found under your Folder options:

1. **From a Windows Explorer window, choose Tools ⇨ Folder Options.** The Folder Options dialog box appears.

2. **Click the View tab.** The View options display, as shown in Figure 10.6.

3. **Select the Show hidden files and folders radio button.**

4. **Click OK.**

In Mac OS X, showing hidden files and folders is slightly more complicated, as you need to adjust a setting in the Mac OS X Terminal application. Follow these steps:

1. **Open the Mac OS X Terminal application.** This can be found in your Applications/Utilities folder.

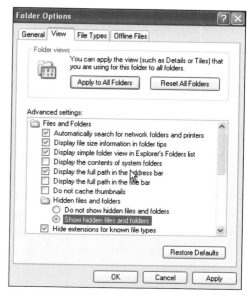

10.6 The View tab of the Windows Explorer Folder Options dialog box

2. **At the Terminal prompt, type** defaults write com.apple.finder AppleShowAllFiles TRUE **and press Enter.**

3. **At the Terminal prompt, type** killall Finder **and press Enter.**

The Mac OS X Finder application restarts, and you can then see all hidden files. To later turn off the display of hidden files, simply follow the same steps again, replacing TRUE with FALSE in step 2.

Once you enable the display of hidden files and folders, open Windows Explorer or the Mac Finder and select your iPod from the list of drives. You should see a folder named iPod_Control at the very top level. This folder contains your iPod's internal database files, as well as all of your actual media content. Specifically, your media content can be found under the Music subfolder, laid out in a series of subfolders, similar to Figure 10.7.

10.7 The layout of the iPod_Control Music folder

Genius You can also manually recover playlists from your iPod using iTunes simply by exporting them to an XML file in your iPod view and then reimporting them into the main iTunes library. See Chapter 1 for more details on exporting and importing playlists.

Despite the name, this folder contains all of your media content with the exception of your photos. Recovering photos from your iPod is covered at the end of this chapter.

You may notice that the files stored in this folder are not named in any useful manner. This is because iTunes renames them when transferring them onto your iPod to ensure that the filenames conform to the iPod's file system. Further, the files are not organized in any way that is logical to a person; they're merely spread out across a series of meaningless subfolders. The good news, however, is that the actual tag information within these files is all completely intact, and in the end, iTunes only cares about the tags inside your files and not the names of the files.

Note Traditional iPod models use a disk format specific to your host computer's operating system. Although Mac OS X can read Windows-formatted iPods, the reverse is not true. This means that if you are trying to recover a Mac-formatted iPod on a Windows PC you must install an additional software application such as MacDrive by MediaFour (www.mediafour.com) to allow your Windows PC to read your Mac-formatted iPod.

So, once you can actually see the files, recovering the content is really as simple as copying it all back onto your computer and then importing it into iTunes as you normally would for any other set of files.

Third-Party Programs for Transferring Music and Video Content

The manual method described earlier in this chapter is the most straightforward and inexpensive method for recovering content from your iPod. If you're in a situation where you've lost your entire iTunes library and simply want to get your content back without any concern for any of your additional library information such as playlists, ratings, and play counts, then the manual method works well and has the advantage of being free.

However, this method is not without its limitations. The first is that the layout of the files on the iPod makes it difficult to restore content selectively. If you need to pull off a single track or a set of tracks, the manual approach is not practical. Secondly, when copying your media content back to your computer manually, only the data that is stored within the actual media files is recovered. This includes most of the important information like track name, artist, album, and genre, but information such as ratings and play counts are only stored in the iTunes and iPod database and not in the actual files. The same thing applies to your playlists.

Fortunately, a number of third-party software applications are available that know how to read the iPod database and not only selectively recover a listing of tracks, but in many cases recover your additional library data as well, such as ratings, play counts, and playlists. Many of these applications also work with the iPhone, iPod touch, and iPad, for which the manual recovery method is not even possible due to the lack of direct disk access.

Note These applications are intended to assist you in recovering your own content from your iPod, a feature that Apple has omitted from the iTunes application in order to discourage piracy. The existence of these third-party tools should not be an encouragement to pillage content from other people's iPods.

The downside is that most of these applications are not free; you can expect to pay around $20 to $30 for a good iPod recovery application. The few free applications that are available are generally quite limited in how much data they can recover and do not necessarily work with all iPod models.

One of my preferred solutions for handling iPod recovery is a program called Music Rescue by KennetNet Software (www.kennettnet.co.uk). This application is available for both Mac and Windows and supports all current iPod models including the iPhone, iPod touch, and even the iPad. The application costs about $20; however, a trial version is available that is fully functional except for a registration reminder screen that comes up intermittently while copying data from your device.

Caution

When looking for iPod recovery applications, always be sure that the application supports the iPod model you're looking to recover your content from and the version of iTunes you're looking to recover your content to. None of these applications is officially supported by Apple, and they usually need to be updated by their own developers when a new iPod model or iTunes version comes along.

Music Rescue offers a number of excellent advanced features over other software applications, including the capability to do a complete one-button recovery of your entire iPod back to your computer, or set up sophisticated rules to copy only selected content back. All additional meta-data, such as ratings, play counts, last-played dates, skip counts, last-skipped dates, and playlists, are copied back during this process as well.

To perform a full recovery from your iPod using Music Rescue, follow these steps:

1. **Download and install the Music Rescue application.**

2. **Connect your iPod to your computer.** If you are using a traditional iPod model, ensure that the Enable disk use option has been selected, as described earlier in this chapter. If you are using an iPhone or iPod touch, you must have iTunes 7.4 or later already installed on the computer.

3. **Open Music Rescue. Any iPod or iPhone devices attached to your computer are shown, similar to Figure 10.8.**

4. **Select your iPod and click QuickRecover.** A QuickRecover welcome screen appears.

5. **Click Continue.** A Recovery Setup screen appears, as shown in Figure 10.9.

10.8 The Music Rescue iPod selection screen

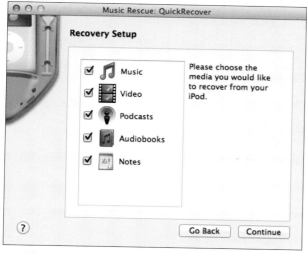

10.9 The Music Rescue Recovery Setup screen

6. **Select the check boxes beside the types of content you want to recover, and click Continue.** A setup screen appears for the first type of content you have selected, as shown in Figure 10.10.

7. **If you want to recover your content to a location other than your iTunes library, select a different location from the Copy To drop-down menu.**

8. **If you do not want your recovered tracks automatically added to iTunes, deselect the Add tracks to iTunes.**

10.10 The Music Rescue Music Setup screen

9. **If you want Music Rescue to also rebuild all of your playlists, select the Rebuild Playlists check box.**

10. **Click Continue to proceed to the next screen.** Similar setup screens appear for any other types of content that you selected in Step 6.

11. **Repeat steps 7 to 10 for each subsequent screen.** When you complete all of the setup screens, a Summary screen appears, similar to Figure 10.11.

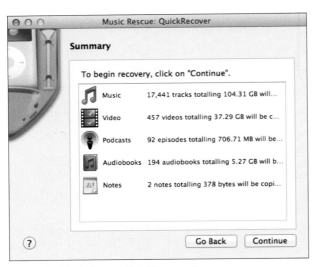

10.11 The Music Rescue QuickRecover Summary screen

12. **Click Continue to begin copying content back to your computer.** A progress screen similar to Figure 10.12 appears.

13. **When the copying finishes, click Continue to close the Music Rescue: QuickRecover window.**

10.12 The Music Rescue QuickRecover Copying progress screen

In addition to performing a full recovery of content from your iPod back to your computer, Music Rescue can also selectively recover individual tracks from your iPod.

1. **Download and install the Music Rescue application.**

2. **Connect your iPod to your computer.** If you are using a traditional iPod model, ensure that the Enable disk use option is selected, as described earlier in this chapter. If you are using an iPhone or iPod touch, you must have iTunes 7.4 or later already installed on the computer.

3. **Open Music Rescue.** Any iPod or iPhone devices attached to your computer are displayed.

4. **Select your iPod or iPhone and click Open.** The main Music Rescue window appears with a list of content on your iPod, similar to Figure 10.13.

5. **From the main Music Rescue screen, you can browse through your iPod content in much the same way as you would in your iTunes library, including your categories and playlists.** Note that Music Rescue also scans your iTunes library for matching items — a green dot to the far right of each item indicates that the item already exists in your iTunes library.

6. **To search for a specific item, type it into the Search box in the top-right corner of the Music Rescue window.**

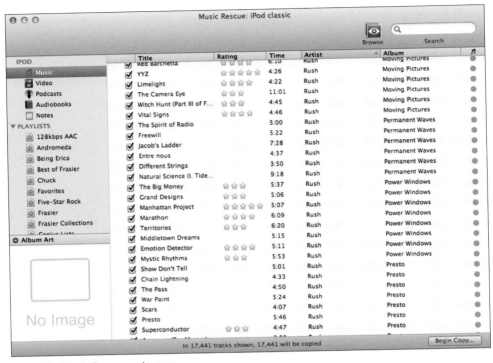

10.13 The Music Rescue main screen

7. **The checkmarks beside each item indicate which items are queued for copying to your computer.** If you want to select only a few items, choose Queue ➪ Unqueue All to clear all checkmarks on the current screen and then specifically select those items that you want copied.

8. **After you select the items you want to copy back to your computer, click Begin Copy in the bottom-right corner.** A media selection screen appears, similar to Figure 10.14.

9. **From this screen, select the check boxes beside each item type you want to copy to your computer.**

10. **To configure the copy settings for a specific item type, click the Configure button beside that item type.** A configuration screen appears, similar to Figure 10.15.

11. **From the configuration screen, choose from the following options to determine how and where your content is copied:**

   • **Copy To.** From this drop-down menu, select either iTunes to copy your tracks directly into your iTunes Music folder and import them into iTunes, or an alternate folder where you want your content copied.

- **Sorting Preset.** Choose Match iTunes to copy your tracks into an album and artist folder structure in the same way that iTunes would store them, or choose an alternate file and folder layout if you want your recovered tracks to be organized differently.

- **Copy previously copied tracks.** Choose whether Music Rescue copies over tracks that already exist in the target location.

- **Add tracks to iTunes.** Select this check box to have Music Rescue automatically add your tracks to iTunes after they have been copied. Note that this is mandatory if you are copying your tracks directly into your iTunes Music folder.

- **Force Metadata.** This option determines whether Music Rescue overwrites the meta-data in iTunes for any tracks that it copies that are already present in iTunes.

- **Rebuild Playlists.** Enable this option to have Music Rescue rebuild your playlists in iTunes using the information on your iPod.

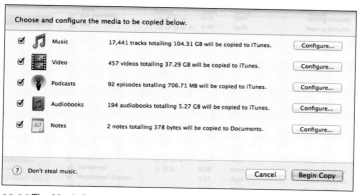

10.14 The Music Rescue media selection screen

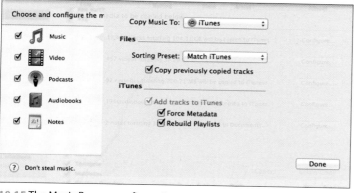

10.15 The Music Rescue configuration screen

12. **Click Done when you finish adjusting these options.**

13. **Click Begin Copy to begin copying the selected items back to your computer.**

Music Rescue also offers a number of more advanced features, such as the capability to recover your Smart Playlists and the ability to build complex rules to quickly select items for recovery, based on search criteria and whether an item is already present in iTunes.

There are a number of other applications that are also available to perform iPod recovery, with some noteworthy ones being CopyTrans (www.copytrans.net), a $20 Windows-only application that can perform either full or selective iPod recovery; iPod Access (www.findleydesigns.com), another $20 application available in both Mac and Windows versions; and Senuti (www.fadingred.com/senuti), an $18 Mac application with a 30-day, 1,000-song trial version available. These applications work quite well and generally perform the same tasks as Music Rescue, although I personally prefer Music Rescue for its cross-platform support, cleaner user interface, quick recovery mode, and advanced selection features.

Note

Searching the Internet for iPod recovery software is going to turn up dozens of options; however, a lot of iPod recovery software does not work as advertised. As with anything else you find on the Internet, it is always wise to do some research before deciding on an application. iPod review sites like iLounge (www.ilounge.com) are generally a good place to get information on reputable applications.

Copying Photos

Although the methods described previously in this chapter work great for recovering your audio and video content, photos are a special case when it comes to the iPod. This is because your photos are stored on your iPod differently from other types of media content.

The first and most important thing to keep in mind with photos on traditional Click Wheel iPods is that iTunes resizes your photos when they are transferred to your iPod, with the largest photo size stored by iTunes being approximately 720 × 480, depending on your particular iPod model. iTunes also scales down photos on iOS devices; however, on the iPad, Retina Display iPhone and iPod touch photos are stored in a more reasonable size of around 3.5 megapixels; older iPhone and iPod touch models still store photos at 640 × 480. For the traditional iPod models, such as the iPod classic and iPod nano, iTunes offers an option to store original full-resolution copies of your photos, which is discussed in Chapter 7; however, this option is not available for the iPod touch, iPhone, or iPad.

If you have stored full-resolution versions of your photos, you can very easily access these by opening your iPod in disk mode through Windows Explorer or the Mac Finder, and simply browsing into the Photos/Full Resolution folder. Original copies of your photos are stored within this folder, organized into subfolders by year, month, and date, and can be copied to your computer in the same way as any other file.

Unfortunately, if you did not opt to store the full-resolution copies of your photos, the best you can recover is a considerably lower-resolution version. For most traditional iPod models with photo support, this is approximately 720 × 480 — the version used for on-TV display. For non-Retina Display iPhone and iPod touch models, this is a 640 × 480 version. To put things in perspective, these equate to approximately 0.3 megapixels. Note that if you have a first- or second-generation iPod nano, which does not have TV output support, you can only recover a 176 × 132 version of your photos. Although photos are stored on the iPad, Retina Display iPhone, and iPod touch models in a better resolution than other devices, they are still scaled down to around 3.5 megapixels.

However, if you find yourself in a situation where you have lost your entire photo collection from your computer but still have it stored on your iPod, a 0.3-megapixel version of a precious memory can be far better than nothing. The photos themselves are stored as uncompressed 16-bit bitmaps in a thumbnail database format on your iPod that is not easily recoverable without third-party tools. Fortunately, however, like other forms of iPod recovery, third-party developers have provided tools to facilitate this.

Two recommended software applications that can perform iPod photo recovery are iPod Access Photo (www.findleydesigns.com), a $13 application available for both Mac and Windows, and CopyTrans Photo (www.copytrans.net), a $20 Windows-only application. Either of these tools can read your iPod, including the iPod touch and iPhone, and recover your photos for you in the maximum resolutions possible. Note that CopyTrans Photo has recently been updated to also provide photo-management support, offering an alternative to iTunes for putting photos onto your iPod.

How Do I Manage Content on an Apple TV?

The Apple TV represents another new direction that Apple has taken with its media products from the traditional iPod models, bringing your media library into your living room. Although Apple still considers this product to be a hobby, the capabilities of the Apple TV have been dramatically expanded. Since the product's initial release in January 2007, Apple TV has moved from a hard-drive based device that synced content from iTunes to a much more inexpensive, second-generation device built around streaming content from your iTunes library. Apple TV also has the capability to allow the consumer to rent movies and access online services, such as Netflix and major sports franchises directly from the device.

Streaming iTunes Content to an Apple TV

Although an Apple TV can function almost completely by itself without an iTunes library on the back end, most Apple TV users are likely to be iTunes users, so streaming content from your iTunes library continues to be an important feature of the Apple TV.

Unlike the original first-generation Apple TV released in 2007, the new second-generation model contains no permanent internal storage to actually sync your content. Instead, it connects over either a Wi-Fi or cabled Ethernet connection and streams content directly from your iTunes library over your home network and from the iTunes Store over the Internet.

The Apple TV connects to your iTunes library through the Home Sharing feature in iTunes, so to set up an Apple TV on your network, you must have enabled Home Sharing on your computer, which you can do by following these steps:

1. **From iTunes running on your computer, choose Advanced ⇨ Turn on Home Sharing.** A screen similar to Figure 11.1 appears. If the Advanced menu instead only contains an entry to Turn off Home Sharing, then Home Sharing is already enabled for your iTunes library and you're ready to go.

11.1 iTunes Home Sharing setup

2. **Type your iTunes Store Apple ID and Password.**

3. **Click Create Home Share.** A confirmation screen appears, advising you that Home Sharing is now enabled.

Note The second-generation Apple TV contains 8GB of internal memory, which is used for caching streamed content to improve performance and cannot be managed directly by the user.

Home Sharing is discussed in more detail in Chapter 12. After you have enabled Home Sharing in your iTunes library, you must also enable it on your Apple TV by using the same Apple ID and password: To do this, follow these steps:

1. **Using the Apple Remote, choose Computers ⇨ Turn on Home Sharing from the main Apple TV menu, as shown in Figure 11.2.** An on-screen keyboard appears similar to Figure 11.3.

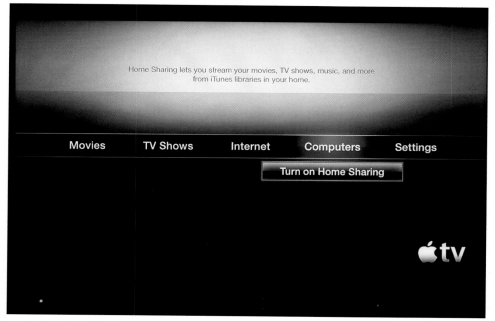

Home Sharing lets you stream your movies, TV shows, music, and more from iTunes libraries in your home.

| Movies | TV Shows | Internet | Computers | Settings |

Turn on Home Sharing

ᔞtv

11.2 Apple TV Home Sharing setup

2. **Using the Apple Remote to select letters, enter your Apple ID and select Submit when finished.** A password entry screen appears.

3. **Again, using the Apple Remote, enter your password and select Submit.** The Apple TV may take a few moments to connect to the iTunes Store to validate your credentials, after which a screen appears asking you if you want to also use this password to rent and purchase content from the iTunes Store, similar to Figure 11.4.

11.3 Entering an Apple ID for Home Sharing

4. **Using the Apple Remote, Select Yes if your Home Sharing account is the same as the iTunes Store account you want to use to rent or purchase content on the Apple TV; otherwise select No.**

Note If you choose to use your Home Sharing account as your iTunes Store account, your password is remembered automatically. If you want to be prompted for your password each time you make a purchase, set up your account manually under the iTunes Store settings.

After you have successfully configured Home Sharing both in your iTunes library and on your Apple TV, your iTunes library should appear listed below the Computers menu similar to Figure 11.5 whenever iTunes is running on your computer and available on the same network. Any additional iTunes libraries configured for the same Home Sharing account and running on your network are also displayed here.

Use For iTunes Store?

Would you like to use the Apple ID ▮▮▮▮▮▮▮▮▮▮ to rent or purchase items from the iTunes Store? Your password will be remembered automatically.

Yes

No

11.4 Using your Home Sharing Apple ID for the iTunes Store

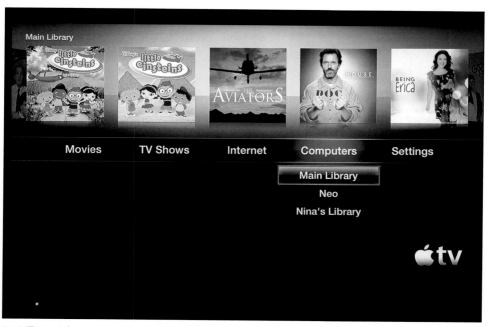

11.5 iTunes Library appearing on Apple TV, named Main Library

Accessing content from your iTunes library works much the same way as it does from any other device. Content is categorized into Music, Movies, TV Shows, Podcasts, iTunes U, and Photos sections with each section further broken down into category-specific subheadings, such as Playlists, Artists, and Albums for music or a list of individual shows and seasons for TV shows.

Using Your Apple TV with the iTunes Store

In addition to accessing content in your iTunes library, the Apple TV also allows you to rent movies and purchase and watch TV shows streamed directly from the iTunes Store using your Internet connection with no Mac or PC required.

Configuring your Apple TV for the iTunes Store

Before you can purchase content on your Apple TV, you must first log in to your iTunes Store account for your country of residence. If you have enabled Home Sharing with your primary iTunes Store account, as described in the previous section, this may have already been done for you. However, if you need to configure a new account or switch to a different account, follow these steps:

1. **From the Apple TV main menu, choose Settings ⇨ General ⇨ iTunes Store.** The iTunes Store Configuration menu appears, as shown in Figure 11.6.

2. **Choose Location.** A list of countries appears.

3. **Scroll to and choose the country for your iTunes Store account.** A checkmark appears next to the selected country, as shown in Figure 11.7.

4. **Press the Menu button on your Apple Remote to return to the iTunes Store configuration menu.**

5. **Select Sign in.** A screen appears for you to enter your Apple ID for the iTunes Store.

6. **Using the Apple Remote to select letters, enter your Apple ID.** Select Submit when finished to proceed to the password entry screen.

7. **Enter your password using the Apple Remote to select letters.** Select Submit when finished.

8. **Select Yes when asked whether you want the Apple TV to remember your password.** Selecting No requires you to enter your password each time you make a purchase from your Apple TV.

9. **Press and hold the Menu button on the Apple Remote to return to the main Apple TV menu.**

11.6 Apple TV iTunes Store settings

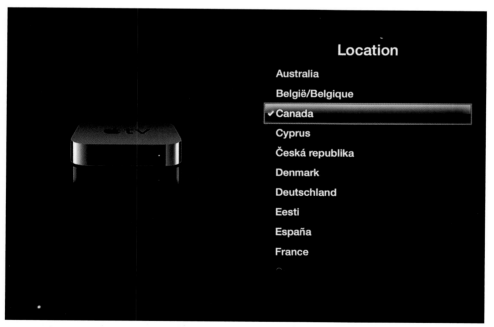

11.7 Apple TV iTunes Store country listing

269

Genius

If you have an iOS device, you can save yourself some time entering text on the Apple TV by downloading the Remote application from the iTunes App Store. Among other things, this application allows you to use your iOS device's keyboard to type information into Apple TV text entry fields. I discuss this application later in this chapter.

After you configure your Apple TV for your iTunes Store account and country, the menus on the Apple TV reflect content that is available in your particular country's store. For example, if TV content is not available on your iTunes Store, then the TV Shows menu does not show any browsing or purchasing options for TV Show content.

Note

You can select different countries in the Apple TV iTunes Store configuration menu to browse the content available in those countries, but you cannot purchase or rent that content unless you have an account for that country. In fact, if you try to purchase from a different country's store, the Apple TV simply gives you an error message and requires you to return to the Configuration menu to set your store to the correct country manually.

Renting Movies with Your Apple TV

One of the big announcements from Apple in 2008 was its entry into the movie-rental business, greatly expanding the role of the Apple TV in the living room. In addition to purchasing movies to keep in your library, iTunes began offering the ability to rent movies for a limited time, similar to the video-on-demand services available from many cable and satellite providers.

Apple TV movie rentals also came with an additional benefit: high-definition (HD) movies. Although iTunes had traditionally only offered standard-definition (SD) movies for purchase, this new announcement introduced the availability of certain titles to be rented in HD resolution for a slight premium over the SD equivalent. Further, many of the HD movies available for rental on the iTunes Store also include a Dolby Digital 5.1 soundtrack, taking advantage of the Apple TV digital audio output capabilities.

Note

By default, movie rentals on the Apple TV are in HD whenever available. You can change this to prefer standard-definition movies in the iTunes Store settings; choose Settings ⇨ General to find the menu.

Movies rented on an Apple TV can only be watched on an Apple TV — they cannot be viewed in iTunes or on an iOS device; however, your rentals are available on any Apple TV signed in with your iTunes Store account, so if you have more than one Apple TV you can watch your rentals anywhere in your home. Apple TV movie rentals are streamed on-demand from the Apple servers rather than downloaded, so you must be connected to the Internet in order to actually watch a rented movie.

Genius

The Apple TV also syncs the playback positions of movie rentals to the iTunes Store so that you can begin watching a movie in one room of your house and then later pick up where you left off on an Apple TV in another room.

Renting movies on the Apple TV is relatively straightforward. Follow these steps:

1. **Using the Apple Remote, navigate to the Movies heading, as shown in Figure 11.8.**

11.8 Apple TV Movies menu

2. **Select Top Movies to see a list of the top-rated and most recent movies in various categories.** A gallery of movie covers and titles appears, similar to Figure 11.9. Other options on the Movies menu allow you to browse titles by specific genres or search for a specific movie by title, actor, or director.

11.9 Apple TV Movies gallery

3. **Using the arrow keys on the Apple Remote, navigate to a movie title and press the center Select button.** A detailed information screen is shown, similar to Figure 11.10.

4. **Select Preview to view a trailer for the selected movie or Rent to rent it.** The More option can be used to display reviews from Rotten Tomatoes and iTunes Store customers as well as a detailed cast and crew listing.

Genius

Pressing the up arrow on the Apple Remote from the movie details screen displays the full movie description. Pressing the up arrow again cycles through additional information views.

Rented movies on your Apple TV are displayed in the Cover Flow view at the top of the Movies screen on the main menu and can be accessed and played from there. This feature replaces the separate Rented Movies menu option found in earlier Apple TV versions.

Note

The Apple TV has a maximum 720p resolution, so even HD content on the Apple TV is not of the same quality as a Blu-ray disc, which is 1080p. This should not be a significant limitation for most users, however.

11.10 Apple TV movie details

Rented movies remain available on your Apple TVs for 30 days, after which they automatically expire whether your have watched them or not. After you begin watching a rented movie, it is set to expire 24 hours after you begin watching it if you purchased it from the U.S. iTunes Store, or 48 hours later if you purchased it from the Canadian or U.K. iTunes stores. If you are in the process of watching a movie when it expires, the Apple TV allows you to continue watching it. The movie is deleted as soon as you exit or finish watching it.

Note Unlike the first-generation Apple TV, the second-generation model only allows you to rent movies from the iTunes Store. To purchase movies, you must buy them by using iTunes on your computer and then stream them from your iTunes library.

Adding movies to your Wish List

You can also keep a Wish List of movies that you might want to rent at a later time. You can add a movie to your Wish List directly from the item information screen. Follow these steps:

1. **Browse to and select a movie that you want to add to your Wish List.** The movie information screen appears.

2. **Choose Wish List, as shown in Figure 11.11.** The item is added to your Wish List and the menu item toggles to read Remove.

3. **Press the Menu button on your remote to return to the main movie information screen.**

11.11 Apple TV movie options

When your Wish List contains at least one item, a Wish List menu option appears on your Apple TV Movies menu, where you can review the contents of your Wish List.

Genius

From the More information screen, you can also select the name of a cast or crew member to see a list of other works available on the iTunes Store for that person.

Note

Your Apple TV Wish List is stored in your iTunes Store account so that you can access it on any Apple TV associated with that account. However, it does not synchronize with your iTunes Store Wish List described in Chapter 2.

Streaming TV Shows to your Apple TV from iTunes in the Cloud

When the second-generation Apple TV was released in September 2010, it was focused on renting movies and TV shows from the iTunes Store. Unlike its first-generation predecessor, you could not purchase content at all on the new device. However, following the introduction of iCloud and the realization that TV show rentals were not catching on with the big networks, Apple changed its strategy with the release of Apple TV Software Update 4.3 in August 2011. TV show rentals were dropped entirely in favor of providing users with access to their entire collections of previously purchased TV shows — possibly hundreds or even thousands of gigabytes worth of content — available to be watched directly from iTunes in the Cloud.

Note

TV show support on the Apple TV is currently limited to iTunes customers in the U.S. only. Apple has not announced when this support will be expanded to include other countries. The TV Shows section is hidden on the Apple TV in countries where TV Show streaming is not supported.

To access and watch your purchased TV shows, follow these steps:

1. **Using the Apple Remote, navigate to the TV Shows heading, as shown in Figure 11.12.**

11.12 TV Shows menu on the Apple TV

2. **Select Purchased.** A grid view of your purchased TV shows appears, similar to Figure 11.13.

3. **Using the arrow keys on the Apple Remote, navigate to a show and press the center Select button.** A list of episodes is shown, similar to Figure 11.14.

4. **Navigate to an episode and press the center Select button to begin watching it.** The episode summary appears while the episode begins streaming playback from iTunes in the Cloud.

Note   Only TV shows that are still available on the iTunes Store are available through iTunes in the Cloud. Content in your iTunes library that is no longer available in iTunes in the Cloud can still be streamed from your iTunes library as described earlier in this chapter.

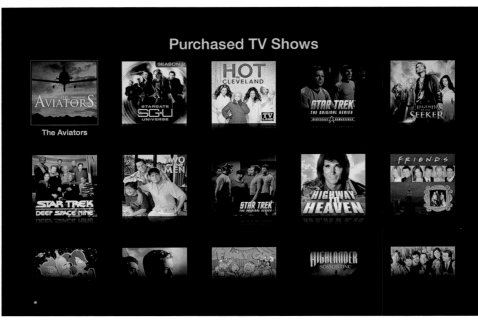

11.13 Apple TV Purchased TV Shows

11.14 Purchase a TV Show episode listing

The Apple TV also allows you to purchase TV shows. You do this in much the same way as you rent movies, as I describe earlier in this chapter, with additional options for purchasing specific episodes, whole seasons, or season passes. Purchased TV Shows are immediately made available for streaming from iTunes in the Cloud. TV Shows purchased on the Apple TV are not automatically queued for downloading to your iTunes library; however, you can download them manually through your Purchase History. (Refer to Chapter 2 for details on how to do this.)

Keeping track of your favorite TV shows

Like the Wish List for movies, the Apple TV also allows you to keep track of your favorite TV shows by adding them to a Favorites List. This list works on the basis of complete shows, rather than individual seasons or episodes, and can be a very useful way to quickly check for new episodes of shows that you follow, particularly when a Season Pass option isn't available.

To add a TV show to your Favorites List, follow these steps:

1. **Browse to and select a TV show title that you want to add to your Favorites.** The TV show's episode listing screen appears.

2. **Select Add Show to Favorites, as shown in Figure 11.15.** The item is added to your Favorites and the menu item toggles to read Remove Show from Favorites.

3. **Press the Menu button on your remote to return to the TV Show listing screen.**

After you have added at least one show to your favorites list, a Favorites menu option appears on your Apple TV Movies menu, where you can review its contents. Your Favorites List also indicates any new episodes within a given show by displaying a red badge count in the top-right corner of the artwork image.

Genius You can rearrange the shows in your Favorites List by holding down the center button on the Apple Remote until the artwork starts jiggling and then using the arrow keys to reposition the current show, or choose to sort alphabetically or by date from the iTunes Store settings on the Apple TV.

Note Your Favorites List is stored online in your iTunes Store account and will appear on any other Apple TVs in your house that are signed in with the same iTunes Store account. Your Favorites List is not accessible from your computer or other devices.

11.15 Select Add Show to Favorites to add an item.

Using the Genius Feature on the Apple TV

The Apple TV provides support for creating a Genius playlist in a similar way as described in Chapter 8 for the iPod. You can create a Genius playlist for a given track from either the track listing or the Now Playing screen:

1. **Locate a track on which you want to base a Genius playlist.** You must select an individual track, although you can also use a track that is currently playing.

2. **Press and hold the center button on the Apple Remote.** A pop-up menu appears.

3. **Select Start Genius, as shown in Figure 11.16.**

A new Genius list is created under the Genius menu in the Music section on your Apple TV, and the selected track immediately begins playing back from the Genius list.

Note Genius lists are not saved nor are they synced back to iTunes or other Apple TVs.

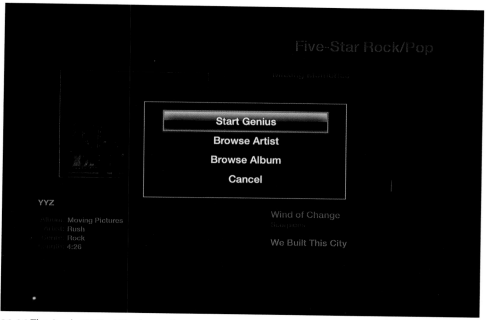

11.16 The Apple TV Start Genius option

Setting up a Video Party Mix

You can also set up a playlist of music videos on your Apple TV and play them either sequentially or shuffled in the same way as a normal playlist. In addition to playing the videos without stopping, the Apple TV provides a small overlay in the bottom-left corner of your TV screen at the beginning of each new video track showing the album artwork, artist, and album name. This feature allows you to create an MTV-style video party mix.

Video playlists are created in the same way as any other playlist, and you can either create them from iTunes or use an On-The-Go playlist. You can even mix video and audio together in the same playlist. Apple TV switches seamlessly back and forth between video playback for your videos and the normal Now Playing screen for audio tracks.

Displaying Photos on Your Apple TV

As with the iPod, iPhone, and iPad, you can also display photos from your computer on your Apple TV by using iTunes. Although the Apple TV displays all of the music, movies, TV shows, and podcasts in your iTunes library, you must specifically choose which photo folders, albums, or events to display on your Apple TV. This feature works a bit differently than it does for an iPod, and you must configure iTunes to make your photo library available to your Apple TV before it can display any of your photos:

1. **From iTunes, choose Advanced ⇨ Choose Photos to Share.** A Photo Sharing Preferences window appears similar to Figure 11.17.

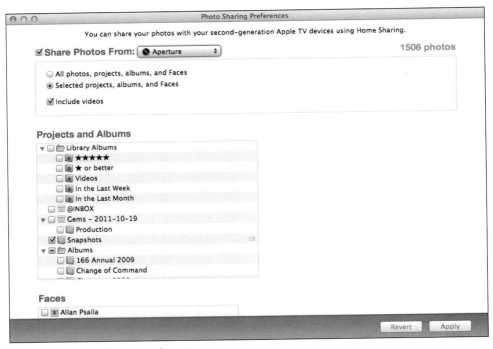

11.17 iTunes Photo Sharing Preferences

2. **Click the Share Photos From check box if it is not already checked.**

3. **From the drop-down menu beside the Share Photos From option, choose from where you want to share your photos.** Compatible applications, such as iPhoto and Aperture for Mac users and Adobe Photoshop Album and Photoshop Elements for Windows users are shown here, if installed on your computer. Alternatively, you can choose to share the photos in your home Pictures folder or select the Choose Folder option to specify any other folder on your computer.

4. **Click the check box beside Include videos to allow your Apple TV to access and play videos in your photo albums.**

5. **Click either All items or Selected items to choose which photos you want synchro-nized to your device.** If you are using a photo-management application, the content structure from that application is displayed, such as albums, events, and faces, if using iPhoto. If you are sharing from a folder, each of the first-level subfolder names appears as albums.

6. **If you have chosen Selected items, click the check boxes beside the selected photo albums or folders that you want to make available for viewing on the Apple TV.** If you are using iPhoto or Aperture, additional options appear here that allow you to choose specific Events and Faces (iPhoto) or Projects and Faces (Aperture).

7. **Click Apply to save your changes.**

8. **Click the Close button to close the Photo Sharing Preferences window.**

Note The photo sharing settings in iTunes apply to all Apple TV devices that are associ-ated with that iTunes library.

The Apple TV also does a great job of displaying your photos as slideshows with 11 very cool slide-show themes, such as the Photo Wall theme shown in Figure 11.18. You can even accompany your slideshows with music from your iTunes library. These settings can be configured directly on the Apple TV when viewing a photo album and are applied to any photo albums that you play as slide-shows. You can also use your photos as a custom screensaver with any of the available slideshow themes.

11.18 Apple TV Photo Wall Slideshow theme

Using Your Apple TV with AirPlay

The Apple TV can also act as an AirPlay client for any of the iTunes libraries or iOS devices on your network, allowing you to stream audio or video playback from iTunes or audio, video, and photos from an iOS device. To configure the Apple TV to function as an AirPlay client, follow these steps:

1. **From the Apple TV main menu, choose Settings ⇨ AirPlay.** The AirPlay configuration screen appears.

2. **Ensure that AirPlay is set to On, as shown in Figure 11.19.**

3. **Optionally, select Set Password to require any connecting iTunes library or iOS device to authenticate before being allowed to stream music through this Apple TV.**

4. **Press the Menu button on the Apple Remote to return to the previous menu.**

After Apple TV is configured, it appears by name in the AirPlay devices list in the bottom-right corner of the iTunes window. AirPlay is discussed in Chapter 4.

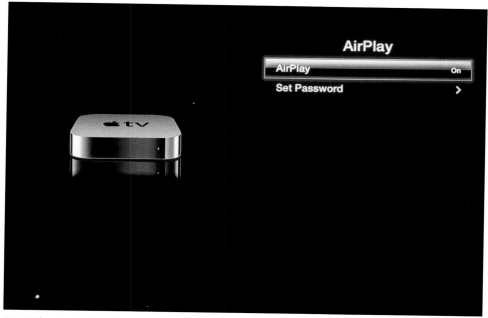

11.19 The Apple TV AirPlay configuration screen

Genius

The iPhone 4S and iPad 2 with iOS 5 or later can also wirelessly mirror the device's screen to an Apple TV using AirPlay.

Note

AirPlay was previously known by the name AirTunes. Although older versions of Apple's hardware and software products may still use the term AirTunes, they are compatible with AirPlay for audio playback.

Using Your iOS Device as an Apple Remote

If you have an iPhone, iPod touch, or iPad, it can also double as a remote control for your Apple TV when you install the free Apple Remote application from the iTunes App Store. This application lets you browse and control the playback of your Apple TV content directly from your iOS device in a manner very similar to the built-in Music and Video applications, including advanced features, such as the ability to search for content all directly from your device.

The Remote app pairs with your Apple TV through the same Home Sharing feature that the Apple TV uses to connect with your iTunes library. Simply enter your Apple ID and password into the remote app. You should see a list of your Apple TV devices and iTunes libraries, similar to Figure 11.20.

Once paired, you can browse through your Apple TV library in the same way as you would browse content stored directly on your device. Selecting content for playback immediately begins playing it on the Apple TV. The Remote application also supports searching, and Genius playlists and can even be used as a touchpad to navigate the menus manually.

One particularly useful feature of the Remote application is as a remote keyboard for typing information into the text-entry fields that appear on the Apple TV. Rather than fumbling with the normal Apple Remote to try to scroll around to spell a word, simply start the Remote application on your iOS device. The data entry prompt from the screen appears on your device, along with a keyboard that you can use to fill it in, as shown in Figure 11.21.

11.20 iOS Remote application

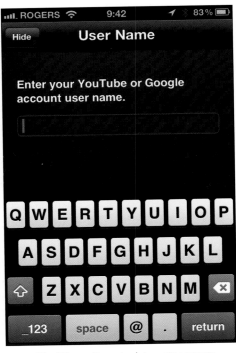

11.21 The iPhone Remote data-entry screen

The iOS Remote app keyboard works on any data-entry field, so you can use it to type passwords or fill in search fields. You can even paste text into this field from another iOS app — a useful feature for entering complex passwords. The only catch is that because the remote uses Home Sharing to access your Apple TV, you have to enter your Home Sharing password by using the Apple Remote control before you can access it from your iOS device.

Using a Third-Party Remote with the Apple TV

The Apple TV can also learn commands from just about any infrared remote. Although users of universal remote controls have likely already taken the opposite approach of teaching the Apple TV commands to their remote, this feature allows any remote to be used regardless of whether it is capable of learning commands — the Apple TV learns the commands directly from the remote.

Another advantage of setting up a third-party remote is that advanced playback controls can be configured beyond those available on the seven-button Apple Remote. The configuration process allows you to have the Apple TV learn additional commands for functions such as play, pause, stop, rewind, fast-forward, previous track, next track, skip backward, and skip forward. Once programmed, the appropriate buttons can be used to trigger these functions directly from your third-party remote.

To configure theApple TV to use your own remote, follow these steps:

1. **Locate either a remote that you are no longer using or a multifunction remote with a device that you are not using.** Many modern TV sets come with basic multifunction remotes to control several devices, such as a cable box, VCR, or DVD player.

2. **Using your normal Apple Remote, from the Apple TV choose Settings ⇨ General ⇨ Remotes.** The Remote Control configuration screen, shown in Figure 11.22, appears.

3. **Choose Learn Remote.** You are prompted to choose an unused device setting on your other remote and then select Start using your Apple Remote to continue. The Learn Remote screen, shown in Figure 11.23, appears to guide you through the process.

285

11.22 Apple Remote configuration screen

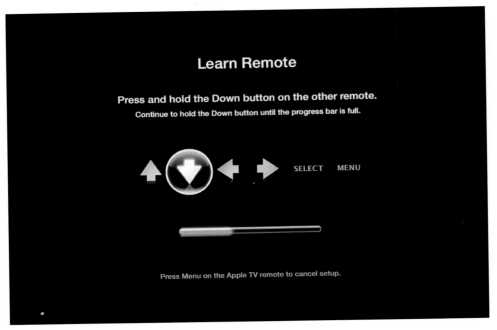

11.23 Apple TV Learn Remote screen

4. **Press and hold each button on your other remote as directed until the progress bar is full.** As you finish each button, the Apple TV automatically proceeds to the next one. When you have programmed the final button, the Apple TV prompts you to name the remote control, as shown in Figure 11.24.

11.24 Apple Remote Name screen

5. **Using either your original Apple Remote or the new remote you have just programmed, enter a name to identify the new remote and choose Done when finished.** The Apple TV displays a screen confirming that you are finished setting up your remote and asks if you want to set up playback buttons, as shown in Figure 11.25.

6. **Choose OK if you are finished configuring the remote to return to the main remote menu or choose Set Up Playback Buttons to configure additional buttons on your remote for use with your Apple TV.** If you choose to set up additional playback buttons, the screen in Figure 11.26 is shown to allow you to set up your Apple TV to respond to additional buttons on your remote. Note that you do not need to program all of the listed buttons. You can use the left and right buttons on your remote to choose which buttons you want to program. Press the Select button on your remote when you finish programming additional buttons.

11.25 Apple Remote Setup Complete

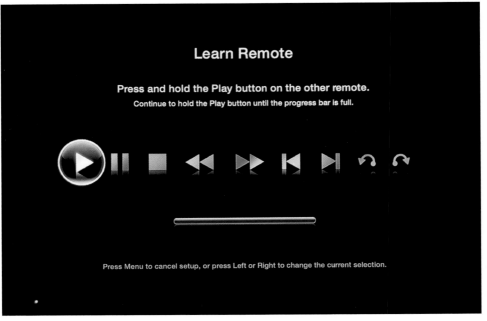

11.26 Apple TV Learn Remote Buttons screen

After you finish programming, you are returned to the Apple Remote Settings menu with your new remote configuration listed. You can select the remote from here to reconfigure, rename, or remove it, and you can even program your Apple TV to respond to additional third-party remotes.

Note

Programming a third-party remote does not disable the Apple Remote.

How Do I Manage a Large iTunes Library?

Although you may only start out with a few dozen CDs and a few hundred music tracks in your iTunes library, with the wide variety of content supported by iTunes, it won't be long before you suddenly find yourself dealing with a much larger iTunes library. Although iTunes handles most of your library management quite seamlessly, some advanced tips and tricks are useful for getting the most out of iTunes when you're dealing with one or more larger iTunes libraries.

Upgrading to iTunes Media Organization

As I discuss in Chapter 1, iTunes began its life several years ago as an application designed solely for managing your music, and in those early days that was the only content it needed to keep track of. Your music tracks were stored in a folder called iTunes Music and organized into folders by artist and album. As iTunes evolved to support new types of content — audiobooks, podcasts, videos, and eventually applications — other content-specific folders were simply added to the existing iTunes Music folder structure parallel to your artists and albums, as shown in Figure 12.1. Further, games for Click Wheel iPod models and applications for iOS devices were stored completely outside of the iTunes Music folder.

12.1 iTunes Music folder organization

iTunes 9 introduced a new file system layout that attempts to put all of your iTunes content on an even footing. References to the iTunes Music folder have all been changed to iTunes Media, and content is now organized by content type within the iTunes Media folder, as shown in Figure 12.2.

This moves the traditional Artist/Album folder structure down into a Music subfolder, puts audiobooks in their own subfolder, and also moves the iPod Games and Mobile Applications folders into the iTunes Media folder. A new folder also appears as part of this structure: *Automatically Add to iTunes*. Files placed in this folder are automatically imported into the iTunes application when it is running, providing a useful drop box for newly downloaded content from other sources.

12.2 iTunes Media Folder organization

If you're starting a new iTunes library from scratch, the iTunes Media organization is used by default. However, because iTunes tends to err on the side of caution when it comes to reorganizing your file system, upgrading from older versions of iTunes preserves the old iTunes Music layout unless you specifically tell iTunes to reorganize your content into the new iTunes Media folder organization. Making the switch is relatively straightforward. Follow these steps:

1. **From the iTunes menu, choose File ⇨ Library ⇨ Organize Library.** A dialog box similar to Figure 12.3 appears.

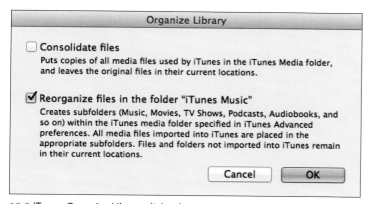

12.3 iTunes Organize Library dialog box

2. **Click on theUpgrade to iTunes Media organization check box.**

3. **Click OK.**

iTunes goes through the files in your existing iTunes Music folder and reorganizes them into the new iTunes Media folder structure shown earlier. Depending on the size of your iTunes library, this process can take anywhere from a few seconds to 2 or 3 minutes.

Note After the Upgrade to iTunes Media organization process completes, you may find that there are still artist and album folders left over in the main iTunes Media folder. iTunes only moves files that are listed in its library database, and any leftover files are likely orphaned files that have been lying around in the iTunes Music folder but are not actually referenced in your iTunes library.

Moving Your iTunes Library to an External Hard Drive

With higher bit-rate music formats becoming more common, as well as iTunes support for movies and TV shows, it's not going to be long before you find that your iTunes library has outgrown the capacity of the hard drive in your computer. At this point, you have two options: Buy a bigger hard drive and deal with the hassle of migrating your operating system over to it, or simply move the iTunes library to an external hard drive.

A common mistake made by many iTunes users is simply copying the entire iTunes Media folder to a new location and expecting iTunes to pick up this change. Unfortunately, this does not work, as iTunes is very specific about where its files are kept and how it manages them. As I discuss in Chapter 1, iTunes references files by their full path names, and so if you move a file to a new drive or partition, iTunes loses track of it, and the result is a broken link in your iTunes library.

Note Mac OS X users can get away with moving files between folders *on the same drive* because of the way that the underlying OS X operating system keeps track of file locations. However, this does not work when moving files to a different drive or partition.

If you have made this mistake and suddenly find that iTunes cannot find any of your tracks, the best solution is simply to move them back to their original location. Provided you have just copied the files over en masse and have not done any major reorganization of your file and folder layout, putting the files back in the locations where iTunes expects to find them should make everything match up again.

The good news is that iTunes provides a method by which you can move your files to a new location through iTunes, ensuring that all of your file locations are updated for the new location in the process.

Note The steps in this section make reference to using an external hard drive, but the same method can be used if you're simply looking to move your iTunes library to a second internal hard drive or a different partition on the same drive.

Specifying a different iTunes Media folder location

By default, iTunes stores its library database and related information as well as your media content in a folder named *iTunes* under your operating system's default *Music* folder. The database is in the main *iTunes* folder while your media content lives in a folder below that named *iTunes Media*.

Note If you've upgraded from an older version of iTunes, this folder may still be named iTunes Music instead of iTunes Media. Older versions of iTunes organized media files differently. Despite the name, however, this folder still contains your podcasts, audiobooks, TV shows, and movies as well as your music.

As I discuss in Chapter 1, the iTunes Media folder is where iTunes places content that you import from CD or download from the iTunes Store, including podcasts and iOS applications. Other files that you import directly into iTunes may also be stored in this folder, or they may have been left in their original locations, depending on your preference settings.

You can change the location of your iTunes Media folder quite easily. Follow these steps:

1. **Open your iTunes preferences and click the Advanced tab, as shown in Figure 12.4.**
2. **Click Change.** A file browser dialog box appears.
3. **In the file browser dialog box, specify a new folder location for your media content.**
4. **Click OK to apply the new settings.**

12.4 The Advanced tab of the iTunes Preferences dialog box

Moving and consolidating your iTunes media

Changing your iTunes Media folder path tells iTunes where to place any new media that you import into your library; however, any existing files already in your library are left in their previous location. iTunes links to these files by their full path name so that it can still find them, but it begins treating them as unmanaged files like any other file outside of the iTunes Media folder.

However, iTunes has a feature designed to reorganize all of your files within your iTunes Media folder, copying in any tracks that are stored elsewhere in the process. Although this feature is primarily designed to allow you to collect any tracks that you may have added to your library from their original locations, it also works very well as a means for transferring your entire library to a new drive. Follow these steps:

1. **In your iTunes preferences, set your iTunes Media folder location to the new drive that you want to store your media on.** More information on this can be found in Chapter 1.

2. **From the iTunes menu, choose File ⇨ Library ⇨ Organize Library.** A dialog box similar to Figure 12.5 appears. Note that prior to iTunes 9, this option was found directly on either the File menu or the Advanced menu.

3. **Ensure Consolidate files is selected and click OK.**

12.5 Organize Library dialog box

External Hard Drives and Laptops

If you're a laptop user who travels often, there's no need to worry about lugging your iTunes media drive around with you unless you really need access to all of your media.

iTunes works just fine without the external drive connected, although, of course, you don't have access to any of your actual media files. Instead, iTunes shows them as broken links, and you may receive the occasional error about a file that cannot be found. Don't worry, as iTunes can pick these files up again as soon as the external hard drive returns.

More importantly, however, if you check your iTunes Media folder location while disconnected, you can see that iTunes has temporarily reverted to the default location on your system drive. This means that you can use iTunes to download podcasts, purchase music, and even import CDs while you're on the road. These tracks are added to the local iTunes folder, where you can manage them normally and even sync them to your iPod or other Apple media device.

Further, you can even use automatic sync with your iPod while travelling. iTunes does not remove a file from your iPod as long as it remains listed in the iTunes library, even if the underlying file is not accessible.

When you return home and reconnect the external hard drive, the iTunes Media folder path should revert automatically to the external path as soon as you restart iTunes, and then you can run another quick Consolidate files operation to transfer any content that you downloaded to the external drive.

iTunes scans through your library looking for files that are stored outside of the iTunes Media folder and begins copying them. In this case, because you have specified a completely new iTunes Media folder location, the result is to copy all of your media to this new location, updating the paths in the iTunes library database in the process.

Keep in mind that the Consolidate files process *copies* your media files rather than moves them. Therefore, you still need to go back and manually clean them up from the original location to free up hard drive space after you confirm that everything is otherwise working properly.

Note

This method may not be desirable if you have chosen not to let iTunes organize your Media folder for you, as this option essentially reorganizes your entire library into the iTunes file-and-folder structure. Unfortunately, there is really no simple way to move a self-organized library to a new drive without reimporting all of your tracks again from the new location.

Moving the iTunes database to a new folder

The iTunes Media folder only specifies where your media content is stored. Your library database and other related support files remain in the default location under iTunes in your *Music* folder. These files generally take up very little space relative to your media collection, so there is rarely any need to move them.

There are, however, cases where storing the iTunes library database in another location may be desirable, such as with an external hard drive that is used with multiple computers, or a shared network location.

Moving your iTunes database is a separate process from moving your iTunes Media folder, and does not change the path in which iTunes looks for your media. Because the iTunes media files are stored by default under the main iTunes folder, I strongly recommend that you move your iTunes Media folder first using the Consolidate files function described earlier in this chapter before moving the main iTunes database.

Moving your iTunes database is relatively easy to accomplish, as long as you're using iTunes 7 or later. Follow these steps:

1. **Shut down iTunes.**

2. **Using Windows Explorer or the Mac OS Finder, copy your iTunes folder to the new location where you want it to be stored.** If your iTunes Media folder is still located under the iTunes folder, you may want to exclude this from the copy to save time, because it won't be used in the new location until you copy it using the Consolidate files function.

3. **Start iTunes while holding down the Opt key (Mac) or the Shift key (Windows).** Keep holding this key until iTunes prompts you with a dialog box similar to Figure 12.6.

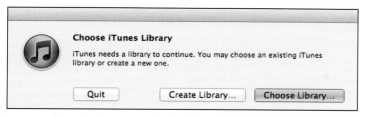

Choose iTunes Library

iTunes needs a library to continue. You may choose an existing iTunes library or create a new one.

| Quit | | Create Library... | Choose Library... |

12.6 The Choose iTunes Library dialog box

4. **Click Choose Library.** A standard file browser dialog box appears.

5. **Browse to the location that you copied your iTunes folder to in Step 2, and select the iTunes folder.**

6. **Click OK.**

iTunes starts up using the iTunes library folder in the new location, and continues to use this new location unless you change it again. Note that if you want to access this iTunes library database from other computers, you must repeat these steps on each additional computer.

Caution

If you choose to store your iTunes library on a network share for access by multiple computers, be very careful to not have iTunes running against the same library on more than one computer at a time. The iTunes database is not designed for simultaneous multiuser access, and corruption can occur in this situation.

Moving Your iTunes Library to a New Computer

Migrating your entire iTunes library to a new computer is actually fairly simple, provided you plan to store your files in the same relative location on each computer. Ideally, if your iTunes Media folder is in its default location on your system drive, then copying your iTunes library to the new computer is really just a matter of copying over the entire iTunes folder from your original computer to the corresponding location on the new computer. Follow these steps:

1. **Optional: Perform a Consolidate files operation, as described earlier in this chapter.**
   This helps to ensure that all of your media files are contained within the iTunes folder.

2. **Shut down iTunes on both computers.**

299

3. **Locate your iTunes folder.** This folder is stored under your Music folder for the current user. See Figure 12.7 for an example.

12.7 The iTunes folder location

4. **Copy the entire iTunes folder and all files and folders underneath it to the corresponding location on the new computer, directly under your Music folder.** You can copy these files by using an external hard drive or USB memory key, by burning CDs or DVDs, or simply by copying them over a network connection between the two computers.

5. **If you receive an error message asking you whether you want to overwrite files in the destination folder, select Yes.** This error can happen if you have already run iTunes on the new computer and created an empty iTunes database. This assumes that you haven't already started adding music to a new iTunes library — in that case you should ensure you have backed up anything from that folder before continuing.

6. **After the copying process is complete, start iTunes on the new computer.** It should pick up the copied library database and all of your content.

Note that your iTunes preferences are not copied from the original computer, and you should revisit your iTunes preferences screens to ensure that these are set the way you want.

If you've stored your iTunes Media folder in another location, the process can be a bit trickier depending on how the new computer is laid out. If you store your iTunes Media folder on an external hard drive, you can still follow the previous steps to transfer your iTunes library database, and then simply make sure that the external hard drive is connected to the new computer.

If you're storing your iTunes library on a second hard drive inside your computer, then you either need to ensure that you copy the iTunes Media folder separately to the same location on the new computer (for example, D:\Music to D:\Music), or perform the Consolidate files steps described earlier in this chapter to move the iTunes Media folder to a new location.

Note Windows users may have problems with using an external hard drive on more than one computer because drive letters may be assigned differently on different machines. You can reassign drive letters manually in Windows by visiting your Computer Management control panel and choosing Disk Management.

Managing Your iTunes Media in Multiple Locations

As your iTunes library grows, one of the more frustrating limitations that you are likely to bump up against is the inability for iTunes to easily handle the storage of your media in more than a single location. Basically, you have one iTunes Media folder in which everything is stored, and although you can move your content en masse to a new location, as described earlier in this chapter, there's really no easy way to split it up. You can certainly choose to not copy files to the iTunes Media folder when adding them to your library, but this is not practical for those situations where your content is already in your iTunes library, and having some of your media stored outside of the iTunes Media folder can make things complicated when you want to relocate that content.

Fortunately, you can use a few tricks in the underlying operating system to help you manage your content across multiple drives or partitions. These are not iTunes-specific features, but instead are ways to trick iTunes into storing or accessing your content elsewhere.

Both the Mac and Windows operating systems support a feature whereby you can link a subfolder to a different file system location — even a completely different drive. In Mac OS X, these are referred to as symbolic links, while in Windows, they're called NTFS Junctions. Regardless of terminology, however, the function is the same: What looks like a normal subfolder in your file system is actually linked to a completely different location.

This concept works with your iTunes library by allowing you to essentially chop off portions of your iTunes Media folder and store them elsewhere. For example, you could take the Movies subfolder from your iTunes Media folder and copy it to a different drive or partition. You would then create a symbolic link or junction in place of the old Movies folder to point to this new location. As far as iTunes is concerned, the Movies folder is still there, but in reality, when it visits that location, it's actually referencing the files on the other drive.

The actual discussion of how to create symbolic links and NTFS Junctions is beyond the scope of this book, although numerous tutorials are available online.

Creating Multiple iTunes Libraries on One Computer

It's not uncommon in many families to have multiple iPod users sharing the same computer, sometimes with widely diverse musical tastes. Although you can easily share the same library and sync it with multiple iPods, as discussed in Chapter 7, this may not work in many cases because the playlists, ratings, and other metadata are also shared across all iPods.

Fortunately, you can manage multiple libraries on a single computer a few different ways.

The first and simplest method is to just use separate user accounts. Your iTunes library is specific to your own user account, and if other users log in on the computer, they get their own iTunes library. In this case, everybody has his or her own self-contained iTunes library database and iTunes Media folder automatically, with no further effort required to manage it.

On the other hand, if you're all sharing a single user account on the computer, this solution may not be practical. In this scenario, iTunes allows you to create and choose different libraries manually. To create a new library for the current user account, follow these steps:

1. **Start iTunes while holding down the Opt key (Mac) or the Shift key (Windows).** Keep holding this key until iTunes prompts you with the Choose iTunes Library dialog box, as shown in Figure 12.8.

Choose iTunes Library

iTunes needs a library to continue. You may choose an existing iTunes library or create a new one.

| Quit | Create Library... | Choose Library... |

12.8 Creating a new iTunes library

2. **Click Create Library.** A standard file browser dialog box appears.

3. **Browse to the folder where you want the new iTunes library to be stored.**

4. **Type a name for the new iTunes library folder.**

5. **Click OK.** iTunes creates a new, empty library at the specified location. To create additional iTunes libraries, simply repeat these steps.

When you restart iTunes, it uses the same library it did last time unless you tell it to use a different one. To change between libraries, follow these steps:

1. **Start iTunes while holding down the Opt key (Mac) or the Shift key (Windows).** Keep holding this key until iTunes prompts you with the Choose iTunes Library dialog box.

2. **Click Choose Library.** A standard file browser dialog box appears.

3. **Browse to and select the folder where your alternate iTunes library is stored.**

4. **Click OK.**

Caution

iTunes preference settings are stored globally for your current user account, regardless of which library you are currently using. This can be especially important for settings, such as the iTunes Media folder location. If you need to keep your iTunes preferences separate, then you must use different user accounts or an iTunes library-management tool, such as the AppleScript discussed in Chapter 14.

Sharing Your iTunes Library on a Network

iTunes provides built-in support for sharing and streaming your media content to other computers on the same network. You can choose to broadcast your iTunes library content for playback by any other nearby iTunes user or enable a new Home Sharing feature introduced in iTunes 9 that allows you to both share and copy content among up to five computers in your home network.

Sharing your iTunes Library for playback by other users

By default, the basic library sharing option in iTunes allows other users to connect to your iTunes library using their own copy of iTunes and browse through and listen to your music. In this mode, remote users cannot actually copy or sync the music — your library is shared in listen-only mode.

Note If you have protected iTunes content stored in your shared library, then the remote computers must be authorized for your iTunes Store account in order to listen to or view that content.

To enable sharing for your iTunes library, follow these steps:

1. **Open your iTunes preferences and click the General tab.**

2. **In the Library Name field at the top of the pane, type a name for your iTunes library.** This is the name that other users see in their list of shared libraries. In Figure 12.9, you can see I named mine Main Library.

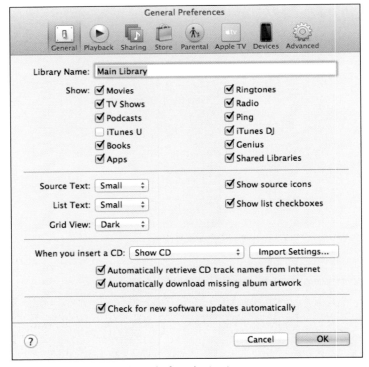

12.9 Name your iTunes library before sharing it.

3. **Click the Sharing tab.**

4. **Click the Share my library on my local network check box to enable it.**

5. **Choose whether you want to share your entire iTunes library or only selected playlists, as shown in Figure 12.10.**

6. **You can also click the Require password check box and type a password if you want to restrict access to your iTunes library.** In this case, users attempting to connect to your iTunes library are required to type this password before they can connect.

7. **Click OK.**

12.10 When you choose to share your library, you need to choose if you want to share all of the library or just parts of it.

Genius

Several tools have been available in the past, including ourTunes, which allowed you to actually copy music from a shared iTunes library. Although such tools are frequently handy for sharing music that you own across several computers in your household, they should, of course, not be used for stealing music from shared libraries that you do not own. Unfortunately, these tools work by reverse-engineering the shared library technology and are therefore frequently broken by iTunes updates. For example, ourTunes does not presently work with versions of iTunes later than 8.

305

Note

After you enable library sharing, other users can see your shared library in their iTunes Source list immediately above their playlists, as shown in Figure 12.11.

Accessing a shared library is handled in the same way as any other iTunes category, and the listing can be filtered and sorted in the same way. Clicking the triangle to the left of the shared library expands it to show a list of playlists from that library. Keep in mind that Cover Flow and Grid views are not available when accessing a shared library.

12.11 An iTunes shared library

Sharing and copying your iTunes library content among multiple computers on a home network

Although iTunes has supported sharing of libraries for several years, as noted earlier these libraries were only useful for playing music on other computers — there was no easy way to actually copy tracks from one iTunes library to another without resorting to digging around in the file system. With the release of iTunes 9, Apple added a new Home Sharing feature that finally allows users on the same network to not only listen to content from more than one library but to actually copy and import that content.

As the name implies, the iTunes Home Sharing feature is intended for users to share music within a family or home environment. All computers must be on the same local area network and must sign in with a common iTunes Store account. Further, as with iTunes Store authorizations, you are limited to sharing content among no more than five computers.

12.12 iTunes Home Sharing option

Enabling Home Sharing is relatively straightforward. If you've just upgraded to iTunes 9 or 10 or started a new iTunes library, a Home Sharing entry should appear in your left-hand iTunes sidebar, similar to Figure 12.12.

To configure Home Sharing, follow these steps:

1. **Select the Home Sharing option from the iTunes sidebar.** A setup screen appears similar to Figure 12.13.

12.13 Home Sharing Setup screen

2. **Type your iTunes Store account name and password.**

3. **Click Create Home Share.** A confirmation screen similar to Figure 12.14 appears, advising you that Home Sharing is now enabled and reminding you that the feature is for personal use only.

4. **Repeat Steps 1 to 3 on the additional computers you want to configure for Home Sharing.** You can set up a maximum of five computers to share content.

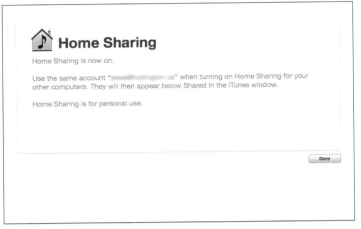

12.14 Home Sharing Setup confirmation

Once enabled, iTunes displays other computers in your Home Sharing network in the Shared library section on the left-hand side of your iTunes window. Home Shared libraries are differentiated from normal shared libraries by a house icon next to the library name, as shown in Figure 12.15.

You can browse through and listen to content from a Home Shared library in the same way as any other shared library. Simply select the shared library and its content will appear in the main iTunes window, similar to Figure 12.16.

From here, you can also copy any tracks from the remote library into your local iTunes library simply by dragging and dropping the tracks into the main Library section on the left-hand sidebar or selecting one or more tracks and clicking Import.

12.15 Multiple shared libraries

Note When copying tracks from a remote Home Shared library, iTunes transfers the media file and its tag information such as name, artist, album, and genre. It does not transfer iTunes-specific metadata such as rating, play count, or last played time.

12.16 Accessing a Home Shared library

By default, content is only transferred between Home Shared libraries manually. You can configure iTunes to automatically transfer specific types of new content added to a remote Home Shared iTunes library. Follow these steps:

1. **Select a Home Shared iTunes library.**

2. **Click the Settings button at the bottom of the track listing.** A Home Sharing Settings dialog box similar to Figure 12.17 appears.

3. **Select the types of content that you want to automatically transfer from the remote iTunes library.** Options are Music, Movies, TV Shows, Books, and Applications.

4. **Click OK.** Any new content added to the remote library in the selected categories is transferred to the current library.

Home Sharing Settings

Automatically transfer new purchases from "Main Library" for:

☑ Music   ☐ Books
☐ Movies   ☑ Apps
☐ TV Shows

Cancel   OK

12.17 Home Sharing Settings dialog box

Enabling automatic transfer only enables content that is added after this setting is turned on. Content already in the remote iTunes library is not copied over unless you transfer it manually.

Note

Home Sharing cannot transfer audiobooks purchased from Audible. You can still import Audible audiobooks manually into other iTunes libraries provided that the other computers are specifically authorized for Audible.

Network Sharing and Synchronizing

iTunes library sharing works well enough for situations where you're really just concerned with letting other users listen to your music or copying it between separately maintained iTunes libraries. However, many users also want a way to share a common set of music that they can sync to their iPod from a single location.

If you have a home network server, you may simply be tempted to put your iTunes library on the server and point each of your computers at it. This solution is fraught with danger, however, because the iTunes library database is not designed for multiuser access, and so you must be very careful to not have more than one copy of iTunes running against it at a time. Another common method is to simply put the iTunes Media folder on a network drive and point each iTunes library at it. This creates less possibility of corruption, but you must again be very careful not to let one of your iTunes libraries reorganize your media files on you, or the other libraries will end up with broken links. Further, new music must be individually imported into each library, because the databases are separate.

Additionally, although iTunes Home Sharing is useful for casually copying tracks between separate libraries, or synchronizing whole categories of content, it does not offer any more granular options for automatically synchronizing only a subset of your content, nor does it provide any options for syncing iTunes metadata between libraries. Third-party software developers have stepped in to provide more flexible solutions for synchronizing iTunes libraries across multiple computers. In this case, each computer has its own stand-alone iTunes library, but a third-party application running on both ends reads the iTunes database and provides a number of additional options, such as syncing by playlist to keep your iTunes libraries up to date with only the content you need.

If you have multiple computers and you're looking for more advanced options for sharing iTunes content among them, check out TuneRanger (www.acertant.com) or Syncopation (www.sonzea.com).

What Can I Do When I Have Problems with My iPod, iPhone, or iPad?

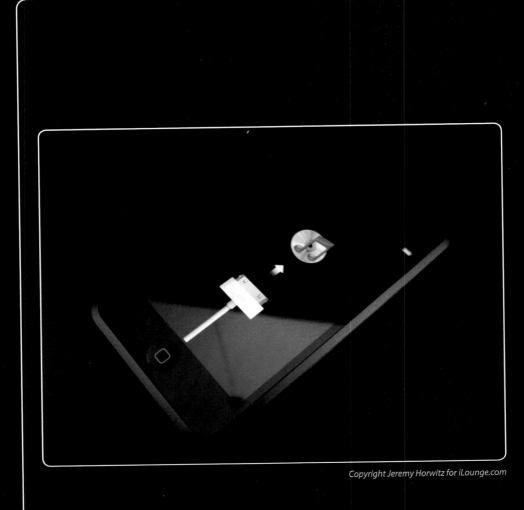

Although Apple's media devices are wonderful pieces of technology, they're also very sophisticated electronic devices, and sometimes you may find that they don't work exactly as they should. A few simple troubleshooting steps can help you to determine whether you can solve your device's problems yourself or whether you should be taking it to your nearest Apple Store for professional help.

Basic Troubleshooting

If you're having a problem with your device, you should start by following basic diagnostic procedures to see if this solves your problem. Many common problems experienced by iPod users are caused by software conflicts on the iTunes computer, USB port or cable problems, or software or database corruption on the device itself.

Reset

The first step is to simply reset your device. This is conceptually the same as rebooting your computer and basically gives your device a clean start. This does not erase any of the content stored on your device but simply restarts it from scratch.

You can reset a traditional Click Wheel iPod by holding down the CENTER and MENU buttons for about 6 to 10 seconds until you see the Apple logo appear. On the iPod touch, iPhone, or iPad this is accomplished by holding down the HOME and SLEEP/WAKE buttons for about 8 seconds, again until the Apple logo appears. On the sixth-generation iPod nano, simply hold down the Volume Down and SLEEP/WAKE button for about 6 to 10 seconds until the Apple logo appears.

Although the Click Wheel iPods are fairly stable and rarely need to be reset, it's not uncommon for the iPhone, iPod touch, or iPad to require a reboot every so often, particularly if you use a lot of demanding third-party applications. Sluggish performance and inexplicable application crashes on these devices are frequently solved simply by restarting the device.

Retry

The second R involves retrying the operation that you're having a problem with. For example, if you're having problems connecting or synchronizing your iPod, try using a different USB port or a different USB cable, if you have one available. Avoid using USB ports on keyboards or USB hubs — connect the device directly to a USB port on your computer.

Another good solution is to try a different computer if you have one available. A computer at a friend's house, or at school or work, can be useful in determining if the problem is with your device or with your computer.

Restart

The third R is to restart your computer and try the operation again. Sometimes simply restarting your computer clears out its memory and resolves any problems you've been having.

If the issue remains after a simple restart, the next step is to try restarting your computer with fewer background applications running — try to start iTunes before you start anything else, and disable other applications that might be causing problems. You can identify and temporarily disable applications that start automatically in Windows by using the MSCONFIG tool. On the Mac, a list of applications that run automatically at startup for the current user account is found in your Account preferences in OS X Snow Leopard and earlier OS X versions or Users & Groups preferences in OS X Lion.

You should also ensure that you are running the latest version of iTunes and the latest software updates for your operating system. You can check for updates for iTunes and Mac OS X by running Apple's Software Update on your Mac or PC, and you can check for updates and patches for Windows by running the Windows Updater tool.

Certain types of applications are known to get in the way of synchronizing your iPod. Virus scanners and disk-management tools can cause problems because they see a traditional iPod as an external hard drive and try to scan it or process it, which may interfere with the capability of iTunes to do so. Likewise, any USB drivers that you may have installed for other devices can easily interfere with your iPod's USB connection, particularly on Windows-based computers. Restarting Windows in Safe Mode is one method you can use to identify whether your problem is caused by third-party software and driver conflicts.

Note Apple provides a Web-based walk-through diagnostic of each specific iPod model at www.apple.com/support/ipod/five_rs.

Reinstall

The fourth R suggests reinstalling iTunes on your computer to clear up any driver-related problems or iTunes connection problems that you may be having. Note that you can uninstall and reinstall iTunes without losing any of your stored media content or your iTunes library — only the iTunes application files are affected when you uninstall. You should always download and install the very latest version of iTunes when doing this, rather than reinstalling your existing version. You can always obtain the latest version of iTunes for either Mac or Windows at the Apple iTunes download page at www.apple.com/itunes/download.

After you reinstall the latest version of iTunes, you should also confirm that your iPod is running the latest iPod firmware. To check this, do the following:

1. **Connect your iPod to your computer.**

2. **Select your iPod from the iTunes Devices list.** The iPod Summary screen appears, similar to Figure 13.1.

13.1 The iPod Summary screen

3. **Click Check for Update.** This tells iTunes to check with Apple to see if a newer firmware package is available for your iPod. If so, iTunes downloads and installs it onto your iPod.

Restore

The fifth R is the final drastic step in the process — to actually restore your device. This effectively reformats your iPod, iPhone, or iPad, returning it to out-of-the-box factory settings and erasing all of the content that you have stored on it.

If you've been using automatic synchronization, all of your content is already stored in your iTunes library and you can easily reload it onto your iPod after a restore. On the other hand, if you're using manual synchronization and do not have all of your iPod's content actually on your computer, then you should look at trying to back up the data from your iPod first — Chapter 10 has more information on how to do that.

Note

Storing your media content solely on your iPod is generally a bad idea because your iPod is a portable device that can easily be lost or damaged. Keep a backup of your content somewhere else, even if it's not on your main computer.

To restore your iPod to its factory settings, follow these steps:

1. **Connect your device to your computer.**

2. **Select your device from the iTunes Devices list.** The Summary screen appears.

3. **Click Restore.** iTunes checks for and downloads the latest firmware for your device, and then proceeds to format the drive and load the latest firmware back on.

When this process is complete, your device is returned to its original configuration and you are taken through the Setup Assistant as you would be for a new device.

Note

In the case of the iPhone, iPod touch, and iPad, iTunes may offer to restore your device's preferences and settings from a previous backup if one exists. If you've been having problems, it may be worthwhile to skip restoring this backup to see if the same problem occurs in a clean configuration. You can always restore the backup later.

Common Problems and Solutions

With the way the iPod and iOS devices work and the wide variety of hardware and software configurations in use, there are a few problems that users commonly run into regardless of configuration. You can solve some of these by going through the standard Five Rs troubleshooting process, but others have slightly different solutions.

Your device is not detected by iTunes

The Five Rs often do you no good if your device isn't even being seen by your computer. Obviously, if your computer doesn't see your device, then updating or restoring it is not going to be an option.

If you're using a traditional iPod model, the first thing to check is whether your iPod appears in Windows Explorer or the OS X Finder when you connect it without iTunes running. If the iPod is showing up as an external drive, but iTunes is not picking it up, then this usually indicates a problem with your iTunes installation or drivers rather than your computer's operating system or hardware. The fact that your computer sees your iPod as a hard drive indicates that the USB communication is working properly. Keep in mind that the iPhone, iPod touch, and iPad devices do not have a disk mode and will not show up outside of iTunes.

On the other hand, if your iPod is not showing up on your computer at all, then this could indicate a problem with your USB port or USB cable, or a driver conflict on your computer. Consider the following:

- **Try a different USB port directly on the computer.** Do not use a USB hub or keyboard port. Plug your device directly into a USB port on your computer. If you're using a desktop PC, try one of the USB ports at the rear of the computer because these are usually directly hardwired to the computer's system board.

- **Try a different USB cable if you have one available.** If you do not have an extra USB cable or know anybody who does, you can visit an Apple Store or local Apple reseller to try one there.

- **Try a different computer.** This troubleshooting step isolates whether the problem is with your device or your computer. If your device appears fine on the other computer — even as a removable hard drive in the case of a traditional iPod — then you can focus on computer-related problems. If the device doesn't appear on any other computer that you try, then there's a good possibility that the device is the problem.

- **Check for any new software or drivers that have been recently installed.** Something as seemingly innocuous as a printer or digital camera driver can create USB driver conflicts that can affect your computer's ability to see your iPod. Uninstalling or rolling back these drivers can often help resolve the problem.

- **Unload any extra software or services.** Some background software applications can also conflict or interfere with your device being properly detected. Quit as many of these applications as possible and try connecting your device. Alternatively, if you're using Windows and a traditional iPod model, try restarting your computer in Safe Mode and connecting your iPod. iTunes won't see it in this mode, but it should at least appear as a removable storage device.

You can also find some very good and specific troubleshooting information for each model of iPod, iPhone, or iPad in the Apple Knowledge Base at www.apple.com/support.

Your songs skip on the iPod or do not play at all

Skipping is another problem frequently encountered by many users. Sometimes you can solve this problem simply by resetting the device, but if it persists, then the likely cause is corrupt or incompatible media files on the iPod.

If this problem is specific to a small number of tracks and these tracks play fine in iTunes, then you should try removing these tracks from the iPod and loading them back on. If you are using manual management, simply delete them directly from the iPod using iTunes, and then copy them back on using drag-and-drop. If you're using automatic synchronization, you can remove them by setting your iPod to only sync checked items. Follow these steps:

1. **Connect your device to your computer.**

2. **Select your device from the iTunes Devices list.** The iPod Summary screen appears.

3. **Select the Sync only checked songs and videos option to ensure that it is enabled, as shown in Figure 13.2.**

13.2 The iPod Summary screen with the Sync only checked songs and videos option selected

4. **Click Apply.**

5. **Locate the affected songs in your iTunes library, and click the check box beside each song to deselect them.**

6. **Select your device from the iTunes Devices list.**

7. **Click the Sync button in the bottom-right corner of the iTunes window.** Doing this removes all unchecked tracks from your device.

8. **Retransfer them onto your device by reselecting them in the iTunes library and syncing your iPod again.**

If you have retransferred the tracks onto your device and they still are not playing properly, then the other possibility is that there is an encoding problem with the tracks themselves. Depending on your device model and firmware version, you may have problems playing MP3 files with non-standard bit rates, or variable bit-rate (VBR) files. Updating to the latest firmware often resolves these problems, but if not, then you may need to encode the affected files again. The simplest way to determine if you have an encoding problem is to try converting the file to your preferred import format using iTunes. Follow these steps:

1. **Select an affected track.**

2. **From the iTunes menu, choose Advanced ⇨ Create AAC Version.** Note that if your default import format is something other than AAC, then this menu option lists that format instead (for example, Create MP3 Version). Chapter 1 provides more detail on import formats and bit rates. iTunes creates a new version of the selected track in the specified format and bit rate.

3. **Transfer the new track to your device.**

Caution

When converting tracks, iTunes creates a copy of each track and leaves the original in place, still taking up space in your library. To conserve space, you should ensure that you go back and delete either the original or the converted tracks when you are satisfied with the results.

Try playing the converted track. If it plays properly, then you may want to convert the remaining tracks that you're having problems with. Note, however, that converting these tracks using iTunes results in a quality loss; whether or not this loss is noticeable depends largely on the original file format, the bit rate chosen, and the quality of your earphones. Ideally, if you have the original CDs available, you should simply rerip the tracks.

Note In rare cases, protected iTunes tracks may end up on your device without the proper authorization being transferred. In this case, these tracks simply do not play. Usually, retransferring additional tracks purchased from the same account solves this problem. However, this should rarely occur, because iTunes does not normally allow tracks to be transferred a device unless they can be authorized.

If a lot of tracks are skipping that did not previously skip, then there could be a problem with the device. Try restoring the firmware, and if this does not fix the problem, then the device likely needs to be serviced.

Advanced Troubleshooting

If all of the standard troubleshooting steps have failed, I have a few more solutions you can try to return your device back to normal operation.

Downgrading your iPod firmware

If you're having a problem that started after a recent iPod firmware upgrade, then it's possible that the problem lies in the new firmware. Fortunately, iTunes keeps older firmware versions that you've previously used on your computer, and you can downgrade your iPod to an earlier firmware version quite easily, although you need to perform a full restore on your device to do so:

1. **Connect your iPod to your computer.**

2. **Select your iPod from the iTunes Devices list.** The iPod Summary screen appears.

3. **While holding down the Opt key (Mac) or Shift key (Windows), click Restore in iTunes.**
   A file browser dialog box appears, prompting you to select a specific software package.

4. **Browse to your iPod Software folder.** In Mac OS X, you can find it under your home folder in *Library/iTunes/iPod Software Updates*. In Windows XP, it is stored in *Application Data\Apple Computer\iTunes\iPod Software Updates* under your home folder, and in Windows Vista, in *AppData\Roaming\Apple Computer\iTunes\iPod Software Updates*.

5. **From the iPod Software Updates folder, select the package you want to restore to your iPod.** Version numbers are normally listed at the end of each package name, as shown in Figure 13.3.

6. **Click OK to begin restoring the older firmware onto your iPod.**

Note Older firmware packages are only available on your computer if you have previously updated or restored your iPod through iTunes. Although Apple does not supply older iPod firmware packages directly, you can find links on the Internet to download them.

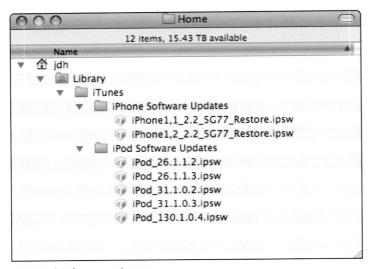

13.3 iPod Software packages

Note iPhone and iPad software packages are located in iPhone Software Updates and iPad Software Updates folders, respectively. Note that in most cases downgrading an iPhone or iPad 3G to an earlier software version is not possible because of the cellular radio firmware.

Starting your Click Wheel iPod in disk mode

Another very useful troubleshooting step for traditional iPod models is to force your iPod into disk mode. This mode bypasses any normal iPod function and forces your iPod to present itself to your computer as a removable hard drive. Disk mode can be very useful for situations where your computer cannot otherwise detect your iPod.

To force your iPod into disk mode, follow these steps:

1. **Hold down the CENTER and MENU buttons for about 6 to 10 seconds until the Apple logo appears.**

Note Despite the iOS style multitouch interface, the sixth-generation iPod nano also supports disk mode. Simply hold the Volume Up and Volume Down buttons after rebooting instead of the MENU and PLAY/PAUSE buttons.

2. **When the Apple logo appears, release the MENU button immediately and hold down the PLAY/PAUSE button until the Disk Mode screen appears, similar to Figure 13.4.**

Once in disk mode, you can try connecting you iPod to your computer to see if it is properly detected. Disk mode can often allow you to restore your iPod in situations where it cannot otherwise be seen by your computer.

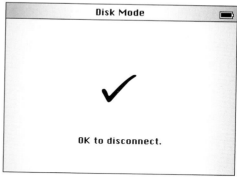

13.4 iPod Disk Mode screen

To return from disk mode, simply reset your iPod by holding down the CENTER and MENU buttons for about 6 to 10 seconds.

Hard-restoring your Click Wheel iPod

In certain cases, particularly with older iPod models, you may find that iTunes still cannot see or restore your iPod, even after you've tried all the other troubleshooting steps, as well as forcing the iPod into disk mode.

In this case, as long as the iPod is visible to your computer as an external hard drive, you can often recover the iPod and get iTunes to recognize it by doing an operating-system-level format. Remember that the iPod is actually just an external hard drive as far as your computer is concerned, and you can therefore treat it like any other hard drive. If iTunes cannot see your iPod or cannot restore it, then there could be something wrong with the hard drive or flash memory on the device that can be fixed by doing a computer-level format.

In this case, simply shut down iTunes and format the iPod through Windows Explorer or Disk Utility (Mac) as you would for any other drive. This erases everything on the iPod, of course, including the iPod's own operating files; however, it also cleans up any file-system issues that may be preventing iTunes from doing its job. After this process is complete, the iPod may not work at all (because the internal operating files have also been erased), but you may now have better luck getting iTunes to complete its restore process and returning the iPod back to normal operation.

Note Despite the iOS style multitouch interface, the sixth-generation iPod nano actually uses the same disk-based interface as the traditional Click Wheel iPod models and should appear to your computer as an external storage device.

These types of issues are less common with the newer iPod classic and iPod nano models, but many a third- and fourth-generation iPod have been saved by performing an operating-system-level format. It's definitely worth a try if you've tried everything else to get your iPod working and iTunes can't get the job done by itself.

Hard-restoring your iPhone, iPod touch, or iPad

The iOS devices do not present themselves as an external hard drive and therefore cannot be hard-restored using the same method as for click wheel iPods. Instead, these devices support a hardware-based DFU mode that can be used to force the device into a restore mode where iTunes should be able to recognize it. To place your iPhone, iPod touch or iPad into DFU mode, follow these steps:

1. **Connect your device to your computer via the USB cable.** Don't worry if it doesn't show up in iTunes.

2. **Hold down both the Home and Sleep/Wake buttons on your device together until your device's screen goes blank.**

3. **When the screen goes blank, release the Sleep/Wake button and continue holding the Home button until iTunes displays a message telling you that it has found your device in recovery mode, similar to Figure 13.5.** Note that your device's screen should remain blank — if the Apple logo appears, then return to Step 2 and try again.

4. **Restore your device using iTunes as described earlier in this chapter.**

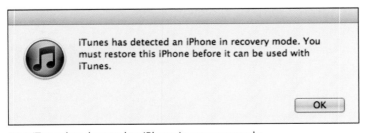

iTunes has detected an iPhone in recovery mode. You must restore this iPhone before it can be used with iTunes.

OK

13.5 iTunes has detected an iPhone in recovery mode.

Note DFU mode bypasses the loading of the iOS operating system entirely — it is a hardware-based restore mode. If iTunes still cannot detect your device in DFU mode even on multiple computers, then chances are that your device is damaged beyond repair.

How Do I Use Scripts to Get More Out of iTunes?

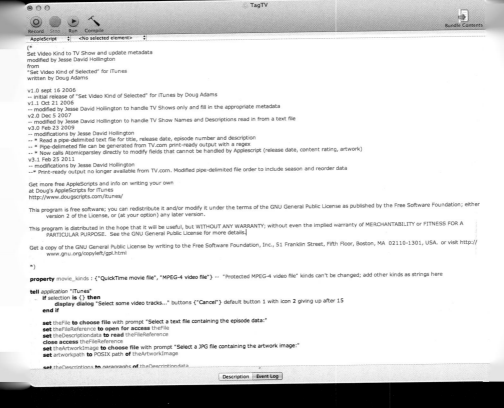

```
TagTV

Record  Stop  Run  Compile
AppleScript    <No selected element>          Bundle Contents

(*
Set Video Kind to TV Show and update metadata
modified by Jesse David Hollington
from
"Set Video Kind of Selected" for iTunes
written by Doug Adams

v1.0 sept 16 2006
-- initial release of "Set Video Kind of Selected" for iTunes by Doug Adams
v1.1 Oct 21 2006
-- modified by Jesse David Hollington to handle TV Shows only and fill in the appropriate metadata
v2.0 Dec 5 2007
-- modified by Jesse David Hollington to handle TV Show Names and Descriptions read in from a text file
v3.0 Feb 23 2009
-- modifications by Jesse David Hollington
-- * Read a pipe-delimited text file for title, release date, episode number and description
-- * Pipe-delimeted file can be generated from TV.com print-ready output with a regex
-- * Now calls Atomicparsley directly to modify fields that cannot be handled by Applescript (release date, content rating, artwork)
v3.1 Feb 25 2011
-- modifications by Jesse David Hollington
--* Print-ready output no longer available from TV.com. Modified pipe-delimited file order to include season and reorder data

Get more free AppleScripts and info on writing your own
at Doug's AppleScripts for iTunes
http://www.dougscripts.com/itunes/

This program is free software; you can redistribute it and/or modify it under the terms of the GNU General Public License as published by the Free Software Foundation; either
    version 2 of the License, or (at your option) any later version.

This program is distributed in the hope that it will be useful, but WITHOUT ANY WARRANTY; without even the implied warranty of MERCHANTABILITY or FITNESS FOR A
    PARTICULAR PURPOSE.  See the GNU General Public License for more details.

Get a copy of the GNU General Public License by writing to the Free Software Foundation, Inc., 51 Franklin Street, Fifth Floor, Boston, MA  02110-1301, USA. or visit http://
    www.gnu.org/copyleft/gpl.html

*)

property movie_kinds : {"QuickTime movie file", "MPEG-4 video file"} --  "Protected MPEG-4 video file" kinds can't be changed; add other kinds as strings here

tell application "iTunes"
    if selection is {} then
        display dialog "Select some video tracks..." buttons {"Cancel"} default button 1 with icon 2 giving up after 15
    end if

    set theFile to choose file with prompt "Select a text file containing the episode data:"
    set theFileReference to open for access theFile
    set theDescriptiondata to read theFileReference
    close access theFileReference
    set theArtworkImage to choose file with prompt "Select a JPG file containing the artwork image:"
    set artworkpath to POSIX path of theArtworkImage

    set theDescriptions to paragraphs of theDescriptiondata

Description   Event Log
```

One of the great features of iTunes is its extensibility through AppleScript and JavaScript on both the Mac and Windows platforms. This direct script integration allows for automated routines and access to features that aren't directly available through iTunes, greatly enhancing the power of iTunes as a media-management application.

that allows many applications in Mac OS X to be controlled and enhanced through the use of scripts that can access features directly within an application. iTunes is no exception, with a comprehensive AppleScript dictionary that allows for sophisticated management of your iTunes library and control of iTunes.

Windows users are not entirely left out in the cold, however, as iTunes can also be extended through JavaScript on the Windows platform. The scripting capabilities are not quite as extensive, and the number of available scripts for Windows users is considerably smaller than for Mac users, but a number of useful scripts still exist to help Windows users manage their iTunes libraries as well.

If you have some experience with AppleScript or JavaScript, then you can also write your own scripts for iTunes quite easily. AppleScript, in particular, is a very user-friendly, natural language-scripting system, and can be quite useful for performing simple library-management tasks like mass-updating information in your tracks that isn't otherwise accessible through iTunes.

Cool AppleScripts for Mac iTunes Users

The best source of AppleScripts for iTunes can be found on a site called Doug's AppleScripts for iTunes at www.dougscripts.com. As of this writing, almost 450 scripts are available to handle a wide variety of different functions, extending the features in iTunes and allowing you to better manage your iTunes library. Many of the scripts are written by Doug Adams, although a number of user-contributed scripts can also be found on his site. With the exception of a few of the more sophisticated scripts, the majority of the AppleScripts available on this site are completely free.

Note
For those users interested in writing their own AppleScripts or modifying existing ones, Doug Adams moderates an AppleScripts for iTunes forum on iLounge.com, where some great additional AppleScripting for iTunes information can be found.

Find duplicate tracks in iTunes

Although iTunes has a built-in feature to show duplicate tracks, this is not particularly useful in a large iTunes library because all it does is show you the tracks — you still have to go through and clean them up yourself. Dupin (dougscripts.com/itunes/itinfo/dupin.php) is a shareware AppleScript for around $15 that automates the process of cleaning up duplicates for you. A lite version is also available for less than $10 that focuses primarily on identifying and eliminating duplicate tracks, omitting some of the more advanced features. Follow these steps to use either of these AppleScripts to clean up your duplicates:

1. **Download, install, and run Dupin.** The main Dupin window appears, similar to Figure 14.1.

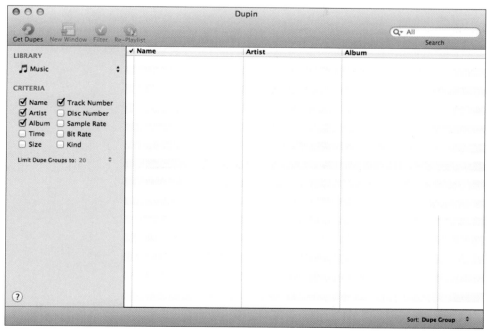

14.1 The main Dupin window

2. **From the Library drop-down menu in the top-left corner, select the context or play-list in which you want to search for duplicates.**

3. **From the Criteria list at the lower left, choose the criteria that you want to use to compare files and match duplicates.** Tracks are only considered duplicates if the properties of all selected criteria fields match between two or more tracks.

4. **Click the Get Dupes button to begin searching the selected context or playlist for duplicate tracks.** Dupin scans your iTunes library in search of duplicate tracks, with the results shown in the main window, similar to Figure 14.2.

5. **Click the Filter button to determine which tracks to keep for each set of duplicates.** The Dupin Filter Controls dialog box appears, as shown in Figure 14.3.

6. **Select the criteria that you want to use for determining which duplicates to keep.**

329

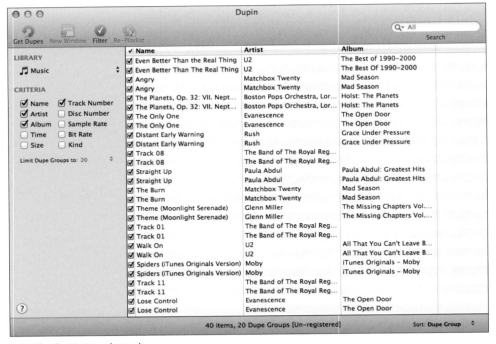

14.2 The Dupin search results

7. **Click the Filter button to determine which tracks to keep for each set of duplicates.**
   The Dupin Filter Controls dialog box appears (see Figure 14.3).

8. **Select the criteria that you want to use for determining which duplicates to keep.**

9. **Click the Filter button.** Dupin scans your list and displays a checkmark next to each item that will be kept. Those without a checkmark will be deleted.

10. **When you are satisfied with the track selections, choose File ⇨ Purge from the Dupin menu to remove the unchecked tracks from your iTunes library.**

Easily use multiple iTunes libraries

Although iTunes allows you to switch libraries manually at startup by holding down the Opt key (Mac) or Shift key (Windows), if you regularly switch between iTunes libraries on the same computer and user account, this can quickly become tedious. Further, as I note in Chapter 12, switching to a different library with iTunes still maintains the preferences from your original library, making it more complicated to truly have multiple independent iTunes libraries.

14.3 The Dupin Filter Controls dialog box

Fortunately, iTunes Library Manager (dougscripts.com/itunes/itinfo/ituneslibrarymanager.php) is a $10 shareware script that addresses both of these problems. First, it prompts you at startup to select an iTunes library, so that you don't have to remember to hold down a key when starting iTunes. Second, it switches to library-specific preference settings, so that you can easily use different iTunes Music folder locations or other preferences unique to each library. To set up and manage multiple iTunes libraries with iTunes Library Manager, follow these steps:

1. **Download, install, and run iTunes Library Manager.** The main iTunes Library Manager window appears, similar to Figure 14.4.

2. **Click Save to back up your current iTunes library before proceeding.**

3. **Type a name for your current iTunes library.** After the backup is complete, your library should be listed in the main iTunes Library Manager window.

4. **To create a new iTunes library, choose File ⇨ New.** iTunes Library Manager displays a dialog box similar to Figure 14.5.

14.4 The iTunes Library Manager window

14.5 The iTunes Library Manager Make New Library dialog box

5. **Type a name for the new iTunes library and choose whether to use your current iTunes preferences settings or create initialized preferences.** If you choose the Create initialized Preferences option, the new iTunes library acts just like a brand-new installation of iTunes, and the iTunes Setup Wizard appears.

6. **Click OK to create the new iTunes library.**

To switch among iTunes libraries in the future, simply load iTunes Library Manager, select the iTunes library that you want to use, and click Load. The current library is backed up, and the chosen library is swapped into its place.

Convert lossless to AAC for your iPod

A common problem among fans of lossless music formats is how to store full Apple Lossless or AIFF files in your iTunes library while automatically syncing a more reasonably sized version to your iPod. iTunes can transcode higher bit-rate formats on the fly when syncing to your iPod, but this feature does not allow you to choose a bit rate or format other than 128 kbps AAC.

A free AppleScript comes to the rescue, however: Lossless to AAC Workflow (dougscripts.com/itunes/scripts/ss.php?sp=losslessaccworkflow) is designed to allow you to convert selected tracks to your preferred AAC format and copy them onto an iPod that is set to manual management. To use this script, follow these steps:

1. **Download Lossless to AAC Workflow and install it into your Scripts folder, according to the provided instructions.**

2. **Ensure that your iPod is connected to your computer and set to manual mode.**

3. **In iTunes, select a lossless track that you want to convert and transfer to your iPod.** You can also select multiple tracks.

4. **Run the Lossless to AAC Workflow (iTunes ⇨ iPod) script.** iTunes converts the selected lossless tracks to AAC files and prompts you for what to do next, as shown in Figure 14.6, with a dialog box.

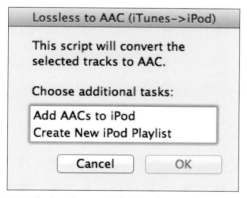

14.6 The Lossless to AAC dialog box

5. **Choose Add AACs to iPod or Create New iPod Playlist.** Add AACs to iPod copies the tracks directly to your iPod; Create New iPod Playlist copies the tracks to your iPod, too, but in a new playlist containing only the newly copied tracks. In either case, the converted tracks are removed from your iTunes library after they are copied to your iPod.

The Lossless to AAC Workflow package also includes a second script that can be used to rip your tracks directly from CD into a lossless file for your iTunes library, and an AAC file for your iPod, all at the same time.

Other cool AppleScripts

The library of AppleScripts at Doug's Scripts for iTunes contains dozens of other cool little scripts that can perform a wide variety of useful functions, and best of all, they're free. Some additional scripts worth looking at include

- **Smarts.** This free script allows you to save the criteria in your Smart Playlists as a template that can either be used as a backup for the original iTunes library or transferred to a different library. This script can be particularly useful for creating "starter" Smart Playlist templates that use common criteria. See Chapter 5 for more details on Smart Playlists.

- **MySpins.** This inexpensive script analyzes your listening habits to identify your most played songs in a variety of ways, such as most played artists, most listened to playlists, and more, for around $5.

- **Join Together.** This script allows you to automatically join multiple individual tracks into a single AAC file, optionally including chapter markers for each track. While its usefulness for music has been largely eliminated by iTunes and the iPod's Gapless Playback features, it may still be of interest to users of older iPod models, as it's a great way to create a gapless listening experience while still being able to skip to specific tracks. It is also extremely useful for dealing with multichapter audiobooks that come as a series of separate files. Join Together is available as both a full-featured free version and a pro version for around $7 with some additional preflight and postop features.

- **DayPart.** This script allows you to set up sophisticated listening schedules with iTunes to automatically play specific playlists or even sets of playlists at different times of the day and on different days of the week. Schedules can include one or several playlists and can include both start and end times. DayPart can even transition between playlists and schedules without cutting off songs in midplay. A free basic version is available that allows you to create a single schedule with up to three playlists; the full version is around $20 and includes unlimited scheduling and playlist capabilities.

- **Tracks Without Artwork to Playlist.** This free script collects any tracks in your iTunes library that do not contain album artwork and groups them together in a single playlist, providing you with an easy way to search out tracks that need album artwork added.

- **No Lyrics to Playlist.** Similar to the Tracks Without Artwork to Playlist script, this script groups all tracks that do not have any lyrics into a single playlist.

- **Embed Artwork.** Artwork that you add to tracks yourself is stored within the AAC or MP3 file tags directly. However, this is not the case with artwork added automatically by iTunes. The free Embed Artwork AppleScript goes through your iTunes library and adds any automatically downloaded artwork into the tags of the MP3 or AAC files.

- **Assign Half-Star Rating.** It's a little-known feature, but iTunes actually supports half-star ratings. Although there is no way to assign these directly through iTunes, this free AppleScript allows you to do this. Note that half-star ratings can be shown in your iTunes library, but do not appear on your media devices — the rating is simply rounded down to the nearest full star.

- **Art to iChat.** This is a neat little free script that automatically updates your iChat Buddy icon with the artwork of the album that you are currently listening to in iTunes. Your original buddy icon is restored when you stop playback or if you're listening to a track that does not contain any album artwork.

- **Super Remove Dead Tracks.** This free script searches your iTunes library for any tracks that cannot be found because of missing files and removes these entries. Any playlists that are left empty as a result are also removed.

- **Gather up the One-Hits.** This free script collects all the one-hit wonders in your iTunes library and collects them in a single playlist.

Many of Doug's AppleScripts can also now be found on the Mac App Store.

Cool JavaScripts for Windows iTunes Users

Although the selection of scripts available for Windows users is far more limited, a number of useful, free scripts for common tasks can be found at http://ottodestruct.com/blog/2005/10/20/itunes-javascripts. Specifically, scripts are available to perform the following useful library-management tasks:

- **Create a playlist of the songs in your library with no artwork.**
- **Create a playlist of the songs in your library with no lyrics.**
- **Create a playlist of the one-hit wonders in your library.**
- **Import lyrics into iTunes.**
- **Reload and update your iTunes library database from the file tags.**
- **Create a list of dead tracks in your library.**
- **Remove dead tracks from your library.**

Appendix A

iPod and iTunes Resources

In addition to print publications like this book, you can find a number of excellent online resources that iPod and iTunes users will find very useful when looking for more information on related products and accessories or the latest technical information. This appendix lists a few of the more popular online sites where you can get technical assistance and find more iPod- and iTunes-related information.

News and Technical Information

The popularity of the iTunes, iPod, iPhone, and iPad has given rise to a large number of Web sites attempting to draw crowds by providing news and support information. Many of these are small sites with very little useful or original material, and you may have a hard time sorting out the good sources of information from all of the fly-by-night operations that are trying to capitalize on the popularity of Apple's media devices. This appendix contains some of the best sources of news, product reviews, and information for iTunes, the iPod, the iPhone, and the iPad.

Apple

www.apple.com

Naturally, as the manufacturer of the iPod and iTunes, Apple provides product information and specifications on the iPod, iPhone, and iPad; a Knowledge Base of technical information; and a set of discussion forums. Its Knowledge Base is very good for established and known problems; however, Apple does not normally post information about unresolved problems, and so it can be difficult to confirm whether or not a problem you are having with your device or iTunes is actually a known issue that has simply not yet been fixed.

Note that although the Apple discussion forums are moderated to ensure that discussions remain appropriate, they are not staffed or specifically monitored by Apple support or engineering personnel, but are designed as user-to-user support forums. Posting support questions in the Apple discussion forums may be useful for getting support from other users, but they are not a conduit for reporting problems to Apple or getting help directly from Apple. One notable area on the Apple Web site is its product feedback page at www.apple.com/feedback. This page allows users to submit feature requests and file bug reports for any Apple hardware or software products. Keep in mind, however, that this is simply a method of reporting problems or suggesting features, and not a support page. Users posting on the feedback pages should not expect a response.

iLounge
www.ilounge.com

Founded one week after the first iPod was announced back in 2001, iLounge (formerly known as iPodLounge) has become the de facto online resource for all things related to iPods, iPhones, iPads, and iTunes. In addition to providing iTunes- and iPod-related news and technical information, iLounge is an excellent resource for information on the seemingly endless supply of iPod- and iPhone-related accessories, with online reviews of thousands of iPod-related products such as cases, earphones, speakers, and applications. Each year before the holiday season, iLounge also publishes a free downloadable Buyer's Guide covering the latest and greatest iPod- and iPhone-related products, accessories, and applications. iLounge also provides the world's largest iTunes- and iPod-specific online discussion forums, with more than 100,000 registered users.

Doug's AppleScripts for iTunes
www.dougscripts.com

If you're a Mac user and you want to get more out of iTunes, you will most definitely want to take a look at Doug's AppleScripts for iTunes. The site features more than 450 AppleScripts that add enhanced functionality to iTunes and iPod management. AppleScripts are discussed in Chapter 14.

iPhone Atlas
www.iphoneatlas.com

iPhone Atlas, run by CNET, is a popular blog for iPhone-related news and information.

Mac Rumors

www.macrumors.com

Although the main site is primarily focused on news and rumors related to Apple's products, the site hosts a very active community forum of users discussing and providing assistance on iTunes, the iPod, iPhone, and iPad.

Macworld

www.macworld.com

Although primarily focused on the Mac computing platform, Macworld also covers iTunes-, iPhone-, and iPod-related news and software reviews.

The Unofficial Apple Weblog

www.tuaw.com

Referred to by the initials TUAW, this weblog is focused on all things Apple, including the Mac, iPod, and iOS platforms. It covers Mac-related iTunes and iOS software announcements and other news.

Content Providers

In addition to the iTunes Store, there are a number of other places where iPod-friendly content can be purchased or legally downloaded for free. Many of these sites offer pricing that is competitive with iTunes, with some offering music on a monthly subscription-based model, and even some free tracks.

Music

Despite all of the new types of content that can now be played in iTunes and on your iPod, these devices are still used primarily for music playback. Online digital music is only increasing in popularity, and there are now dozens of sites offering legal iPod-ready music tracks for sale or even free download. iLounge also maintains an up-to-date listing of free music sites.

iTunes

If you're looking for free music, keep in mind that iTunes frequently offers free tracks of the week and other similar promotions. iTunes offers a "free on iTunes" page that is sometimes linked from the main store page or that you can search for. Further, some Internet sites, such as www.itsfree downloads.com and freeitunesmusic.blogspot.com, track weekly free iTunes downloads with links to them.

Free video content can also be found on the iTunes Store. Single episodes of TV shows are frequently made available for free as teasers, and iTunes has recently begun offering short movie featurettes for free download similar in concept to the extras found on many traditional DVDs.

3hive (**http://3hive.com**)

This site provides free MP3 tracks offered by record labels as samples to promote full album purchases.

mfiles (**http://mfiles.co.uk**)

This site provides free downloads of classical music in MP3 format.

Amazon.com (**www.amazon.com**)

As an alternative to the iTunes Store, Amazon.com provides DRM-free music for sale in the MP3 format. At this time, Amazon's digital music services are not available outside of the United States.

eMusic (**www.emusic.com**)

This subscription-based service allows you to download a fixed number of tracks each month for a monthly subscription fee. Tracks are in the MP3 format and unprotected by digital rights management. Unlike other subscription-based services, such as Napster (which are not iPod compatible), eMusic tracks are yours to keep even after you cancel your subscription. eMusic also offers an ad-supported variation on its service, where tracks can be downloaded for free by adding an advertising toolbar to your browser.

Podcasts

Podcasts are a great source of free music from many independent artists. Simply search the iTunes Store for music-related podcasts, and you can find numerous podcasts being published by music reviewers, radio stations, and even some artists.

Downloadable Video Content

A search for iPod-ready video downloads on the Internet turns up hundreds of links to questionable sites offering premium video content for free download, almost all of which is copyrighted content not licensed for distribution through these sites. At this time, the only legitimate source of television and movie content that is iPod ready is for purchase from the iTunes Store itself. However, many free independent and educational videos can be found in the various video podcasts and iTunes U collections throughout the iTunes Store.

Streaming Audio and Video

Users of iOS devices also have options for streaming audio video content from a number of online services. In most cases, content cannot be saved locally and an active Internet connection via Wi-Fi or the cellular network is required. Also note that some apps and services may specifically require a Wi-Fi connection.

- All iOS devices include a YouTube application for accessing and streaming video from YouTube. A free Vimeo app is also available from the App Store.

- Users in the United States and Canada with a Netflix subscription can access any of its rental content using the free Netflix app available for the iPhone, iPod touch, and iPad.

- U.S. iPad users have access to a number of official apps from television and movie networks, such as the ABC Player and PBS apps that provide ad-supported access to selected television content. Hulu Plus and HBO To Go apps are also available for their subscribers to watch content on the iPad, and many TV networks in other countries have also begun offering similar applications.

- Numerous streaming radio apps are available, such as Pandora, Slacker Radio, Rdio, Spotify, and Last.fm that provide streaming access to a large online collection of audio. Note that some of these require a subscription and are not all available in all countries. Some of these apps now even allow users to play music tracks while offline by storing them locally on the device.

- Many radio networks and local radio stations are also now providing their own streaming audio applications that can be found on the App Store.

Appendix B
Third-Party Software

In addition to iTunes, there are a number of third-party tools and utilities discussed in this book for enhancing your iTunes experience. For your convenience, a listing of these tools is provided here for each topic.

Adding lyrics

Adding lyrics to your iTunes library is covered in Chapter 3. Here are suggested links for third-party software, with some basic information about each one:

iArt

- www.ipodsoft.com
- For Windows only
- Priced around $10 (as of this writing)

SongGenie

- www.equinux.com
- For Mac only
- Priced around $30 (as of this writing)

GimmeSomeTune

- www.eternalstorms.at/gimmesometune
- For Mac only
- Free

Tagging videos

Tagging videos is discussed in Chapter 3. Here are suggested links for third-party software, with some basic information about each one:

AtomicParsley

- www.atomicparsley.sourceforge.net
- For Mac, Windows, and Linux
- Free

MetaX

- www.kerstetter.net
- For Mac and Windows
- Free (Mac), $10 (Windows)

Parsley is Atomically Delicious

- www.them.ws/pad/
- For Mac only
- Free

Adding album artwork

Adding album artwork is discussed in Chapter 3. Here are suggested links for third-party software, with some basic information about each one:

CoverScout

- www.equinux.com/us/products/coverscout/index.html
- For Mac only
- Priced around $40 (as of this writing)

iArt

- www.ipodsoft.com/site/pmwiki.php?n=IArt.HomePage
- For Windows only
- Priced around $10 (as of this writing)

Add-on visualizers

Add-on visualizers are covered in Chapter 4. Here are suggested links for third-party software, with some information about each one:

JewelCase

- www.opticalalchemy.com
- For Mac only
- Priced around $10

G-Force

- www.soundspectrum.com
- For Mac or Windows
- Prices range from free to around $20

WhiteCap

- www.soundspectrum.com
- For Mac or Windows
- Prices range from free to around $20

SoftSkies

- www.soundspectrum.com
- For Mac or Windows
- Prices range from free to around $20

Converting audiobooks

Audiobooks are covered in Chapter 6. Here are a couple of suggested links for third-party software, with some information about each one:

Audiobook Builder

- www.splasm.com/audiobookbuilder
- For Mac only
- Priced around $10

MarkAble

- www.ipodsoft.com
- For Windows only
- Priced around $18

Accessing Mac-formatted iPods on Windows machines

This topic is discussed in both Chapters 7 and 10. Here is a link to a good piece of software to accomplish this task:

MacDrive

- www.mediafour.com
- For Windows only
- Priced around $50

Video conversion

Video conversion is covered in Chapter 9. Here are suggested links for third-party software, with some information about each one:

HandBrake

- www.handbrake.fr
- For Mac or Windows
- Free

MPEG Streamclip

- www.squared5.com
- For Mac or Windows
- Free

EyeTV

- www.elgato.com
- For Mac only
- Priced around $80 as a stand-alone application (usually bundled with hardware tuners)

Recovering iPod content

Recovering iPod content is discussed in Chapter 10. Here are suggested links for third-party software, with some basic information about each one:

Music Rescue

- www.kennettnet.co.uk
- For Mac or Windows
- Priced around $15

CopyTrans

- www.copytrans.net
- For Windows only
- Priced around $20

iPod Access

- www.findleydesigns.com
- For Mac or Windows
- Priced around $20

Senuti

- www.fadingred.com/senuti
- For Mac
- Priced around $19

iPod Access Photo

- www.findleydesigns.com
- For Mac or Windows
- Priced around $13

CopyTrans Photo

- www.copytrans.net
- For Windows only
- Priced around $20

Synchronizing iTunes libraries

Synchronizing iTunes libraries is covered in Chapter 12. Here are a couple of suggested links for third-party software, with some basic information about each one:

TuneRanger

- www.acertant.com
- For Mac or Windows
- Priced around $30

Syncopation

- www.sonzea.com
- For Mac only
- Priced around $25

Index

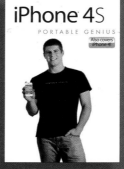
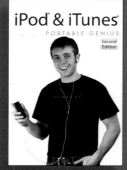

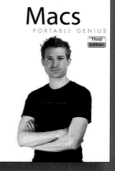